Kenneth Burke and His Circles

Kenneth Burke and His Circles

Edited by
Jack Selzer and Robert Wess

Parlor Press
West Lafayette, Indiana
www.parlorpress.com

Parlor Press LLC, West Lafayette, Indiana 47906

© 2008 by Parlor Press
All rights reserved.
Printed in the United States of America

SAN: 254-8879

Library of Congress Cataloging-in-Publication Data

Kenneth Burke and his circles / edited by Jack Selzer and Robert Wess.
    p. cm.
 Based on papers presented at a conference held at University Park, Pa. from July 10-12, 2005.
 Includes bibliographical references (p.   ) and index.
 ISBN 978-1-60235-067-0 (acid-free paper) -- ISBN 978-1-60235-066-3 (pbk. : acid-free paper) -- ISBN 978-1-60235-068-7 (adobe ebook)
 1. Burke, Kenneth, 1897-1993--Criticism and interpretation. I. Selzer, Jack. II. Wess, Robert.
 PS3503.U6134Z69 2008
 818'.5209--dc22
                          2008024442

Cover Image: "Retro Scroll" © 2007 by Aleksandar Velasevic. Used by
    permission.
Cover design by David Blakesley.
Printed on acid-free paper.

Parlor Press, LLC is an independent publisher of scholarly and trade titles in print and multimedia formats. This book is available in paper, cloth and Adobe eBook formats from Parlor Press on the World Wide Web at http://www.parlorpress.com or through online and brick-and-mortar bookstores. For submission information or to find out about Parlor Press publications, write to Parlor Press, 816 Robinson St., West Lafayette, Indiana, 47906, or e-mail editor@parlorpress.com.

Contents

Abbreviations of Works by Kenneth Burke   *vii*

Introduction   *ix*
    Jack Selzer and Robert Wess

1 From Acceptance to Rejection: Kenneth Burke, Ralph Ellison, and *Invisible Man*   *3*
    Bryan Crable

2 An Interview with Ben Belitt: On Kenneth Burke's Bennington Years   *27*
    Michael Jackson

3 Denis Donoghue's Kenneth Burke   *40*
    Miriam Marty Clark

4 Burke's McKeon Side: Burke's Pentad and McKeon's Quartet   *49*
    Robert Wess

5 Essentializing Temporality, Temporizing Essence: The Narrative Theory and Interpretive Practice of Kenneth Burke and Wayne Booth   *68*
    Greig Henderson

6 Style and the Defense of Rhetoric: Burke's and Aristotle's Competing Models of Mind   *86*
    James Kastely

7 Aesthetic Power and Rhetorical Experience   *96*
    Gregory Clark

8 The Romantic in the Attic: William Blake's Place
in Kenneth Burke's Intellectual Circle   *109*
   Laura E. Rutland

9 Leveraging a Career with Kenneth Burke: The
Politics of Theory in Literary Studies   *120*
   Cary Nelson

10 Kenneth Burke and the Claims of a
Rhetorical Poetry   *129*
   Melissa Girard

11 The "Logological Organizing" of Corporate
Discourse: A Burkean Case-Study Analysis   *149*
   Peter M. Smudde

12 Still the King of Queens? Kenneth Burke,
The Rhetoric of Religion, and the Theorizing
of Rhetoric and Religion Now   *161*
   Benjamin Bennett-Carpenter

13 The Revelations of "Logology": Secular and
Religious Tensions in Burke's Views on Language,
Literature, and Hermeneutics   *174*
   Christine E. Iwanicki

14 Burkean Perspectives on Prayer: Charting a Key
Term through Burke's Corpus   *201*
   William T. FitzGerald

Works Cited   *223*
Contributors   *237*
Index   *241*

Abbreviations of Works by Kenneth Burke

ACR: *Auscultation, Creation, Revision*
ATH: *Attitudes Toward History*
CP: *Collected Poems*
CS: *Counter-Statement*
GM: *A Grammar of Motives*
LSA: *Language as Symbolic Action*
PC: *Permanence and Change*
PLF: *The Philosophy of Literary Form*
RM: *A Rhetoric of Motives*
TBL: *Towards a Better Life*

Introduction

Jack Selzer and Robert Wess

The Special Collections Library at Penn State in many respects operated as the innermost circle for the conference on Kenneth Burke and His Circles, which was held at University Park, Pennsylvania from July 10 through July 12, 2005. It was simultaneously the Nineteenth Penn State Conference on Rhetoric and Composition, and the Sixth Triennial Conference of the Kenneth Burke Society.

A dozen exhibit cases in an anteroom adjacent to the Special Collections Library (and watched over by a bust of Kenneth Burke created by Virginia Burks) supplied "representative anecdotes" for the entire conference. In one case Marika Seigel displayed material artifacts related to her study of how Burke's famous comment about "a little fellow named Ecology" developed not only out of Burke's fertile brain but also out of Burke's engagement with the field of ecology that was nascent in 1937, when his comment appeared in his *Attitudes Toward History* (150). Seigel showed articles from the 1935 *Newsweek* issue that meditated on the Dust Bowl and on the environmentally unfriendly farming practices that were then associated with the agricultural crisis. She directed conferees to Paul Sears's 1935 book *Deserts on the March*, one of the most important early books in the field of ecology—and a book that was reviewed prominently in *The New Republic*, a periodical that Kenneth Burke consumed avidly each week. Drawing on those materials, Seigel's exhibit demonstrated that key concepts in *Attitudes Toward History*, among them "the comic corrective" and "efficiency," developed out of Burke's close interest in those texts and events and people.

In another exhibit case, Jordynn Jack offered an array of artifacts associated with Burke's service in the late 1920s to the Bureau of Social Hygiene in New York. Supported by John D. Rockefeller and supervised by the legendary Colonel Arthur Woods, the Bureau was created to reduce social vice, and Woods employed Burke as a researcher and ghostwriter for his 1931 Yale University Press book *Dangerous Drugs.* Having noted references to the Bureau in Burke's personal correspondence, having documented the particulars of Burke's work there, and having researched the Bureau carefully through a study of primary manuscripts, newspapers, and contemporary periodicals, Jack showed conferees salient passages in *Dangerous Drugs,* made telling connections between the Bureau and Burke's work more generally, and demonstrated intertextual connections between Burke's experiences at the Bureau and segments of his 1935 book *Permanence and Change*—notably those related to the important concept of "piety."

In a third exhibit case, organized by Jay Jordan, work by and about Dell Hymes was available for inspection. Hymes—one of the creators of the field of sociolinguistics during the 1960s and 1970s—pursued his studies as he did in part because of his personal experiences with Burke and Burke's writings, beginning when Hymes took a graduate course from Burke at Indiana University late in the 1950s. The case drew attention to key passages in Burke's *Language as Symbolic Action* that were especially vital to Hymes, presented correspondence between Hymes and Burke, and even drew the living and breathing Dell Hymes himself to comment on the connections between his work and Burke's—for Hymes was attending the conference as a keynote speaker.

In other cases were displayed evidence of Burke's engagements with various other intellectuals and intellectual circles: with R. P. Blackmur (by Rosalyn Eves), with Bennington College (Scott Wible), with educational theorists (Jess Enoch), with John Crowe Ransom (David Tell), with Marxism (Ned O'Gorman), and with Allen Tate (Ann George). Two cases offered evidence of Burke's connections with poets and poetry, and with music: the first contextualized Julie Whitaker and David Blakesley's then-forthcoming edition of Burke's *Late Poems, 1968–1993,* and the other, prepared by library staff member Jeannette Sabre, showed how Burke's music and music criticism emerged both from his critical writings and from his family relationships. And a final case exhibited sculpture by Burke's son Michael, in the form of a metallic "book" with pages inflected by some concepts of his father's and by Michael's own unique vision, materials, and technique.

Introduction   xi

After conferees explored the exhibits, they went next door to hear a presentation about the Kenneth Burke Papers housed at Penn State—the basis for most of the exhibits. Sandra Stelts, Curator of Rare Books and Manuscripts and long-time custodian of the Burke collection, offered background on the Papers—their acquisition over the years beginning with the visionary leadership of Charles Mann, their history and reach, and their current arrangement. Just as important to the participants, she explained how those papers had supported the research projects captured in the exhibits (including the published articles by Seigel, Jack, Jordan, George, Tell, and many others). And she invited participants to explore the archives themselves. Several took her up on the offer: the Reading Room was crowded in the days following the conference.

The Papers, amazing in their comprehensiveness and sheer volume, are the most significant repository of materials related to Burke's career in existence. As the library description indicates,

> The Kenneth Burke Papers contain the personal and professional papers of the philosopher of language Kenneth Duva Burke. Spanning over eight decades, from 1906 to 1993, the multifaceted papers illuminate not only the personal and intellectual life of Burke, but also the lives of his correspondents, many of them major twentieth-century figures. [. . .] The Kenneth Burke Papers consist of two collections. The first Burke collection, Burke-1, dating from 1906 to 1961, was purchased by The Pennsylvania State University Libraries from Kenneth Burke in 1974. Although it includes a few manuscripts, it is primarily a correspondence file of letters written to Burke. It measures twelve linear feet. The Pennsylvania State University Libraries purchased the second Burke collection, Burke-2, from the Kenneth Burke Literary Estate in 2005. This collection dates from 1950 until Burke's death in 1993, with the bulk of its correspondence written between 1960 and 1987. Burke-2 contains Burke's later correspondence (including many carbon copies of Burke's own letters), news clippings, article reprints, a few typescripts, many poems, and several

photographs. Burke-2, more than double the size of Burke-1, measures twenty-five linear feet.

A third group of papers, known informally and locally as Burke-3, includes additional letters, manuscripts, and other documents rescued by Burke's family from his Andover home late in the 1990s, as well as a recent acquisition: the correspondence between Burke and William Rueckert. Considered in their entirety, the Kenneth Burke Papers constitute a rough intellectual biography of Kenneth Burke; they document the manifold intellectual associations that Burke developed and sustained from his boyhood until his death. As early as January, 1916, Burke and his lifelong friend Malcolm Cowley had agreed informally to keep their correspondence (Jay, *Selected Correspondence* 19), and Burke consequently kept a massive, historically significant file of his dealings with a fantastic host of people, famous and more ephemeral, throughout his long life. Those who explore the archive learn of his engagements with the Greenwich Villagers of the 1920s (among them William Carlos Williams, Allen Tate, Marianne Moore, Gorham Munson, Matthew Josephson, Jean Toomer, Katherine Anne Porter, Malcolm Cowley, James Sibley Watson, the Provincetown Players, and Austin Warren), with central 1930s figures from the political left (among them Joseph Freeman, Sidney Hook, Granville Hicks, Dorothy Day, James T. Farrell, and Waldo Frank), and with notables throughout the remainder of his life—Richard McKeon, Robert Penn Warren, Stanley Edgar Hyman, I. A. Richards, Ralph Ellison, Theodore Roethke, Howard Nemerov, A. R. Ammons, Denis Donoghue, Wayne Booth, Hugh Dalziel Duncan, Edmund Wilson, Francis Ferguson, William Empson, John Crowe Ransom, and so forth. There is lots of "so forth": the list of names provided here provides barely a hint of the breadth and depth in the correspondence; the contents provide a vehicle for understanding Burke's connections to just about every scholarly and critical and artistic (and social scientific and political) movement of substance in the twentieth century: Dada, Freudianism, surrealism, pragmatism, estheticism, socialism, communism, Southern agrarianism, new humanism, New Criticism, neo-Aristotelianism, General Semantics, the new rhetoric, structuralism, post-structuralism, deconstruction—there is no place to stop. . . .

Given the wealth of primary materials and multiple dimensions of Burke's life and work, and given that Burke has passed into history, no wonder scholars have begun to study his works and his impact in terms of the circles that he frequented. If two decades ago the emphasis was more on understanding The Man and His Work, more recently attention has shifted to the communities that shaped Burke and were shaped by him: individual snapshots focusing on Burke alone have been replaced by group photographs (so to speak) that place Burke among a variety others, including in many cases personal friends. That scholarly work inspired the conference theme, Kenneth Burke and His Circles, which attracted over 150 participants. Before turning to the circles explored in the chapters in the present volume, all of which are based on presentations at the conference, we should mention that other participants explored Burke in relation to, among other topics, language theory, rhetorical criticism, scientific illustration, feminism, drugs, ecology, and ethics; and in relation to, among others, Mikhail Bakhtin, Henri Bergson, Michel Foucault, C. Wright Mills, Gregory Bateson, Sir James Frazer, Lucretius, and Nietzsche. Everything from Burke's short fiction and music criticism, from *Counter-Statement* to *The Rhetoric of Religion,* came under close scrutiny; there were papers on *Towards a Better Life,* Burke in digital media, Burke at *The Dial,* Burke's music criticism, Burke's critical methods and methodologies. Conference participants, themselves from a variety of fields (literary criticism and theory; rhetoric and composition; communication studies; religion; American studies; the social sciences; cultural studies), implicated themselves in Burke's circles: the interchanges at sessions and at conference social events were animated and interanimated.

This book is a representation of that intellectual event. The papers offered here provide a sampling of many of the best presentations. The first chapters focus on relationships between Burke and some of his closest personal friends. Only time can tell whether the circle of Burke's personal acquaintances will attract the attention of literary and cultural historians as much as some other circles in the past, such as Samuel Johnson's circle in eighteenth-century Britain. In any event, a full account of Burke's circle of personal relationships would intersect significantly with many strands in the history of American culture in the twentieth century, as is hinted in the chapters by Miriam Marty Clark, Bryan Crable, Michael Jackson, and Robert Wess, which explore Burke's friendships with, respectively, Denis Donoghue, Ralph Ellison, Ben Belitt, and Richard McKeon. Indeed, Burke himself sometimes defined his different selves in terms of different personal relationships. Wess quotes from two letters in which Burke depicts himself as divided between a literary side (Malcolm Cowley in one letter, William Carlos Williams in the other) and a theorist side (McKeon in both letters). Burke thus suggests the value of refining our understanding of his work through careful study of the friendships that helped to animate his life as he animated the lives of others.

Crable's chapter is part of his larger project on race, rhetoric, and identity that examines major issues in American cultural life through the lens of Burke and Ellison. Burke's relationship with Ellison has received considerable attention (not only is there a book on the subject by Beth Eddy, but there are also numerous studies of Burke's influence on Ellison, prompted largely by Ellison's own expressions in print of his indebtedness to Burke); but Crable supplements these studies by going beyond the published record to look closely at their friendship as it appears in unpublished correspondence not only between the two of them but also between them and their mutual friends, especially Stanley Edgar Hyman. This attention to a personal relationship stretching over many decades illuminates Burke's observations about race in *A Rhetoric of Motives* and contextualizes his late essay on Ellison's *Invisible Man*. Crable's narrative of this friendship also explains convincingly why Burke waited over three decades to respond to Ellison's classic novel despite the closeness of their relationship in the decade before its appearance.

Clark's and Jackson's chapters take us to a different part of American culture, the world of poets. In Jackson's chapter, unlike any of the others, we hear about Burke in the words of one of his friends, Ben Belitt, who both wrote and translated poetry. Belitt was preparing a book collecting all his poetry when Jackson interviewed him in 1997 about his relationship with Burke.[1] Fourteen years younger than Burke, Belitt first met him in the 1930s through their mutual connection to *The Nation,* and their relationship continued during their days as colleagues at Bennington. Belitt's recollections include anecdotes about Burke, but perhaps what they most reveal is the influence Burke could have through the force of his example: "He taught me to never be afraid of adventure," recalls Belitt, "both as a poet and in the people I wanted to write about" (36).

While Clark's chapter considers Burke's relationship with Donoghue, it nonetheless contributes more generally to the study of Burke's "influential, if sometimes fraught, friendships with American poets" (45). Though not a poet himself, Donoghue has a place in this study because the Burke who animates Donoghue's work gives us a glimpse of the "terms of Burke's engagement with twentieth-century American poetry" (45). Interesting in itself, Donoghue's Burke thus has an interest and significance beyond Donoghue's critical stance. In the course of the essay, Donoghue's Burke even broadens to become A. R. Ammons's as well, when Clark turns her attention to "Information Density," a poem Ammons dedicates to Burke. Moreover, as defined by Donoghue, what poets found in Burke gives us, as Clark puts it, "an alternative way of understanding Burke's place in contemporary critical and theoretical conversation" (42). In this alternative, Burke appears as a humanist rather than either a Marxist (as Frank Lentricchia would have it) or a post-humanist (Cary Nelson).

Wess's chapter turns to yet another part of American culture, the philosophical thought characteristic of much of the twentieth century. Friends from their days together as students at Columbia, Burke and the philosopher McKeon kept in touch until McKeon's death in 1985. Correspondence indicates that Burke regularly looked forward to testing his theoretical ideas against McKeon's considerable philosophical expertise. Wess suggests, moreover, that their thought can be profitably examined together from the standpoint of parallels between Burke's pentad and McKeon's quartet, both of which serve to generate philosophical perspectives. This quartet also distinguishes general philosophical orientations characteristic of different historical periods, so that it helps to reveal the significance in the history of philosophy of the twentieth-century's "linguistic turn," the phrase that became shorthand for the widespread emphasis on language in twentieth-century Anglo-American philosophy, an emphasis evident in Burke as well as in McKeon.[2] The quartet's historical side pinpoints some of the philosophical problems and solutions available within the context of the "linguistic turn," as shown in Wess's McKeonesque defense of Burke's "Our Attempt to Avoid Mere Relativism," the concluding section of "Terministic Screens," where Burke, after de-privileging terminologies by showing that they are "deflections" as much as "reflections" by virtue of being "selections," seems to retreat to a foundationalist position by privileging his own terminology of selection, reflection, and deflection.

Greig Henderson also considers one of Burke's friends, Wayne Booth, but the personal relationship between Burke and Booth is not a consideration in his essay. Instead, taking as his starting point the

Burkean premise that every way of seeing is also a way of not seeing, Henderson considers Joyce's *Portrait of the Artist as a Young Man,* a text analyzed by both Burke and Booth. Henderson locates their differing analyses in the context of narrative theory, where a decades-long conversation among narrative analysts has produced a rich repertoire of analytic strategies, a striking feature of late twentieth-century literary studies in America. Henderson thus helps us to see Burke and Booth as distinctive voices in the circle of this conversation, their differences producing different analyses of Joyce's *Portrait.* In Henderson's closing pages, though, a third way of analyzing *Portrait* emerges, one different from both Burke's and Booth's, and readers may differ over whether this third way is itself to be viewed as another way of both seeing and not seeing, or something more.

Later chapters turn from Burke's circle of personal friends to wider circles. An autodidact, Burke emerged out of no particular academic circle, but he was instead influenced by work in multiple fields, where he read eclectically and extensively. Attempting to explain why reviewers and editors often had trouble placing Burke's work, his friend Stanley Edgar Hyman once explained famously that Burke "has no field, unless it be Burkology" (359). Burke thus comes out of a circle of his own making.

Among the first authors likely to come to mind in any attempt to compile an author list for the library of Burkology is Aristotle, whose relation to Burke is fundamental to James Kastely's chapter. Burke, of course, never simply mimes Aristotle or anyone else; instead he mines people for whatever serves his purposes, often rewriting them, as when in *A Grammar of Motives* he rewrites philosophical texts in pentadese. Kastely focuses on one area of contrast between Burke and Aristotle to forge a perspective on the centrality for Burke of "style." His principal Burke text is "Semantic and Poetic Meaning," first published in 1938 and reprinted in *The Philosophy of Literary Form.* (Gregory Clark, it should be added, also discusses this essay and explicitly links his chapter to Kastely's in acknowledging his indebtedness to Kastely for calling his attention to it.) As Kastely notes, Burke's polemical antagonist in this essay is logical positivism. Positivism's "semantic ideal would attempt to *get a description* by the *elimination* of *attitude,*" whereas Burke's "poetic ideal would attempt to *attain a full moral act* by attaining a perspective *atop all the conflicts of attitude*" ("Semantic" 147-48). This distinction between the "semantic" and the "poetic" is not for

Burke a mutually exclusive binary opposition, perhaps most importantly because of the fundamental impossibility of positivism's project. As Burke explains,

> We should also point out that, although the semantic ideal would eliminate the *attitudinal* ingredient from its vocabulary (seeking a vocabulary for events equally valid for use by friends, enemies, and the indifferent) the ideal is itself an attitude, hence never wholly attainable, since it could be complete only by the abolition of itself. To the logical positivist, logical positivism is a "good" term, otherwise he would not attempt to advocate it by filling it out in all its ramifications. (150)

For Burke, then, "[s]tyle [. . .] [is] the *beneath-which-not,* as the *admonitory and hortatory act,* as the *example* that would prod continually for its completion in all aspects of life" (161-62). Even positivism is hortatory in advancing the "goodness" of positivism. But Kastely's purpose is neither to rehearse Burke's now dated polemics with positivism, nor, even less, to identify Aristotle with positivism. Rather, it is to show that Burke's conception of style in the 1930s is not only much more expansive than Aristotle's but also that this expansiveness can help us today to combat threats to the "growth of a democratic mind adequate to deal with the current world of significantly differing perspectives" (95).

Gregory Clark similarly concerns himself with the expansiveness of Burke's conception of rhetoric but not by contrasting Aristotle to Burke. Rather, Clark contrasts a rhetoric based on logic to a rhetoric based on aesthetic experience. "Semantic and Poetic Meaning" supports this argument, as suggested by the fact that Burke first called it, in its opening sentence, a rhetorical defense of rhetoric (138), and then valorized poetic meaning over semantic and identified poetic meaning with the aesthetic (150). Clark features an extended example of listening to a radio broadcast of a jazz performance the night after September 11, 2001 to show how Burke's aestheticized rhetoric reveals the rhetorical power of art to unify individuals in a culture, as de Tocqueville suggested, that fosters isolation rather than community. In recounting this radio broadcast, Clark offers an instance of the rhetorical effects that he analyzes.

While Aristotle is among the first names likely to come to mind in any attempt to imagine the authors in the library of Burkology, William Blake is equally likely to be among the last. Yet, as Laura Rutland's chapter shows, Blake actually figures significantly in both early and late Burke texts. In Burke's novel *Towards a Better Life,* the protagonist, John Neal, writes a story featuring an epistolary narrator who quotes Blake obsessively, while in the "Prologue in Heaven" in *The Rhetoric of Religion,* "The Lord" is characterized as Blakean. Rutland's chapter attends most closely to Blake's appearance in the novel, but she also associates Blake's antinomianism with Burke's to suggest that the Blakean strain in Burke alerts one to Burke's decades-long struggle to combine antinomian skepticism about order with recognition of its necessity. One can't live without order, yet one must always be alert to its dangers.

Burkology has, of course, made its way, in varying degrees and ways, into the literature of a number of academic fields. Burke's circles of influence, however, have also been surprisingly limited in some fields. In no field is this more true than English, where Burke has long been known but has never been as influential as one might expect, or even as influential as he should be, considering the field's needs. Cary Nelson's chapter deftly identifies varying resistances to Burke in this field from the heyday of the New Criticism in the middle of the twentieth century down to the present. The more recent resistances receive far more attention than the early ones, as Nelson, speaking from within English, suggests ways to use Burke to forge perspectives by incongruity within the field that can help it to foster the reflexivity it needs now more than ever. This need, moreover, is hardly limited to this field but extends to American culture in general. Alluding to Burke's famous essay on Hitler in *The Philosophy of Literary Form,* Nelson proposes that because the press generally resists "writing pieces about 'The Rhetoric of Bush's Battle,' it is up to us to do so. The culture desperately needs reflexivity about all that seems contained or naturalized" (128).[3]

Melissa Girard's essay also examines the resistance to Burke, particularly the resistance stemming from the New Criticism's sharp distinction between poetic and non-poetic discourse, based on its privileging of the "intrinsic" internalities of literary language over the "extrinsic" conditions of its production, reception, and transformative cultural effects. Her essay has the added value of going beyond Burke's theorizing about such matters to consider his own poetic production. She astutely pinpoints ways that Burke's conception of poetry as an act of communication, rather than a socially isolated autonomous utterance that can only be "overheard," informs his writing of poetry. Especially valuable are her insights into Burke's "perspective by incongruity" strategies in his "Flowerishes." Burke's poetry has not received nearly as much attention as his critical work, so that Girard's essay is a welcome step toward righting this imbalance.

By contrast to Nelson's and Girard's chapters, those by Peter Smudde and Benjamin Bennett-Carpenter comment on academic areas where Burke's influence has been extensive. Smudde is concerned with public relations, a sub-specialty in the area of Speech Communication, where Burke's influence has been greater than in any other academic field. Aside from giving some indication of the extensive work in this sub-specialty that draws on Burke, Smudde notes that Burke himself links *Attitudes Toward History* to public relations. Smudde draws on his own experience as a General Motors employee in examining a specific case in which the production of corporate discourse, always a team effort, is best seen as organized, not according to any corporate pre-defined plan, as is the case in much corporate discourse, but according to Burke's logological paradigm. From the standpoint of logology, a level of motivation becomes apparent that standard discussions of public relations typically overlook.

Bennett-Carpenter's chapter calls attention to the extensive current work now being done in the area of rhetoric and religion, where Burke's *The Rhetoric of Religion* remains the basic text over four decades after its publication. Booth reappears in this chapter, this time as one who also works in this area and is deeply influenced by Burke's text, with its seminal interpretation of relations between rhetoric and religion. Judging from Bennett-Carpenter's account, current work in this area tends to put the primary emphasis on rhetoric rather than religion: the *rhetoric* of religion rather than the rhetoric of *religion,* to borrow a Burke device. Burke's primary interest, Bennett-Carpenter argues, is not the divinity but the linguisticality of religious words. In the course of his argument, Burke's six analogies between words and the Word in the first chapter of *The Rhetoric of Religion* receive the most detailed attention.

Christine E. Iwanicki's chapter overlaps with Bennett-Carpenter's insofar as Iwanicki is also concerned with the religious theme in

Burke. The difference is that whereas Bennett-Carpenter is content to demonstrate that Burke studies the linguisticality rather than the divinity of religious discourse, Iwanicki wonders why Burke is so preoccupied with such discourse in the first place. Even more importantly, she wonders whether this preoccupation undermines the insights into the materiality of language and human relations that Burke offers elsewhere, when he's not considering religion. Without ever embracing the religious theme herself, Iwanicki proposes in the end to position Burke's preoccupation with religion within a broad circle of modern thought in which, given events such as the Holocaust, religious chatter may seem better than no chatter at all.

William FitzGerald's chapter rounds off the collection by reminding us of the many ways that Burke animates our discussions through the force of his coinages and new definitions—"identification," "terministic screens," and "perspective by incongruity" are just a few that come readily to mind. The prevalence of these terms and others are perhaps the most concrete examples of the extent of the circle of Burke's influence. FitzGerald then suggests that this circle can be broadened even further if more attention is given to some of Burke's terms whose significance has yet to be fully explored. "Prayer" is the example that FitzGerald examines.

His account begins with "Secular Prayer—or, extended: Character-building by Secular Prayer," a neglected section of Burke's "Dictionary of Pivotal Terms," in *Attitudes Toward History*. While FitzGerald sees prayer playing the role of "symbolic gesture of communion or solidarity toward an audience" (206), one might alternatively suggest that "character-building" is prayerful precisely because it is such a gesture of solidarity. That would be consistent with the entry for "Identity, Identification" in the same "Dictionary." Be that as it may, FitzGerald's careful reading of this section demonstrates that it deserves much more attention than it has received heretofore. FitzGerald also shows that when "prayer" later reappears in *The Philosophy of Literary Form*, its meaning is narrowed to define "a paradigmatic communicative act" (207). The power of FitzGerald's nuanced analysis is perhaps greatest when he turns to the disappearance of "prayer" in favor of "rhetoric" in *A Rhetoric of Motives*, Burke's most complete theorizing of communication. Burke's analysis of "prayer" in *Attitudes* and *Philosophy of Literary Form*, FitzGerald suggests, is best seen as a bridge connecting the prominence of rhetoric in *Counter-Statement* (the "Lexicon Rhetoricae") and its return to prominence in the *Rhetoric*. "Prayer" helps us to see why, when Burke returns to rhetoric, he epitomizes its function in the prayerful "call for help" and its perfection in "pure persuasion." FitzGerald concludes with insightful comment on prayerful moments in Burke's poetry and prose.

Although Burke is no longer with us, he will no doubt continue to have fresh things to say to us, not only as scholars bring archival materials to the light of publication but also as they find new meanings in familiar texts by looking at them in the context of the circles that animated Burke and that he animated himself. We now have intriguing collections of Burke's correspondences with Malcolm Cowley, William Carlos Williams, and William Rueckert to enjoy and examine, but hundreds of additional Burke letters (as well as manuscripts, no doubt[4]) are there to be discovered, digested, shared, and debated. Because of those archives and the scholars who will be drawn to them, our appreciation of Kenneth Burke and his circles is likely to widen and deepen: and Burke himself is likely to remain close to the center of many of them.

Notes

1. The jacket for this book, *This Scribe, My Hand: The Collected Poems of Ben Belitt*, includes blurbs from Kenneth Burke along with Harold Bloom, J. D. McClatchy, and Howard Nemerov. Burke's is first: "Written with beauty, poignancy and skill. Like a gambler who can tell the cards by the feel: he has that kind of touch." Burke died in 1993, so this comment must have originally been written for one of Belitt's earlier books.

2. The phrase "linguistic turn" comes from Richard Rorty's seminal collection of essays in Anglo-American philosophy, first published in 1967 and most recently republished with a retrospective essay in 1992.

3. An example of what Nelson calls for may be found in Robert L. Ivie's "The Rhetoric of Bush's 'War' on Evil" (*KB Journal*, 1.1 [Fall 2004], online at www.kbjournal.org). Ivie uses Burke's "Rhetoric of Hitler's Battle" as a model for analyzing Bush's current rhetoric.

4. James Zappen, who attended the conference, has recently located a yet unpublished Burke essay amid the Burke papers still at Andover.

Kenneth Burke and His Circles

1 From Acceptance to Rejection: Kenneth Burke, Ralph Ellison, and *Invisible Man*

Bryan Crable

Responding to an interviewer's question concerning friendships between writers, Ralph Ellison once noted:

> Writers of different backgrounds and generations often disagree because they seek to make unique works of art out of the subjectivity of diverse experiences which are connected objectively by duration and by issues arising from within the social scene in which they find themselves. If friendships between writers are not strong enough to overcome these built-in sources of conflict and competition, they fail, but if the relationship has been fruitful it finds continuity in the works of art that came into being during the quiet moments of antagonistic cooperation which marked the friendship. (Ellison, Stepto, and Harper 419)

Judging from the ensuing conversation, the relationship that Ellison had in mind was his friendship with fellow African-American novelist, Richard Wright.[1] However, the words might have just as easily referred to Ellison's relationship with another notable American writer and critic, Kenneth Burke.[2] Certainly the "diversity of experiences" that he notes would fit: Burke, after all, was sixteen years Ellison's senior, and his background—growing up as a young white man in Pittsburgh—significantly differed from that of Ellison, who came of age in the increasingly segregated Oklahoma Territory.[3]

Despite these contrasting origins, Burke and Ellison forged a connection that spanned some fifty years of American literary and social history, from 1942 until Burke's death in 1993. This longstanding friendship thus witnessed the publication of some of their most significant works—including Ellison's epic *Invisible Man,* his essay collection *Shadow and Act,* and Burke's two volumes on motivation, *A Grammar of Motives* and *A Rhetoric of Motives.* Burke's influence on Ellison's writing has been well-documented by scholars in literature, American studies, and African-American studies.[4] By contrast, however, relatively little has been written about the friendship that helped give these books life. To the extent that attention has even focused on their personal relationship, it has largely been limited to two sources. The first is Ellison's 1964 introduction to *Shadow and Act,* which acknowledges "special indebtedness" to Burke, whom Ellison credits as "the stimulating source of many of these [essays]" (*Collected* 60).

The second is an essay written by Burke, "Ralph Ellison's True-blooded *Bildungsroman,*" included in a 1990 collection celebrating Ellison's life and work.[5] This essay is typically described as the best source on the existence and character of the friendship, for—although it is almost exclusively focused on the plot of Ellison's novel—the essay is framed as a personal letter from Burke to Ellison, given its opening salutation, "Dear Ralph," and its warm closing line, "Best luck, to you and Fanny both, K.B" (359). Moreover, the essay contains a striking quote: "The demands local to your story [*Invisible Man*] ruled out that biographical strand in which not only did *we* back you, but you could and did get us to look for traces of unconscious Nortonism in our thinking" (359).[6]

Largely on the basis of this evidence, scholars invariably take this essay for what it appears to be: a personal letter, from Burke to Ellison, later published as part of a celebratory collection.[7] However, these scholars have missed something crucial; indeed, I contend that this letter *is not what it seems,* despite its formal similarities to a private letter. First, the essay was written nearly forty years into the friendship, hence it should not be taken as a faithful reflection of the early stages of the relationship. More importantly (and contrary to scholars' assumptions), it was written specifically for inclusion in the collection—and thus was *always* intended as a public, not private, document. Adding to its public character, the "letter" passed through a series of revisions (revisions by Burke himself, by Ellison, and by the editor of the collection) prior to its publication.[8] These situational factors make it impossible, I argue, to take it at face value, as a simple (or unvarnished) reflection on their longstanding relationship.

This is not to say that I would dismiss the essay altogether. On the contrary, I contend that—if we read the essay within the context of the Burke-Ellison friendship—this late "letter" from Burke takes on a new, surprising significance. This essay, I argue, is best understood as the fulfillment of Burke's promise to read and respond to *Invisible Man*. This reading of the essay also helps explain why, thirty-plus years after the novel's publication, the bulk of Burke's essay simply offers a dramatistic reading of *Invisible Man*. However, this new interpretation of Burke's "letter" requires that we look beyond its formal characteristics, and instead place it within the context of the (truly) private correspondence between Burke, Ellison, and their mutual friend, Stanley Edgar Hyman.[9]

Reading their friendship through these letters, and not through later reminiscences, we can also appreciate the discipline and struggle that Ellison's opening quote underscores, the "antagonistic cooperation" that spurred both toward groundbreaking works of art and criticism—though, given the duration and complexity of this relationship, a complete chronicle of this friendship moves well beyond the scope of Burke's late "letter" to Ellison. Consequently, for the purposes of this essay, I will solely focus upon three critical points in the Burke-Ellison relationship: 1942, the birth of this friendship; 1945, the exchange which decisively altered the relationship; and 1952, the publication of Ellison's "epoch-making" novel, *Invisible Man*.[10] The context provided by these unpublished letters between Burke, Ellison, and Hyman reveals the hidden significance of Burke's late essay—disclosing the story of a friendship marked not only by conflict, but also by a productive, and heartfelt, sense of communion.

1942: Birth of a Friendship

By all accounts, the intellectual relationship between Burke and Ellison began three years before the two even met. Indeed, a 1964 letter from Burke's longtime friend Malcolm Cowley reported that, at a meeting of the American Academy and Institute of Arts and Letters, "Ralph Ellison ascribed his birth as a writer to you" (Jay 351). This statement is supported by a 1977 interview with Ellison, where he explicitly identified Burke's famous essay, "The Rhetoric of Hitler's Battle," as a formative influence on his thinking about politics, language, and literature (Ellison, Reed, Troupe, and Cannon 148).[11] Ellison was in the audience as Burke read the essay to the League of American Writers in 1939 (Jackson, *Ralph Ellison* 181, 256; though Jackson wrongly places the date as 1937), and was immediately struck with the depth of Burke's analysis, as well as his courage in the face of a hostile audience. Following this encounter, in 1941, Ellison published an essay in the journal, *Direction,* which Burke was closely affiliated with (Jackson, "The Birth" 329)—but neither occasion resulted in further contact.

Ultimately, their introduction was sparked partly by Ellison's acquaintance with Hyman, whom Ellison met in his capacity as editor for *The Negro Quarterly.* Ellison initiated their correspondence, inviting Hyman to review some books for the journal (Hyman to Ellison, 24 June 1942, RE). Ellison and Hyman soon developed a personal relationship on the basis of this professional contact, fueled by their mutual admiration of Burke. Replying to one of Ellison's comments about Harry Slochower's work, Hyman wrote, "I know him slightly, having met him through his neighbor Kenneth Burke (who, as you have probably guessed, is my critical hero and mentor)" (Hyman to Ellison, 19 July 1942, RE). In his first surviving letter to Hyman, likely written in late July, 1942, Ellison echoed his praise of Burke:

> No, I am not at all suprised [sic] that Kenneth Burke rates high with you, having noticed similarities in your approaches to art. But, perhaps, most of all because he is also a hero of my own (I have just about exhausted myself in trying to obtain a personal copy of *Counterstatement* [sic]), and I'm never able to understand critics who don't admire him.[12]

The friendship between Ellison and Hyman subsequently deepened, and they began to meet frequently in New York, socializing and discussing art and politics. During this same period, though they had previously exchanged letters, the pace of the Hyman-Burke correspondence substantially increased. The triangle was completed when Ellison and Burke finally met face to face. The occasion of their introduction was recorded by Hyman in a letter to Burke:

> My friend Ralph Ellison, with whom I have a weekly lunch devoted principally to expounding the revealed word of Burke, tells me that you will be in town Sat-

urday at Harry Slochower's wedding, where he is to
have the privilege of meeting you. I am very anxious
to see you, not having done so in two years, and am
hoping you will have some spare time Saturday either
before or after the wedding to go out for a meal or
some drinks with me and perhaps Ralph. (Hyman to
Burke, 16 December 1942, KB)

This initial contact was obviously quite positive, as ensuing letters between Hyman and Burke are filled with references to Ellison. Indeed, in the months following this weekend, Burke sent Ellison and Hyman two of his earliest (and hardest-to-acquire) books; Hyman received a copy of Burke's novel, *Towards a Better Life,* while Ellison received his longed-for *Counter-Statement* (Hyman to Burke, 16 March 1943, KB; Burke to Hyman, 25 March 1943, SH). Responding to this gift, Ellison wrote Burke for the first time: "Here are my very belated, but no less gracious, thanks for *Counterstatement* [sic]. When it came I was in the mist [sic] of a sick spell, which I am trying to shake off up here with maple syrup and fresh air. Sorry we were unable to get together before you went back to N.J. as I had many questions to ask you" (Ellison to Burke, 28 May 1943, KB). In addition to offering thanks, Ellison reported excitedly reading Burke's work on Coleridge, as well as an early section from Burke's *Grammar:* "Am just beginning to grasp the implications of your five terms and am becoming impatient to get into your opus in progress. It promises something stable in a world too much in flux" (Ellison to Burke, 28 May 1943, KB). Thus, in 1943, just as Ellison's career as a critic and writer was beginning to blossom, we see that he was extensively reading Burke's work—and that the two were developing a personal and intellectual connection, one rooted in a common love of ideas and literature.

Following this initial burst, Burke and Ellison ceased exchanging letters, though the Burke-Hyman correspondence continued unabated—primarily because Ellison, responding to the events of World War II (and in danger of being drafted), enlisted in the Merchant Marines (Hyman to Burke, 24 September 1943, KB). As detailed in Hyman's letters, Ellison, Hyman, and Burke attempted to meet several times during the fall of 1943, though they were only successful once, in early December (Hyman to Burke, 8 October 1943, KB; Hyman to Burke, 12 November 1943, KB; Hyman to Burke, 30 November 1943, KB). Since Ellison left New York on a Merchant Marine ship soon after (in mid-December, 1943), for the next year he and Burke communicated only through Hyman (e.g. Hyman to Burke, 14 January 1944, KB).

At this point in time, we should note that the nature of the Burke-Ellison friendship was clearly defined—as were the roles that both men played within it. Burke was accorded a certain privilege within the relationship; he was already an established writer (unlike Ellison or Hyman), and was one of Ellison's primary inspirations in the field of criticism and literature. It is not surprising, then, that the Burke of the early 1940's would view himself as Ellison's mentor—and that, based on their differences in status, Ellison would willingly accept the complementary role.

Befitting his position as elder scholar, Burke was generous with his young protégé, not only by giving him a copy of *Counter-Statement*, but, even more substantially, by recommending Ellison for a Rosenwald Fellowship in the winter of 1944 (Ellison to Burke, 23 November 1945, KB; cf. Ellison, *Collected* 521). This award came at a critical point in Ellison's career, as he had just been forced to take recuperative shore leave—and was beginning work on his first novel (Ellison, *Collected* 471, 521–22). Hyman's congratulations to Ellison on the Rosenwald reflected his (and Burke's) longstanding support of Ellison's efforts: "Stuff is finally turning your way, as it should, and all of us [. . .] are pleased as hell. Kenneth sends his congratulations, and he and I are planning to have calling cards made reading 'Early Ellison Fans'" (Hyman to Ellison, May 30, 1945, RE). At the same time, it also reinforced the difference in status between Burke and Ellison: "We don't see too much of Kenneth who keeps pretty busy up here [in Bennington] with his own work. [. . .] I do have a couple of his students in my criticism class, however, which is a very funny sensation, like the time I met you. That is, I expect to talk the jargon, not hear it" (Hyman to Ellison, 30 May 1945, RE). Hyman's account thus positions Burke as the source of the ideas espoused by both Ellison and Hyman—and simultaneously defines Ellison as simply another of Burke's students.

All this would soon change; the summer of 1945 found both men poised to begin important new projects. Burke was awaiting the publication and review of his massive treatise, *Grammar*, but was already contemplating the follow-up, *Rhetoric*. Ellison, similarly, had just witnessed the publication (in *The Antioch Review*) of one of his most important early essays, "Richard Wright's Blues," a response to and defense of Richard Wright's autobiography, *Black Boy*. Like Burke, though, he had already moved on; even as the article moved to print, Ellison was writing the striking opening passages of *Invisible Man*. However, Ellison's essay would soon threaten the heretofore-accepted patterns and roles of their friendship.

1945: A Change in the Relationship

Writing Hyman soon after his arrival in Vermont in the summer of 1945, Ellison reflected upon both his novel-in-progress and his recently-published essay:

> We've been here for a week now, where I'm working like hell on my novel. I started a letter to you just before we left the city but somehow it got left; perhaps because I was unable to get a copy of the current *Antioch Review* with my Wright piece, which I wanted you and Kenneth to see. Let me know if you haven't seen it, so that I can pick one up or order one when I return. (Ellison to Hyman, 21 August 1945, SH)

Though the essay was very favorably received in literary circles, the essay was also an immediate hit with Ellison's friends. Hyman applauded Ellison's work: "I thought your piece on Wright, incidentally, was terrific, the best critical writing of yours I have ever read. I agree with almost everything you say, would have written it myself if I could" (Hyman to Ellison, 19 October 1945, RE). Libbie Burke offered similar praise in a letter to Shirley Jackson: "Ralph Ellison's pamphlet on Wright is positively the best, the most profound, the wisest thing I have ever seen on the black-white issue. [. . .] He is really seeing things from a higher level."[13] In a later letter, Hyman passed Libbie's praise along to Ellison (Hyman to Ellison, 24 November 1945, RE).

On the heels of the essay's critical success (and at Hyman's request), Ellison was invited to lecture at Bennington College. Hyman wrote Burke of the occasion, and asked him to come up for the weekend, noting "it is the social highlight of the Bennington season. [. . .] Ralph would be overwhelmed, and we would have a high good time" (Hyman to Burke, 27 October 1945, KB). Burke apologetically declined the invitation, since he was still planning the structure and content of the *Rhetoric*. In closing his response to Hyman, though, he added:

> Tell Ralph I continue to ponder the article he sent me. Reading it again, I find myself beset by a whole new line of thought. I guess I didn't read it right the first time. Now it seems to suggest a paradox. I.e., Wright is able to protest fully as a *Negro* by separating himself out as an *individual;* but such a protest, by the nature of the case, resists *organization*. What would Ralph say? (Burke to Hyman, 30 October 1945, SH)

In a follow-up letter to Burke, Hyman commented, "I passed your message onto Ralph when he was here, he promised to write you anent it hotly, and then apparently forgot what you said. Anyway he called the other day when I was out and had Shirley read the paragraph to him over the phone. So you will probably be hearing from him, or may have already" (Hyman to Burke, 24 November 1945, KB). Ellison's letter to Burke was already in the mail; ranging far beyond Burke's comment, Ellison's rejoinder consisted of five, single-spaced pages of commentary on literature, Ellison's work in progress, and the psychological and social impact of the American racial divide.[14]

Ellison's lengthy answer also included substantial discussion of his indebtedness to Burke. Though initially expressing thanks simply for the Rosenwald recommendation, Ellison wryly reflected on the insufficiency of such a statement, noting instead that:

> my real debt to you lies in the many things I've learned (and continue to learn) from your work and that perhaps the greatest debt lies in your courage in taking a counter-position and making your "counter-statement." But then the problem arose of whether one really has the right to thank a thinker for having courage, and would not that be a misunderstanding and an embarrassment? For when a man, in battling for his life, has given birth to works which enlighten and inspire, is it not a mistake to confuse the matter and attempt to thank him? It's like thanking him for being a human being. (Ellison to Burke, 23 November 1945, KB)

Ellison consequently suggested another, more artistic expression of his gratitude: "I am writing a novel now and perhaps if it is worthwhile it will be my most effective means of saying thanks. Anything else seems to me inadequate and unimaginative" (Ellison to Burke, 23 November 1945, KB). Given what we now know of Ellison's work during this time, it is clear that the novel in question was *Invisible Man* (cf. Ellison, *Collected Essays* 471–85)—and thus that Ellison's celebrated first novel not only draws upon Burkean terminology, but was *conceived by its author as a means of repaying his intellectual debt to Burke.* The connection between Burke and Ellison's novel cannot, then, be confined to structure or terminology; expanding the focus of current scholarship on this connection, we can see the novel itself as an offering to Burke, the most appropriate means for Ellison to show the impact Burke had on his thought and career.

However, tempering his enthusiastic praise of Burke's work was a counter-statement of Ellison's own, directed toward Burke's position on the difference between racialist and universalist perspectives. When examining the situation of black Americans in a culture founded on white supremacy, Ellison argued, the two perspectives are not so easily untangled:

> I certainly agree with you that universalism is desirable, but I find that I am forced to arrive at that universe through the racial grain of sand, even though the term "race" is loaded with all the lies which men like Davidson warm their values by. [. . .] I, for instance, would like to write simply as an American, or even better, a citizen of the world; but that is impossible just now because it is to dangle in the air of abstractions while the fire which alone illuminates those abstractions issues precisely from my being a Negro and in all the "felt experience" which being a Negro American entails. (Ellison to Burke, 23 November 1945, KB)[15]

As a result, Ellison's letter initiated the first serious intellectual disagreement or argument between the two men. Though Ellison consistently quoted Burke to make his points clear, his letter ultimately articulated a position quite different from Burke's own: "to throw away the concern with the racial [. . .] emphasis would for me be like cutting away the stairs leading from my situation in the world to that universalism of which you speak" (Ellison to Burke, 23 November 1945, KB).

Further, Ellison seized the opportunity to address the pathologies inherent in the perspectives and motives of white Americans—a topic contemporary scholars term the psychology of whiteness, the impact of anti-black racism on the development of white identity. Though Ellison would soon become well known for this sort of analysis (especially in the essays collected in *Shadow and Act*), the letter provided a glimpse of some of his earliest thoughts on the subject:

> How well I understand that possibility of civil war that you mention! But don't you see the war exists already and its effects are in many ways more serious than any mere shedding of blood. It has warped our culture, truncated our ability to think deeply and broadly and schooled us to drop bombs on a defenseless city. [. . .] Violence is coming at any rate and perhaps if the conflict in our society is resolved we'll be so sobered that we'll think twice before starting another war. (Ellison to Burke, 23 November 1945, KB)

Following an extended discussion of his novel-in-progress, Ellison closed the letter with his response to Burke's initial question—and with a correspondingly scathing attack on the American Left:

> But getting back to Wright (and your note to Stanley), I think that what you have here is not just an arbitrary resistance to organization, but a problem in allegiance [. . .] when it comes to breaking worn-out allegiances we Americans have a gangster psychology. For even when an organization goes bad, or when it persecutes us or maims us spiritually, we feel a strange need to keep silent about it [. . .] We are afraid to stand alone or speak alone. (Ellison to Burke, 23 November 1945, KB)

Burke's response to this letter, and to Ellison's arguments, was initially rather ambiguous. He wrote Hyman soon after that he had received Ellison's reply, commenting, "Ralph wrote me. And a very good letter it was. So good that I'll have to write him an essay for an answer" (Burke to Hyman, 4 December 1945, SH). However, his assessment of the letter, and of Ellison's perspective, was not wholly appreciative: "If he never yields more than half to his temptation (quite justified!) to become an intellectual Garveyite, he'll go on getting better and better.

And he's damned good already" (Burke to Hyman, 4 December 1945, SH).¹⁶ Here we see Burke offer a racially charged characterization of Ellison—that Ellison's position is tantamount to racial separatism, and, as such, is a position that is not yet fully (dialectically) matured. Adding to the ambiguity of Burke's reaction, though Ellison eagerly awaited a reply, the promised response was slow in coming (Ellison to Hyman, 12 December 1945, SH).

Burke's response to Ellison thus opened with an apology for the delay. Burke also thanked Ellison for the praise of his work, but expressed discomfort with Ellison's position on race. Though granting the legitimacy of Ellison's argument, Burke wrote that, universalism aside, the issue for him was tied to individual (and not racial) motives:

> Whatever indignities and fears I have suffered, I have always had the feeling that I suffered them as an individual; hence that the problem of repair was primarily an individual problem. [. . .] The indignities and fears you suffer, you suffer not as an individual, but as member of a race. (Burke to Ellison, 16 December 1945, RE)

However, Burke acknowledged that this difference in outlook arose, in part, from their difference in race. Reflecting on his own racial identity, Burke noted, "If I often forget that I am a white man, and burn merely from the sense of my inadequacies as an individual, it is only because I am not surrounded by a set of customs that continually reminds me of my color" (Burke to Ellison, 16 December 1945, RE). As a result of this fundamental difference in perspective, Burke concluded, white and black intellectuals are charged with two radically different responsibilities. Ellison, in taking up the question of race—and in "intensify[ing] racial thinking"—was living up to his responsibility; the white intellectual, Burke wrote, must instead "do all that he can to mitigate the magic of race," by striving "to weaken the magic of any such classification" by color (Burke to Ellison, 16 December 1945, RE). The true dilemma, Burke admitted, is that these two tasks necessarily result in black and white scholars espousing contradictory positions on the issue of race and racism—which, he noted, sets people of goodwill at permanent odds.

At the same time, Burke argued, when the subject is the artistic treatment of the problem, the artist's race is irrelevant. The American racial divide must be addressed through equally complex artistic representations of whiteness and blackness; the alternative is a literature which flatters, seduces, or titillates, but does not lead to greater human understanding. As a result, Burke agreed with Ellison that Richard Wright's work was inadequate (because of its simplistic aesthetic), but found Ellison's stated approach too intellectualist to meet the multiple demands of the situation. Burke consequently offered advice to Ellison on his novel's protagonist, describing the ideal as

> a figure who is beset even by the temptations of his own words, who finds that an attempt to improve himself is by implication a treachery against his people, that attempts to quiet his people are mainly serviceable to white landlords, indeed, who finds a contradiction at every turn. He would be ashamed of being tough, and ashamed of being tender. He would do far less than he wants to do; and whatever he does do, his motivations are distrusted not only by those whom he would help, but even by himself. (Burke to Ellison, 16 December 1945, RE)

Before ending the letter, Burke returned to his initial question on "Richard Wright's Blues." He rejected Ellison's preference for a terminology of allegiance over one of organization—and his corresponding critique of the Left—as blind to its conservative consequences. Racialist critiques of Communism are problematic, Burke wrote, because "there is something unsatisfactory about remaining silent. But there is something much more unsatisfactory in selling one's grievances to an audience which loves to hear of them for wholly reactionary reasons" (Burke to Ellison, 16 December 1945, RE). In short, Burke argued, African Americans' attacks on racism in the Left simply collaborate with the worst elements of white American industrial society.

Perhaps to minimize the discomfort he felt about these topics, Burke ended the letter apologetically: "If any of this sounds dumb, at least I meant well" (Burke to Ellison, 16 December 1945, RE). However, I believe that the full significance of this exchange cannot be seen through an examination of content alone. Instead, the letters should be understood as symbolic acts in and of themselves, acts that, taken together, form a pattern of statements and counter-statements. True to Burke's conception of the "counter-statement," Ellison's letter repeatedly rejects Burke's positions on race, but is most certainly grounded in Burkean terminology. In like fashion, Burke's letter responds to Ellison's statements, offering parallel counter-statements—most notably in his redescription of Ellison's fictional protagonist. Taken as such, the letters indicate (and help create) a decisive change in the previously-accepted patterns and roles of the Burke-Ellison relationship.

With this exchange, we see that, in the summer of 1945, Burke no longer functioned simply as a mentor for Ellison, an unquestioned source of vocabulary and ideas. Ellison's letter instead positioned him as an "intellectual sparring partner" (to borrow a term from *Shadow and Act*), one whose ideas are as open to debate as any other; within these letters, intellectual exchange—as between two equals—took the place of the hero worship that dominated the early correspondence.[17] Further, Ellison, far from remaining a young aspiring writer, staked a claim to his own position in the debate over race, even if this position grew out of a very Burkean framework.

Consequently, I believe that the Ellison of this 1945 exchange was no longer simply content to see himself as a follower of Burke, one among others. Rather, he attempted to honor Burke in the only fitting way: by crafting a unique perspective, and a corresponding terminology, from the materials Burke provided him. However, the depth and complexity of this perspective would not become fully evident until the publication of Ellison's novel. Though he was not to know this in 1945, the appearance of the novel would have an immediate, and more dramatic, impact upon his relationship with Burke.

1952: *INVISIBLE MAN*'S ACCEPTANCE AS REJECTION

The stretch of time between 1945 and 1952, the publication date of *Invisible Man,* marks one of the closest periods in the Burke-Ellison relationship. Their differences of opinion on matters of race were of little import, it seems, as the two men were in regular contact, both face to face and via the post. Indeed, they were close enough that Hyman suggested Burke's farm, in Andover, New Jersey, as a possible site for Ellison's wedding to Fanny McConnell (Hyman to Burke, 18 July 1946, KB). Burke, in turn, invited the Ellisons to accompany Hyman and Jackson on a visit in August, 1946: "We'll be expecting you both, and with the Ellisons. Tell Ralph I'd write him in person; but have once again misplaced the address you gave me. [. . .] Hope to be seeing you all soon. And do impress it upon Ralph that we very much hope they'll come too" (Burke to Hyman, 29 July 1946, SH; cf. Burke to Hyman, 21 July 1946, SH; Ellison to Burke, 23 September 1946, KB).

Perhaps a harbinger of events to come, the Ellisons made another trip to Andover the following winter, though this visit was less successful—and less genial—than the previous one. Soon after, Burke reported dissatisfaction with Ellison's behavior: "Ralph and Frances E. were out. Thought it was a good session (The Blackmurs & Berrymans were also here). But haven't heard a peep from him since th[en] which may or may not indicate vast preoccupation or vague disgruntlement, but certainly does not indicate vast graciousness" (Burke to Hyman, 8 January 1947, SH). Ellison finally wrote Burke in August, noting that "until quite recently I've found it next to impossible to write letters—which explains why you haven't heard from me. I did manage to use the telephone and was thus able to keep in touch with Stanley, but with you this wasn't possible; so I had to contend with my vain resolutions and bad conscience" (Ellison to Burke, 25 August 1947, KB). Ellison's letter apparently mollified Burke; no more is said of this incident.

Ellison's next proposed visit to Andover was precipitated, at least in part, by Burke's citation of "Richard Wright's Blues" in his *Rhetoric*. According to Hyman, Ellison disapproved of Burke's interpretation:

> I also saw Ralph, who wants to see you and talk over your butchery of him in Red Taurus [*Rhetoric*]. I said the three of us should get together in town (do you ever come in Fridays?) or he and I would drive out to Andover some day (he just bought a station wagon) and beard you. I would advise you to grow a quick beard. (Hyman to Burke, 10 October 1950, KB)[18]

Although the proposed visit fell through when Hyman's son was injured in an accident (Hyman to Burke, 9 November 1950, KB; Burke to Hyman, 12 November 1950, KB; Hyman to Burke, 15 November 1950, KB; Hyman to Burke, 28 November 1950, KB), efforts were more successful the following summer. After much consultation, it was agreed that the Ellisons would visit Andover on Saturday, August 25, Hyman and Jackson would arrive the next morning, and all four would leave on Monday (Hyman to Burke, 17 July 1951, KB; Burke to Hyman, 28 July 1951, KB; Hyman to Burke, 31 July 1951, KB; Hyman to Burke, 14 August 1951, KB; Burke to Hyman, 20 August 1951, KB; Hyman to Burke, 22 August 1951, KB; Libbie Burke to Fanny Ellison, dated "Wed," RE).

Though the weekend reunion took place, Burke again indicated his dissatisfaction with the result—this time because the Ellisons left Andover much earlier than expected. Burke expressed his feelings to Hyman in a postscript: "The Ellisons were presumably disgrunt! Livnlearn!" (Burke to Hyman, 11 October 1951, SH). Hyman apparently did not share Burke's sentiments, as his response made light of Burke's complaint: "I don't understand what you mean by the Ellisons being 'disgrunt.' Not so far as I know. Please explain. Poor old Burke, he was quite a gay fellow until these general delusions of persecution caught up with him" (Hyman to Burke, 18 October 1951, KB).

Perhaps alerted by Hyman to Burke's discontent, Fanny Ellison tried to smooth the matter over in a letter to Libbie. She emphasized that their early departure had a perfectly innocent explanation, that it did not indicate any hostility toward the Burkes: "We would have liked to have stayed out for the remainder of the week we were there, but as I explained, Ralph had to return to the city and as it turned out it was good that I did too" (Fanny Ellison to Libbie Burke, 30 October, 1951, RE). Fanny also underscored the close nature of their friendship: "There aren't many places that we go, nor many people whom we see—six families in all—but these six, among whom are you and Kenneth, are very important to us and it is always a joy to see you and share in your hospitality and friendliness" (Fanny Ellison to Libbie Burke, 30 October 1951, RE).

Though these apologies seemed to suffice, this last incident was soon followed by an even more consequential—and lasting—disruption in the Burke-Ellison relationship. In early 1952, Ellison's *Invisible Man* debuted to extensive critical praise. The book was originally dedicated (as discussed above) to Burke; however, his response to Ellison's magnum opus clearly discouraged its author. In a letter to Burke following its publication, Hyman commented, "I saw Ralph Monday, and he was awaiting Delphic word from you" (Hyman to Burke, 16 April 1952, KB). Based on all available evidence, Hyman's invocation of the Olympian gods likely does not exaggerate the importance Ellison placed on Burke's opinion. However, Burke did not take the bait, so Hyman's next message again broached the subject: "Ralph says he still hasn't had word from you" (Hyman to Burke, 22 April 1952, KB).

Prompted by Hyman's letters, Burke finally sent his belated congratulations to Ellison—although, even then, his remarks were restricted to a short postcard. Burke noted that, though he had not yet finished the book, the opening was familiar from early excerpts,[19] and that the entire publicity effort pointed to "a very friendly press" (Burke to Ellison, 23 April 1952, RE). Burke deferred further judgment until later, ruefully stating, "Am in a jam at the moment, but hope to write you fairly soon about your book" (Burke to Ellison, 23 April 1952, RE).

Ellison evidently waited for another letter, one containing Burke's final pronouncements on the novel's merit. Months later, Burke's promised follow-up still unsent, Ellison expressed disappointment, though notably not to Burke himself (Ellison to Hyman, 17 November 1952, SH). Burke, for his part, maintained a distance between himself and Ellison. Hyman, obviously concerned for the fate of the friendship, urged Burke to break his silence: "Today Ralph receives the Nat'l Book Award gold medal for 1952 fiction, and I hope you will write him a letter. He is still quite hurt that you never wrote more than a postcard on his novel" (Hyman to Burke, 27 January 1953, KB).

Burke's reply changed the subject, but Hyman continued to stress the importance of the issue: "I am glad to see all the mists vanish, except the one about Ralph, where I still think you are wrong, and losing a good friend for reasons of disagreement that can be peaceably handled in the community of honest men. As for your unconcern with the forms of rejection, what kind of symbowelic actionist are you?" (Hyman to Burke, 25 February 1953, KB). This last appeal—or perhaps the prospect of the end of the friendship—clearly touched a chord in Burke, as evidenced by a contrite aside: "(Psst. I'll be good, and write to Ralph. My aloofness has been due not to grouch, but to fact that I still haven't done my lessons. And if you knew how I have been beset, you'd know why I haven't done my lessons. Also, you'd know that I'll be quite some time yet. But I'll get around to it, that I will.)" (Burke to Hyman, 3 March 1953, SH).

Though Hyman expressed considerable relief (Hyman to Burke, 17 March 1953, KB), hidden in Burke's apologia is a startling revelation—a full year after its publication, *Burke still had not read Ellison's novel*. Another exchange with Hyman, several months later, confirms the fact; Burke coyly asked Hyman's permission to read Jackson's latest novel prior to finishing "the second two-thirds of Ralph's" (Burke to Hyman, 2 June 1953, SH). Hyman granted Burke's request, though he noted, with good-natured disapproval, "Finishing Shirley's book before Ralph's may not be political, but it certainly shows a discouraging preference for large type and wide margins" (Hyman to Burke, 9 June 1953, KB).

Although the subject subsequently disappeared from Burke's correspondence with Hyman, it reappeared in a 1957 letter from Burke to another scholar, George Knox. The letter was sent in response to one of Knox's articles, which discussed the work of several black writers, including Ellison. After thanking Knox for sending him the essay, Burke offered an unexpected and jarring reflection on his friendship with Ellison:

> You should send an offprint of the Negro [article] to Ellison, if you haven't already. I don't have his present address, but I think I can get it for you if you want it. I used to see him on and off; he and his wife have been out here a few times; but I got so irritated with an ass-kissing job he did on Eliot in an interview, I still haven't finished his *Invisible Man*. (Mainly, of course, it was a matter of being busy. But I think I'd have finished it anyhow had I not felt prima-donnishly irritated by the Eliot line.). (Burke to Knox, 16 July 1957, KB)

Two points are quite significant in this letter—one sharply different in tone than those written to their mutual friend, Hyman. First, we see that Burke fails to even claim Ellison as a current friend; his language both relegates the relationship to the past and classifies the relationship as relatively superficial, a surprising development in and of itself, given their (at that point) fifteen-year relationship. However, Burke also admits in this letter—*over five years after its publication*— that he never finished the novel. When we consider that this book was conceived as a way of honoring Burke and his influence, this admission is simply astonishing. Further, when we recall that Burke read every word written by Hyman and Jackson (regardless of his own workload), these points indicate that Burke's abandonment of *Invisible Man* was no mere accident; as he suggests in the letter to Knox, it was most certainly a deliberate act.

Though the evidence thus indicates that Burke intentionally put the novel down, the motive behind this decision is less clear. As we have already seen, Ellison and Burke had several differences of opinion on matters of race—and the Ellisons' visits to Andover seemed to do more harm than good to the relationship. However, several letters from Burke suggest that his act was motivated by something else entirely: feelings of jealousy and abandonment. Their relationship began with Burke serving as Ellison's cherished mentor; a few short years later, Ellison had achieved an almost overnight celebrity, making Burke's continued guidance unnecessary. The rush of acclaim for Ellison's novel seems to have generated little but resentment in Burke. He clearly felt that Ellison, having achieved success, was leaving his mentor behind—which hurt even more because Burke's own work was then receiving only a fraction of the attention given Ellison's. In a letter to Hyman, Burke strongly hinted that this was the source of his discontent:

> Heard Ralph's phonogenic voice on radio the other day. Missed first part—but from point at which I tuned in, he seemed to be faring quite well. In his joyous world of T. S. Eliots and Harvey Brights and Irving and Hows, he doesn't need the likes of me to say him yea. (Incidentally, the situation being what it is today, I think he has a good chance of being "groomed" for a role of considerable politico-cultural importance. I say this in all seriousness.) (Burke to Hyman, dated "January 1953," SH)

This reference to Ellison's potential "politico-cultural importance" suggests that Burke was reacting more toward Ellison's celebrity profile—and its connection to the burgeoning civil rights movement—than toward the artistic achievement represented by the novel. Moreover, Burke's letter indicates that he read Ellison's interviews, and was hurt when Ellison pointed to Eliot as a central influence—leaving Burke out of account.

Although Burke's letter to Knox, characterizing Ellison's interview as "ass-kissing," seems extreme, he does point to something crucial. In his 1950s interviews, Ellison frequently cited Eliot as an influence on his writing; Burke's name, by contrast, was largely absent (and remained so, in Ellison's interviews, until the 1970's). Burke certainly did not take the matter lightly; following these statements, Burke had little to say to or about Ellison for several years—and, even then, his hostility toward Ellison remained fully evident (e.g. Hyman to Burke, 1 September 1959, KB; Burke to Hyman, 4 December 1962, SH). I believe it is quite justified, then, to read jealousy and hurt in Burke's silence on and abandonment of the novel.

Indeed, subsequent correspondence from Burke reinforces this interpretation. A few years after Burke's letter to Knox, Hyman wrote Burke that he was reviewing Ellison's *Shadow and Act,* and that he had "credited it all to you, including things you might want credited to someone else" (Hyman to Burke, 3 November 1964, KB). Burke's reply revealed that his feelings of rejection remained in full force: "I'd be much amused to see what I get credited and discredited for, in re R*lph *ll*s*n—for I'm morally (in a nasty way) certain that said Astericks will be furious" (Burke to Hyman, 6 November 1964, KB). Even a decade after the novel's publication, Burke clearly felt that his influence on Ellison's work had been ignored—and, worse, repudiated by Ellison himself. Writing Ellison a year later, after the publication of *Shadow and Act,* Burke's congratulations to a friend likewise reflected the stirrings of jealousy: "Meanwhile I rejoice to see you getting so much acclaim; but I could rejoice even more if I were getting some too" (Burke to Ellison, 21 October 1965, RE).

A month later, Ellison proposed a visit to Andover as part of a television documentary on his life and work. Burke first attempted to dissuade Ellison from the project, claiming that the house would not be a suitable location for a show honoring Ellison. Though he still openly displayed a measure of envy (references to "Ellison Year" and "thy glory"), when Ellison insisted, Burke tried to reframe his actions: "I write these words, to assure you that my droopings represented not lack of joy in your advancement, but fears lest the project at this point fail to meet the Producer's explanations" (Burke to Ellison, 1 November 1965, RE). Soon after, Burke gloomily wrote Hyman of the impending event: "Ralph Ellison is coming here today with a TV crew. Channel 13 is doing a show in which he is the primus donnus" (Burke to Hyman, 6 November 1965, SH). Although the videotaping apparently went quite well (Burke to Ellison, 12 November 1965, RE), Burke's strained tone reappeared soon after, in a letter congratulating

Malcolm Cowley on an award: "Jeez, I thought that this was to be Ralph Ellison Year" (Burke to Cowley, 11 November 1965, KB).

When read together, Burke's letters from the ten-plus years following the publication of *Invisible Man* paint a very clear picture of disappointment, hurt, and jealousy over Ellison's success. Although Burke's work eventually began to receive more recognition in the late 1950s and early 1960s, he never experienced the sort of success—let alone instant success—that Ellison achieved with his first novel. Further, Ellison's seeming abandonment of his early mentor did not sit well with Burke—and Ellison's interviews discussing the influence of Eliot, Hemingway, and Twain did nothing to improve the situation. Given all available evidence, I believe that this is the best explanation for Burke's puzzling silence on *Invisible Man*. Burke was unwilling (or unable) to transcend his feelings of jealousy over Ellison's success, and thus refused to give the critical attention to the novel that Ellison clearly desired. As a result, and despite Hyman's efforts to mediate the conflict, Burke and Ellison drifted apart. Though Hyman remained close friends with both Ellison and Burke until his sudden death in 1970, he was never able to fully resolve their quarrel. As a result, the three men would never again share the close relationship they enjoyed throughout the 1940s and early 1950s.

Conclusion: Burke's Promise Fulfilled

Obviously, it is impossible to limit the account of such a complex relationship to these three periods in a fifty-year relationship, without sacrificing some of the details. Though there clearly is more to the story of the Burke-Ellison friendship than their dispute over *Invisible Man*, these three moments in time help us grapple with the personalities, struggles, successes, and failures of these two giants in American theory and criticism. Moreover, they suggest a new interpretation of Burke's late essay, "Ralph Ellison's Trueblooded *Bildungsroman*."

At first glance, as discussed in the introduction to this essay, Burke's contribution to the edited volume seems to be relatively straightforward: it is a letter from Burke to Ellison, discussing the significant elements of *Invisible Man* from a dramatistic perspective. However, this description alone should puzzle the reader: why, over thirty years later, would Burke write a letter to a close friend analyzing the plot of his novel? One answer might be that the letter, and its content, was from earlier in the relationship, just after the novel's publication. The correspondence between Burke, Ellison, and Hyman suggests that this is simply not the case. First, the essay itself was not written earlier than November, 1982 (Ellison to Burke, 7 November 1982, KB; Burke to Ellison, 26 December 1982, KB). Moreover, and more significantly, we know that Burke had not even read the novel by 1957—so he could not have written a detailed assessment of its plot and structure soon after the novel's publication. However, if we relinquish that explanation, we are simply faced with another question: if "Ralph Ellison's Trueblooded *Bildungsroman*" was an essay written long after the novel's publication, why did Burke write it in the form of a letter?

These questions, I believe, can only be adequately answered if we place the essay in the context of the unpublished correspondence between these three men. When taken together with this correspondence, I argue that we arrive at a new interpretation of Burke's late essay. I see it as neither a simple letter, nor a critical essay on Ellison's novel, but, more specifically, as the letter that Ellison waited for, and Burke never wrote: the letter offering Burke's assessment of the artistic merits of *Invisible Man*. The essay therefore is Burke's offering to Ellison, the fulfillment of a thirty-year-old promise to read and respond to his friend's first novel. Burke himself provides support for this thesis, in a brief letter he wrote to Ellison when the essay was finally completed: "'Tis done. I'm shipping it to Yaley-Waley tomorrow. It's not too good—and it's not too bad either. But I owed it to you, and I dare hope you'll like it" (Burke to Ellison, 16 August 1983, RE).

As can be seen from this note, Burke felt that he had an obligation to Ellison, and that the essay could somehow discharge that obligation. Given what we know of their history—and lacking evidence of any other debt Burke owed Ellison—I believe that Burke's essay represents a symbolic redemption, an opportunity Burke seized to make good on a pledge to a friend. Only by writing an essay devoted specifically to Ellison's novel could Burke prove to Ellison that he had read it, and that he found it to be powerful, intelligent, and worthy of its considerable acclaim; the letter that he should have written about *Invisible Man* in 1952 became the 1983 "letter" to a friend, devoted to the novel. "Ralph Ellison's Trueblooded *Bildungsroman*" thus signals Burke's approval, and his acceptance of Ellison's artistry, thirty years later than expected; its form and content attempt to make up for Burke's earlier symbolic rejection of Ellison and his work. Since both were critics, little wonder that it was only through criticism that the bond could be reaffirmed, the old debt canceled. Little wonder also that the letters Burke and Ellison exchanged in the 1980s are some of the warmest each man ever wrote to the other, a testament to the "quiet moments of antagonistic cooperation" that produced some of the finest writing of both men's careers.

Notes

1. For an insightful discussion of the tumultuous friendship between Ellison and Wright, see Jackson, "The Birth."

2. Such a reference would be even more appropriate, given that "antagonistic cooperation" is a Burkean phrase used to define and discuss dialectic.

3. For more on Ellison's childhood, and on the changes in Oklahoma's race relations, see Jackson's biography, *Ralph Ellison: Emergence of Genius*.

4. For sustained discussions of the intellectual relationship between Burke and Ellison, see Adell; Albrecht; Eddy; O'Meally, "On Burke"; Parrish (117–22); Pease; Holmes (266–69); Jackson, "The Birth" (326, 329, 336), *Ralph Ellison* (e.g. 39, 180–82, 203, 218, 229, 256, 271, 288, 294, 306, 309, 315–16, 326, 335, 351–55, 361, 380, 387–90, 395–96, 406, 419); Scruggs (e.g. 105–06, 108, 110, 117–18); and Wright (67–69). Brief treatments of the Burkean phrasings woven into Ellison's work can be found in Forrest (308–09, 314); O'Meally, "The Rules" (255, 267); and Whitaker (389–90, 394–95).

5. Other than this late text, Burke's body of work references Ellison only once, in *A Rhetoric of Motives* (193), where he quotes (without specific attribution) Ellison's essay, "Richard Wright's Blues," but makes no mention of their personal relationship.

6. As noted by Lewis, Burke's "we" might easily be expanded to include not only himself, but their mutual friends Stanley Edgar Hyman and Shirley Jackson—and, perhaps, the entire climate of Bennington College in the 1940s. Burke's use of "Nortonism" refers to a central character in *Invisible Man*—the rich, Northern, white industrialist whose donations to the Invisible Man's school are merely another form of anti-black racism.

7. This is the case even with extensive treatments of the Burke-Ellison relationship. For example, Eddy refers to it as a "letter to Ellison" (18), while Pease—although he places it within an extended dialogue over *Invisible Man*—simply notes that "in 1985, Burke published a private letter to Ellison" (74).

8. Indeed, these revisions even involved Burke's discussion of the plot points of the novel. For more on the solicitation and writing of this "letter," see the following correspondence: Kimberly Benston to Kenneth Burke, February 28, 1982, Kenneth Burke Papers; Ralph Ellison to Kenneth Burke, November 7, 1982, Kenneth Burke Papers; Kenneth Burke to Ralph Ellison, December 26, 1982, Kenneth Burke Papers; Kenneth Burke to Ralph Elli-

son, May 20, 1983, Kenneth Burke Papers; Ralph Ellison to Kenneth Burke, June 20, 1983, Kenneth Burke Papers; Kenneth Burke to Ralph Ellison, August 16, 1983, Ralph Ellison Papers; Kenneth Burke to Kimberly Benston, September 24, 1983, Ralph Ellison Papers. The Kenneth Burke Papers are housed in the Rare Books and Manuscripts Collection, Pattee Library, Pennsylvania State University. The author is grateful to Sandra Stelts, the Penn State Libraries, and the Burke Literary Trust for their help and for permission to quote from these unpublished manuscripts. All letters from Burke, but also indicated as from this collection, are carbon copies of original letters sent to others. Subsequent letters from this collection will be parenthetically indicated "KB." The Ralph Ellison Papers are housed at the Library of Congress, Washington, D.C. The author is very grateful to John Callahan, literary executor of Ellison's estate, for his assistance and his permission to quote from a portion of these unpublished manuscripts. All subsequent letters from this collection will be parenthetically indicated "RE."

9. Since the three men (and their spouses—Shirley Jackson, Fanny Ellison, and Libbie Burke) formed a close-knit relationship during the 1940s, frequently spending time together arguing, writing, and socializing, both Burke and Ellison reflect on each other—and on their friendship—in their letters to Hyman. Additionally, Hyman, like Burke, is singled out in Ellison's introduction to *Shadow and Act;* he identifies Hyman as someone "with whom I've shared a community of ideas and critical standards for two decades" (Ellison, *Collected* 60). Although little has been written about this fascinating three- (or, more properly, six-) sided friendship, brief reflections on its importance can be found in Lewis (34–37), Jackson, "The Birth" (336), and Burke ("Ralph Ellison's" 359). Tantalizing clues can also be found in Oppenheimer's comprehensive (but gossipy) biography of Shirley Jackson, *Private Demons* (e.g. 81, 103, 105, 113, 157, 181–82).

10. This essay is thus part of a larger, book-length project, which presents the complete chronicle of this friendship as part of a Burkean-Ellisonian theory of race, rhetoric, and identity. Another section of this project can be found in my essay, "Race and *A Rhetoric of Motives:* Kenneth Burke's Dialogue with Ralph Ellison."

11. Scholars who dig further can find more clues regarding Ellison's intellectual relationship with Burke. Ellison draws explicitly and implicitly upon Burkean theory in his fiction—witness, for example, the famous reference to "seeing around the corner" from *Invisible Man* (e.g. 15), as well as that to "perspective by incongruity" in the working notes for his unfinished follow-up, *Juneteenth* (352). He also offhandedly mentions many Burkean concepts in his essays and interviews: "purpose to passion to perception" (*Collected* 218); form as audience psychology (*Collected* 305; Ellison, Reed, Troupe, and Cannon 148); symbolic action (*Collected* 502, 772; Ellison, Stepto, and Harper 428; Ellison and Carson 22); language as "equipment for

living" (*Collected* 543); the dramatistic nature of social life (*Collected* 629); courtship and social relations (Ellison, Stepto, and Harper 419); comedy (*Collected* 647); "perspective by incongruity" (*Collected* 655); and the drama of Constitutions (*Collected* 773–74).

12. Ralph Ellison to Stanley Edgar Hyman, hand-dated "ca. 1942-'43," from the Stanley Edgar Hyman Papers, Library of Congress, Washington, D.C. The author wishes to express deepest gratitude to Phoebe Pettingell Hyman for her valuable insight and her permission to quote from these unpublished manuscripts. All subsequent letters from this collection will be parenthetically indicated "SH."

13. Libbie Burke to Shirley Jackson, hand-dated "December 1945," from the Shirley Jackson Papers, Library of Congress, Washington, D.C. All subsequent letters from this collection will be parenthetically indicated "SJ."

14. The constraints of this essay prevent me from exploring fully the rich nature of this text. A future essay, focused more specifically upon a Burkean-Ellisonian theory of race and rhetoric, will attempt to do justice to this complex letter.

15. Here Ellison refers to a recently-published essay by the "Southern Agrarian" Donald Davidson. Within the article, Davidson characterizes the "Negro spiritual" as simply derived from the European-influenced "white spiritual," denying that African-Americans had any significant influence on American music and culture.

16. Burke's characterization of Ellison refers to Marcus Garvey, the vocal advocate of separatist politics for African-Americans in the early part of the twentieth century.

17. As a result, these letters are more reminiscent of the Ellison-Hyman correspondence than the early Burke-Ellison correspondence.

18. Although no record remains regarding Ellison's objections to the *Rhetoric*, several possibilities arise. One certainly would involve Burke's characterization of Ellison as "The Negro Intellectual" (*Rhetoric* 193). Another, and one which will be explored in a later essay, involves Burke's renewed discussion of the difference between individual, specific, and universal motives; though it seemingly takes up Ellison's own themes from the 1945 letter, Burke recontextualizes Ellison's words. The emphasis becomes one of guilt and disloyalty rather than a false (because white) universality. For more on this point, compare Ellison's November 23, 1945, letter to passages in the *Rhetoric* (193–95).

19. Burke's letter specifically mentions excerpts previously published in *Accent*. However, in a keynote address at the 2005 Kenneth Burke Society Triennial meeting, Burke's youngest son Michael recalled Ellison reading the "Battle Royal" scene in the living room at Andover, prior to its appearance in the novel. A letter from Burke in 1957 corroborates this memory (Burke to George Knox, 16 July 1957, KB).

2 An Interview with Ben Belitt: On Kenneth Burke's Bennington Years

Michael Jackson

In the Fall of 1997, I spoke with poet Ben Belitt (1911–2003) at his home in the Old Firehouse on Paran Creek in North Bennington, Vermont. The primary purpose of this interview was to learn more about Kenneth Burke's tenure at Bennington College from 1943 to 1961.

Ben Belitt was Professor Emeritus of Language and Literature at Bennington College. In October 1998, the Louisiana State University Press published *This Scribe, My Hand: The Collected Poems of Ben Belitt*. Belitt's prior books of poetry are *Possessions* (1986), *The Double Witness* (1977), *Nowhere But Light* (1970), *The Enemy Joy* (1964), *Wilderness Stair* (1955), and *The Five-Fold Mesh* (1938). His many books of translations include *Selected Poems 1923–1967*, by Jorge Luis Borges; *Four Poems by Rimbaud: The Problem of Translation; Poems of Five Decades: 1925–1970*, by Pablo Neruda; *Selected Poems of Rafael Alberti;* and *Poet in New York: Federico García Lorca*. His most recent book of critical essays is The *Forgèd Feature* (1995). Belitt was a Guggenheim Fellowship recipient in 1945.

As a young assistant editor at *The Nation* in the 1930s, Belitt often solicited book reviews from Burke and prodded Burke to meet deadlines. During this period, Belitt would frequently mingle with Burke and other intellectuals associated with *The Nation* at Eda Lou Walton's apartment at 61 Morton Street, New York City. In a letter to Burke dated May 18, 1952, Belitt confesses that these early encounters with Burke "shook me out of my Jeffersonian daydream."

From 1948 to 1961, Belitt and Burke were colleagues at Bennington College. Even as a colleague, Belitt says that he was "so much in awe of [Burke] that I would never go rousting about and wasn't as intimate with him as I might have been." Belitt says that Burke's rigorous and creative endeavors in criticism helped to "replenish whatever it is that I expended" in poetry and translation. Belitt used a passage from *Permanence and Change*[1] as the epigraph to an early series of sonnets entitled "In Time of Armament." Their relationship seems to have been one of mutual respect. In a letter dated March 20, 1945, Belitt thanks Burke for "endorsing my Guggenheim dossier."

In the following interview, translation is Belitt's primary strategy by which to conjure the Bennington Burke. "I've been involved in the whole gory battlefronts of translation," says Belitt. As one who has both translated poetry and has had his poetry translated, Belitt is sensitive to dictionary-based, literal translation. "Anyone who writes with a deaf ear for what's happening in English and gives you what's happening in the dictionary—If you've been a victim of that as a poet yourself, you say 'for god's sake lay your hands off it.'" When Belitt translates another poet's work into English, he feels that "two voices should be heard. . . . The English is mine; the poem is his." In "translating" for us Burke's Bennington years, it is as if Belitt weaves three voices: One voice focuses directly on Burke and Bennington College; another reveals glimpses of Belitt's own oeuvre; and still another urges us to recognize Burke's strong influence on Belitt's work.

Belitt had prepared a statement to open our interview:

> I first encountered Burke in New York through Eda Lou Walton. My acquaintance with Eda Lou Walton was a lucky dividend of her sponsorship of college poets at both NYU and elsewhere. She was the watchful curator of a magazine devoted to the surveillance and publication of college verse in the early 1930s. In 1932 she wrote me at Virginia to say that my "contributions to *College Verse* are the best poems I've seen in some time" and invited me to call on her on my visit to New York during the summer of that year. Thereafter, during a subsequent interval of residence in New York as assistant literary editor of *The Nation* (1932–1937), I was her neighbor on 61 Morton St. and frequent guest of her seances for a striking fellowship of poets and intellectuals connected with *The Nation*, which included Louise Bogan, Leonie Adams, William Troy, and Kenneth Burke, among others. While still a graduate student at the University of Virginia (1932–1935), I had already marveled at

celebrities legendary to me at a distance: it was Eda Lou who first gave me access to Leonie and Louise on paper and as palpable presences, and who eventually dazzled me with a copy of *Attitudes Toward History* in 1937—which she regarded as a breakthrough for progressive philosophy in America and a prophecy of things to come in a revolution of American taste. She associated Burke with her own search for contemporary check-points and a changing of winds blowing from the Left—and she was determined to jolt me out of the academic complacencies of graduate study at the University of Virginia. As it turned out, she also hastened my abandonment of a PhD thesis-in-progress on Chekhov and Katherine Mansfield and my unexpected candidacy for a stint as Assistant Literary Editor of *The Nation*. As it happened, Troy and Burke were both regular critics for *The Nation* as well as guests at the soirees on Morton Street; and Bill and Leonie were also members of the faculty at Bennington College when the vacancy at *The Nation* occurred. It was the triad of Bill and Leonie and Eda Lou Walton that opened up for me the pages of *The Nation* as prentice/reviewer; and my apprenticeship there unexpectedly landed me on the staff of *The Nation* itself in 1936. By yet another trick of coincidence, Burke (who had joined the faculty of Bennington College in 1943) was in his ascendancy when I returned to teach there in 1948 after a five-year absence.

In 1948, the Bennington scene was nothing short of luminous with talents of unprecedented proportion: there was a pantheon of poets, including Stanley Kunitz, Theodore Roethke, Howard Nemerov, and myself; and a duo of critics in the pairing of Stanley Edgar Hyman and Kenneth Burke. At the time, Kenneth was lodged in one of the two cottages reserved for personnel on the move: I at Cricket Hill and Kenneth at Shingle Cottage at the turn of the road to North Bennington. At the innermost circle were Kenneth and Howard and Hyman, whose periodic poker sessions and carousals were already inscribed in the mythology of Bennington as a fellowship of Homeric proportions. My own contacts with Burke were very casual by comparison: a neighborly give-and-take of visits from Shingle to Cricket and Cricket to Shingle for conversational exchanges and the transaction of Collegiate and pedagogical business.

On the whole I would say that Kenneth's conversational approach was memorable for its improvisational character—monologues punctuated by uproarious laughter and self-mockery, direct hits of conviction and wonder, silences, repositionings, surrenders. On yet another occasion when I accompanied Eda Lou and her adoptive protégé, Henry Roth, on a visit to Kenneth in Andover as on-looker and over-hearer, I was left to wonder at the *dailiness* of conjugal rusticity. At his best, however, I had the sense of unsparing intellectual assault and a tilting with possibility that turned all answers into reversals of quest and initiative. His concern was with the potentiality rather than the finality of things; with ricochet rather than arrivals. His totem-animal was Coleridge's water-spider that "wins its way up against the stream by alternate pulses of active and passive motion to gather strength for a further propulsion."

I think whatever Kenneth did in the classroom, these things could be both a strength and they might be a weakness. I was often left to wonder at a public talk or something whether the audience appreciated what was going on because his purpose, as I say, wasn't to dazzle, but this constant agitation, this propulsion moving this way and that, like the water spider. Keats called it "negative capability." And I think that's the real clue to the spirit of his attack on matters of great seriousness and complexity.

MJ: Did Burke give a lot of public talks in Bennington?

BB: I would say that he didn't obtrude himself. In faculty meetings with the rest of us, he didn't try to revise or to challenge whatever it is we had in common. I think he chose rather to be watchful and more silent than vocal and to give the initiative to the faculty or another colleague. So there was nothing spectacular about his sense of "here I am at Bennington; it's progressive; it's a college that many are concerned about"; he was reclusive.

MJ: You said you would sometimes talk to him about pedagogical concerns?

BB: I can't remember; they were just routine things. And he was perfectly content to treat them as such; he didn't try to constantly assert his dominance in intellect; in fact Bennington was really a secondary area of his predations. And he came here to teach and also to work as it were on the connections that were whirling in his mind; then Burke was always exploring the realm of a book that was in progress; we all did that. I did that. Of course, it was way above the heads of the sophomore or junior or senior, but we all did that. We were aloft and the whole idea was to exceed oneself as a teacher and to get the students to exceed themselves, and the courses were memorable for that very reason. Later in life students would tell you, "I never really exerted myself in the realm of ideas and issues and values as I did when I was a student at Bennington" because there was nothing cautionary about our sense of what was appropriate. And there was always something very private about one's creation of a course and one's own movement in the realm of ideas and issues.

MJ: So you approached the design of a course as you would approach a book?

BB: Yes, but also we felt that it wasn't an academic kind of retelling of the content of this or that. But that it was the whole depth and passion of inquiry. There was something very intellectual and passionate going on there at the same time because this was the means by which the teacher was discovering his own identity and the means by which the students also came to create their identities. And that's about the secret of what Bennington was doing—identity-making. And that's not too far from what Keats was saying, that poetry is identity-making. They were not academic pedagogies; there were real reasons for our own inquiry into the things that were moving us directly into what we would then turn to on our own, and that was encouraged.

MJ: Burke also talked about identification, didn't he?

BB: That sounds so academic, doesn't it? But there was this dance going on; and there is this restlessness, as I say, love of ricochet, bouncing this off of that. I keep thinking of basketball: There is a team—and that's what you're watching—then someone breaks from it and moves toward some objective and that's what you watch—that's also the game. It's not a departure from the basketball team and the court to move toward the basket. That's the whole point of it. And the whole point of ours was to touch and to activate the energies of those who came to listen, but remained to participate.

MJ: There was a flux of faculty coming and going, wasn't there?

BB: Yes, but on the whole there wasn't too much of that, just "experimentation" with teachers. At least the group we had tended to stay. But also the college could always spot from afar volatile talents and would invite them here for sojourns, and that was particularly the case during the war years, when people like myself were away. So we got Auden here and we got others who came and went. Malcolm Cowley was here and had these contacts also with Kenneth. I wasn't around; I was, as I say, nonacademic and had these other concerns. I was busy on something I call "The School of the Soldier"[2] which has to do with the preparation of complex people for direct expenditures in acts of warfare and violence—basic training. And I had to find a way to say that this was an important thing: action and not language as action was what you had to accept as the whole function of your activity there.

MJ: One reason rhetoricians like Burke is that he also concentrated on the relationship between language and action. Jack Selzer has described him as an aesthete early in his career in New York (Selzer 19), but. . . .

BB: Oh yes, there's a whole thing of mine—a collection of poems—that's coming out in the Fall I call "The School of the Soldier" in which I try to convince myself and force myself to say that the important thing is "pure act" that was not verbal but physical. The government would place a gun in your hand and then send you out on a mission of murder. Basic training does what it can, but you couldn't survive that unless you had certainly totally changed your character—which I did so effectively that when I was dismissed from the army I wouldn't go back to Bennington for two years. I didn't want anything to do with words or anything to do with Bennington.

MJ: Burke said that during the First World War he wasn't accepted due to health reasons.

BB: Does he comment on that?

MJ: I don't know, but he said he was stuck somewhere, perhaps Pittsburgh, making gauges to measure gauges (Foss et al. 155).

BB: Well I had a broken knee from the age of 19 in college and they said, "Well, it's up to you." I was inducted right here in Bennington in 1942 and went to basic training the first morning of '43. Bennington had been turned into a farm and all that was their way of being basic. And so basic training in Bennington became "basic studies." That was the operative word. And then we all tried to adapt the circumstance and the landscape of Bennington to the mission that we could connect with a country at war. But of course Burke wasn't here, so it doesn't figure. Burke doesn't hit the place, I gather, until 1943. But again, this is from me ricochet; I had known Burke—looked at and listened to him worshipfully at a distance as a protégé of Eda Lou's. And also they were very close to Bill and Leonie. And Bill and Leonie, along with Kenneth, were very well known and highly esteemed at the time for very good reason. That's why I had to go through a very circuitous route to orient myself; I was trying to make a map that leads to where we can talk about Burke.

MJ: Your understanding of the relationship between words and actions, which you learned from the war, seems quite relevant to Burke's concern with language as symbolic action.

BB: Oh yes, I don't know if you've read them, but I've spent most of my life as a translator, a whole series of ten or fifteen books of translations, as well as two books of essays in which you can just see I mention Kenneth now and then, particularly this whole concept of perspectival incongruity. I mean his terms are the ones which still are the operative ones for me. And also my preoccupation with Coleridge is a consequence of Burke's respect for him. And also, when he was teaching the rhetoric of religion, I was teaching a course called Literature and Belief, which had to do with a secular consideration of the Old and the New Testament—a very important venture. One of the essays in my book is based in this course. This is what I was saying earlier: I would reconstruct my identity or my priorities in the classroom. And that was not only allowable, but it was really the secret of the extra dimension of student accomplishment and achievement at Bennington, and not characteristic of most colleges.

MJ: So you would prepare a class lecture?

BB: Oh yes, very much so. But you don't just lecture a course at Bennington. You then induce this kind of scurrying. It's a basketball court. So you then sort of lead the chase and when you have set into that kind of pedagogical motion the minds in front of you and the attention, and also the participation, which is the real proof of it, then you've got it. It would fall on deaf ears and nothing would happen in most of the conventional graduate classes. Anything I was studying at the U. of Virginia was burdensomely pedantic. So it wasn't pedantry we were after, but identity—my identity and you couldn't stop that because there was this constant element of risk, the whole secret of Bennington and the whole secret of the movements on the basketball court is you're working on a team, you've had relations with them, and then you cut forward through the resistance of the opposing team. . . . I hope that doesn't trivialize it. It's a matter of the secret of what initiative is and what it comes from and also it debunks the idea that initiative is really self-seeking and egotistic. It is a sense of working against the possibility of spectacular losses and rebuffs.

MJ: When we talked on the phone, you said it surprised you when Burke got interested in the rhetoric of religion.

BB: Well yes, totally. Nothing before had given any hint—just as it surprises me, I wonder what the hell did Burke know about music? How could he have been a music critic for both *The Dial* and *The Nation*? Have you read any of the reviews he wrote as a music critic? I'd be very curious about that, to see whether he was tactical and philosophical. I don't know what he was after in his criteria of the judgment of musical utterance; language, that's different, because any language of poetry involves musicality. You can't function without accepting that interpenetration.

MJ: When you were assistant editor of *The Nation,* did you ever edit Burke's music reviews?

BB: I was there when he was writing for it, but I don't remember his music reviews. At the instruction of Krutch [the editor] I would make these arrangements with the reviewers and attend to the mechanics of transacting those connections. And during those years, if you read *The Nation,* you'll find that it's full of reviews by me and also articles and also notes on the theater and motion pictures, which Krutch turned over to me. So they allowed me pretty free range and it was an exceptional opportunity for me. If you look up some of those issues from 1936 and 1937, you'll see that there are all sorts of reviews of poetry, novels, fictions, and also some articles that created debate in the pages there. I wrote one piece on vanity publishers and poetry, which went on for some time in the course of which someone threatened to sue *The Nation* for defamation of character.

MJ: I've heard of these, where you pay to have your work published; I think they still do that, don't they?

BB: Oh yes, so I did that, and I was also very much interested in drama and theater, and the new forms of documentary—photography, Paul Strand, and new things that were on the rise, motion pictures. And that carried through to after I was discharged from the army. There I landed into a military police battalion. And then I went through all that business, until they discovered later when we had joined forces with Russia that they needed people in languages, so I was sent to study Russian at Cornell. Then I went back to the army, but during preparation I injured my back climbing obstacles or something. After that I was very angry at the army for dismissing me; I said, "You still taught me Russian." But they said, "No, you have to realize that we'd be best served if you didn't associate with us." So by my own choice, I went to the signal corps in Queens, New York, and they hired me and I helped to revise a whole manual on photography in the field. Then finally I was associated with an historical project—all the film coming in from the fronts was screened in Queens at that center, a photographic center for the army. And we each had a segment that we identified and put together and I did a twenty-three--reel film on the Battle of the Bulge. So I did all kinds of weird things. And Eda Lou, again, is the one who jolted me out of it.

MJ: Jack Selzer has suggested that Burke's interest in music corresponded to his early interest in and emphasis upon form.

BB: Oh, form, yes. What is form? Because, again, most of the criticism of Kenneth Burke is that he is so form-less. I mean he expatiates; and carries it out into space and risks it and doesn't conclude anything in the way that people obsessed by a formulation write books cunningly or willfully or whatever to accomplish preconceived aims. There are no preconceptions in Burke. In my latest book, I have a series of four essays on poetry and quantum mechanics. That kind of venture, I learned from Burke. To risk it that way and not to dominate the question I raise but to try the risks of entering an area which was not one's obsession. So I wish you'd read some of that. The last two essays in the book have mostly to do with the application of all things quantum to Gerard Manly Hopkins. Now that kind of freewheeling and yet perilous venture was in the spirit of Kenneth Burke; he is my master. And that happened from the very first time I set eyes to *Attitudes Toward History*. I was drowning in the words, but the whole thing was full of excitement and also revelations. And as I said, I taught Literature and Belief and that first essay in the book is really most of what I began with, but also I was making my criteria of how it is you enter an area of dispute or uncertainty. This is something Burke made me feel comfortable in. Of course uncertainty is the thing he is so adept in using to positive advantage. That's what Keats meant by negative capability: withholding any kind of sense of working towards a completion of a task, but reconnoiter, that's the thing. But in the deepest sense that was where Burke was very, very present within me. I haven't read all of his work, but the ones that mattered to me most—*Attitudes Toward His-*

tory, Permanence and Change, A Grammar of Motives—those criteria are the ones that stayed with me and replenished whatever it is that I expended.

MJ: When Burke left Bennington, why did he leave?
BB: I don't know. Can you tell me?
MJ: No, I don't know either.
BB: And when did he die?
MJ: In 1993, I think.
BB: Oh, in 1993—a hale old age!

We move out onto his deck overlooking Paran Creek.

BB: In my Belief and Literature course we'd say, "Well, what is belief?" And someone might say, "You believe in the novel when you are reading it." Or "I believe in the Bible." "Then start reading it and see what comes from just its composition rather than what is prescribed by theological propriety." In fact, that's what you avoid. So all of that was a very Burkean thing, and he was doing it at the time and I said [laughing], "What's he doing teaching my course?" He taught me to never be afraid of adventure, both as a poet and in the people I wanted to write about; you see, there was quite an assortment. And also very much in the literatures of Spain and Italy and their contemporary poets of the highest magnitude that I translate—without any sense of doing something impertinent or rash. And, of course, you had to study the languages, too.

MJ: When you taught Literature and Belief and Burke taught Rhetoric of Religion, did you have students who were taking both of your classes?

BB: I don't know. But he never talked about that with me. His relation to me, again, was very helpful and admiring—he wrote some blurbs on the jackets of my books of poetry and that was very genuine and very private. But that was why I was in Bennington, because Leonie and Bill who saw me at work on *The Nation* recommended a person who hadn't taught! I didn't know for sure but thought I'd try it. And that's why I felt so at home in the spontaneities of discovery that were part of Kenneth's thinking: He'd take an ounce of anything and come back with unthinkable returns because you didn't expect the conclusions to be what they were or, again, he would point to more problems. He'd seethe all of the time. They were a hard-drink-ing bunch, too, Kenneth, Stanley, and particularly Howard Nemerov. They would have these kabals, and they would gamble until early in the morning, and then they would go off and get high—Howard has a poem about their going up into the mountains and stripping and dunking into the mountain stream. It's a wonderful poem, a poem of some length, a narrative poem expressing all of that willful breaking of regulations:

> Our easy bones groaned, our flesh baked
> on one side and shuddered on the other; and each man
> thought bitterly about primitive simplicity
> and decadence, and how he had been ruined
> by civilization. (from "A Day on the Big Branch," by Howard Nemerov)

MJ: What kind of rapport did Burke and Auden have?

BB: Well, I don't know. Auden came when I went to the war; he replaced me and stayed for only a semester or so. Again, the reputation of Bennington was such that it always drew this kind of venturesome expert.

At this point, Belitt and I were "distracted" by the splendid autumn foliage along Paran Creek. After some talk of the view, we found ourselves on the topic of translation:

BB: I've been involved in the whole gory battlefronts of translation—I believe that two voices should be heard because one voice is using English and is inseparable from it. The Spanish poet would never have dreamt of initiating his project in the English language—and once you have given a flat dictionary rendering, it doesn't get you anywhere.

MJ: Joseph Brodsky addresses this phenomenon in a series of English poems about his parents who died before he began working in English and who couldn't speak any English themselves. He was very self-conscious about the fact that these poems were composed in English. Like the Spanish poet, the Russian parents didn't expect to be translated into English.

BB: Of course he didn't. And also, once you begin to be moved and set up a pulsation, the rhythms that are native to the English word have nothing to do with the accidents that happen to be a part of Spanish; the English is of longer or shorter duration, is full of vowel sounds or consonant sounds which have impact that are, of course, no reduplication of the autonomous thing. Language compels autonomy: anyone who writes with a deaf ear for what's happening in English and gives you what's happening in the dictionary—If you've been a victim of that as a poet yourself, you say "for god's sake lay your hands off of it." I got a call from a poet in Canada—an Argentine poet—who said "please deliver me." He wants an English translation of his poetry and he's been the victim of this other thing that happens.

MJ: How do you decide whether to translate a poet's work?

BB: Well, we have to see how we get on together, and whether the work is something that brings out of me that sort of expenditure; I can't force it. I do it because the English is mine; the poem is his. Again, this is the poetics of uncertainty. Isn't that what Burke is doing? It's in his veins. But then again, have you read his poetry?

MJ: I haven't seen much of it.

BB: It's awful. It's so surprisingly trivial. He loved to be a poet; he wanted above all things—and he insisted on publishing—and I gather there's something called a "collected poems" and I don't know what that would come to because one volume was, to say the least, not disappointing but dismaying. It was so far from what you would think. Sometimes you would follow the great critics through what they did as poets to get a sense of their excitement and also their initiative. Funny because in a way, Burke entered all sorts of areas and territories that he himself was not really involved in. But turn him loose in the realm of theory and idea and he *is* a poet. That's what I sensed: someone with this capacity for self-demolishment and self-advancement.

MJ: What are you working on now?

BB: Well, in the Fall of 1998, Louisiana State University Press will publish my collected poems. The title is *This Scribe, My Hand*. This title is a quotation from Keats, which I used in an epigraph to a poem.

MJ: Is "School of the Soldier" in the collected poems edition?

BB: Yeah, it is; but it was first published in 1949. I wrote it really during the first few months of basic training, simply to keep my head together. I had to find some way of saying it's right for me to wish to be a pure piece of action, and I'm grateful for those who take me out on the drill field and say by the numbers, "left face, right face, do this, do that," mindlessly as a whole effective volume, an entity which can only accomplish directives, but the intent is the destruction of a hated enemy. You can make a case for it and I do, but it's a kind of mistake and, as I say in the end, it's really an act of self-destruction, a suicide that I was doing. Still, it's what I needed to do to go on as a private in the ranks; I never rose above private first-class studying languages.

MJ: You said that Burke has commented on some of your books of poetry?

BB: Oh yeah, I have a couple of letters. Have you seen any letters of his? They are, again, self-mocking, in that they adopt some of the clichés of the highway and work against them; he wanted to say something that gives perspective by incongruity. That's exactly what they do; he's incongruously plainspoken. Sometimes you would think his letters were so disappointing in that he would talk just like a clown, but the clown thing is all a very serious venture. And that's in the picture, too—the clown, as well as the athlete and the basketball player, something involving a team. Inside the very discipline of the group is the breakaway and the unforeseen contingency of what happens that day to a trained athlete in a public exhibition: "Well, he did good today," or "he didn't do it today . . ."

Notes

1. This series of sonnets appears in *The Five-Fold Mesh*. The epigraph is the final sentence in *Permanence and Change:* "And in this staggering disproportion between man and no-man, there is no place for purely human boasts of grandeur, or for forgetting that men build their cultures by huddling together, nervously loquacious, at the edge of an abyss."

2. This poem first appeared in *Quarterly Review of Literature* 5.1 (1949) and reappeared in *This Scribe My Hand*.

3 Denis Donoghue's Kenneth Burke

Miriam Marty Clark

On New Year's Day, 1980, Kenneth Burke wrote to his friend Denis Donoghue that he had just returned "from the field of battle, the MLA meeting" held in San Francisco a few days before. "On the way back," he writes, "at some time around three or so o'clock at the time where the plane was, in darkest AM, I was a-reading Donoghue anent Ashbery, in a darkened plane, except for a bead of light bearing down upon thy text alone, while at my side there slept (as safe as a *Comus* virgin) an unknown, untouchable, darling seat-companion—and never cd. I have been more grateful for an opportunity to commune with a study of *attitudes* that don't lead to *action*."[1]

The bead of light falls not on the text alone, of course, but also on Burke's witty self-construction: aged warrior, mid-night reader, would-be romancer of the red-eye flight. Burke's use of Donoghue using Burke—the comic theme of the letter—has its context in a friendship that spanned a quarter of a century from the mid-1960s into Burke's old age, an association amply documented in the letters of the Burke archive and in Donoghue's published recollections.[2] Burke's centrality to Donoghue's thought is evident in the number and variety of citations across Donoghue's many books. The younger critic—indebted to "Cher Maitre!" as he calls him in a September 27, 1975, letter—borrows titles, passages for epigraphs, terms, phrases, mottos. "When in Rome, do as the Greeks" may be his most frequently cited tag (*CS* 119); it turns up again and again in his books and essays where it captures both the antinomian spirit he reveres and Burke's acute grasp of the human terminological situation. Donoghue reviewed Burke's books as they were reissued, reflected—under changing light as the twentieth century advanced—on Burke's terms and ideas, and returned again and again to Burke as a vital presence whose work shapes his way of reading, thinking, and talking about literature.

So what was Burke reading that night at the end of 1979? It was almost certainly Donoghue's review of John Ashbery's *As We Know*, an essay that appeared a few weeks later in the *New York Review of Books* and again in Donoghue's 1987 collection *Reading America*. "Normally," Donoghue notes in that brief essay, "attitudes are preparations for acts, but in some cases, as Kenneth Burke has pointed out, they are substitutes for the corresponding acts." This "recession from acts to attitudes" has uses for Ashbery, Donoghue notes: "it provides 'an open field of narrative possibilities' instead of a single story he is no longer disposed to endow with authority. So long as his poems do not tell stories as privileged interpretations of what happened," he adds, "they make spaces to move around in" (*Reading* 307–8).

Although this review is a minor piece and was not written for a specialized audience of literary critics and theorists, it is highly consistent with Donoghue's extended critical project: an argument in behalf of poetics and a *re-valuation* of aesthetics as indispensable to human freedom, ethics, and social justice. But it's not just Burke's response that makes this particular essay interesting to me. Written in the middle of a period of intensive reassessment and ideology critique of Burke that runs from the English Institute in 1977 (see White and Brose) through the publication of Cary Nelson's influential essay in 1989, the review presses a humanist reading of Burke, one that contrasts strikingly with the Marxist and post-humanist positions at stake in Jameson, Lentricchia, and Nelson.

Cary Nelson marks the distinction between humanist and post-humanist readings of Burke incisively, if without subtlety. "Put baldly," he writes, "the issue is whether one sees the symbol-using animal in Burke as an independent agent or as a figure occupying the role of agency within a verbal drama that is in a sense already written for us" ("Writing" 157). That he, like Donoghue, addresses Burke's thinking in terms of narrative possibility makes the differences between the two very clear; for a moment the essays seem to stand face to face. If Donoghue's Burke stands for open possibilities, freedom, unconstrained agency, space to move among narratives in resistance to the claims of any "single story," Nelson's "counter-Burke" reckons its opposite, a culturally constructed agency enclosed within an already written story.

It's not my intent to quarrel with either reading; for one thing, these two Burkes derive from different sources—Donoghue's from the early and middle work, particularly *Counter-Statement* and *Towards a Better Life*,[3] Nelson's from *The Rhetoric of Religion* and the essays of the late sixties and seventies—and they serve markedly different purposes. But the moment invites some resistance to the abrogation of old terms by new ones, the simple burial of humanist under post humanist readings. Nelson relegates Donoghue and Wayne Booth to an old school of Burke scholars—"Marie Nichols, Bernard Brock, Leland Griffin, and Lloyd Bitzer" ("Writing" 157)—dismissing their readings as humanist, trivializing, and reductive. What gets lost in this transaction, in Donoghue's case at least, is not only a series of astute engagements of Burke's terms and ideas but an alternative way of understanding Burke's place in contemporary critical and theoretical conversation.

Donoghue's humanism encompasses a set of closely related commitments elaborated in his work of the last two decades: to the virtuality of art, the belief that art has no representational responsibility toward the world or being but exists purely to be perceived;[4] to the irreducibility of human experience to material conditions; to the force of the imagination not only in the cause of pleasure and individual freedom but also for social justice and common good; and to the validity of individual consciousness and introspection against widespread critical devaluations of "inwardness" (*Being* 71). If these commitments place him directly at odds with theorists like Jameson and Nelson, they emerge not in isolation but in dialogue with a wide range of thinkers of the last half century, from R. P. Blackmur, Suzanne Langer, and Herbert Marcuse to Derrida, De Man, Habermas, De Certeau, Bourdieu, and Emmanuel Levinas. For Donoghue as for many critics of the 1990s, Levinas opens a conversation as deeply provocative as it is challenging. Donoghue wrestles with Levinas's rejection of literature as occasion for ethical encounter but finds in him important support for his own belief in the moral and ethical value of interiority. "The inner life," he quotes Levinas in *Totality and Infinity* (58), "is the unique *way* for the real to exist as a plurality" (*Being* 71).[5] On the next page, he goes on to cite a later passage in which the dangers of collectivity are more fully elaborated. "One begins with the idea that duality must be transformed into unity," Levinas writes, "and that social relations must culminate in communion. This is the last vestige of a conception that identifies being with knowledge, that is, with the event through which the multiplicity of reality ends up referring to a single being and where, through the miracle of clarity, everything that encounters me exists as coming from me" ("Other" 164). If the terms of his encounter with Levinas—like those with Marcuse and Bourdieu—reflect Donoghue's longstanding commitment to the ethical and political significance of subjectivity, they also parallel his much more extended conversation with Burke.

Reading against the powerful draw of unity and universality in Burke's elaborations of dramatism,[6] Donoghue finds in Burke a similar (if very differently oriented) regard for multiplicity and interiority. From *Counter-Statement* through *A Grammar of Motives* and beyond it, what interests Donoghue most is Burke's grasp of how literary forms act to sustain multiple realities. As Burke's ideas are deployed across wider and wider fields of culture, Donoghue presses the case that Burke is foremost a literary critic. This is not simply a declaration of his own literary critical stakes; it's a measure of Burke's importance in a world where literature, for its powers of contradiction and counter-statement, and against the encroachments of popular culture, plays a vital role in individual and cultural well being. It is literature that resists the complacencies of materialism, reckoning the inner life as the space of freedom, invention, resistance, responsiveness, ethical action—the things that refuse and stand against the culturally imposed stories. The beauty of literature, Donoghue observes in *Speaking of Beauty*, "seems to entail resistance to the official designations of reality. [. . .] Society makes statements and sends forth instructions, edicts, laws, definitions of reality. Literature makes counter-statements, Greek when official designations are Roman." What's at issue here is not simply a reassertion of subjective power—humanist vs. post humanist—but substantially raised stakes for *poetics* as a field of moral and social significance. Literature, Donoghue continues,

> makes these counter-statements not discursively but formally: as particular forms to be apprehended, achievements of invention and style, the right words in the right order, proprieties of cadence and invention. That is why it cannot be reduced to the journalism of themes or the commonplaces of social practice. *Works of literature are forms of composition rather than forms of designation.* (*Speaking* 114, emphasis added)

Donoghue approaches the matter from a somewhat different angle in an essay on Alistair MacIntyre's *After Virtue*. Concerned with the interminable and unsettled character of contemporary moral debate, MacIntyre searches unsuccessfully, Donoghue notes, for "a common stock of concepts and norms which all may employ and to which all may appeal" (MacIntyre 252).[7] Donoghue notes that the same situation is true in literary criticism: "At present," he writes, "no school of criticism holds power, except among its scholars" (*Adam's* 129). This claim might simply offer a parallel story—chaos everywhere—attended by a comparable dismay. Instead he embarks on a different line of reasoning—most immediately informed by William Empson but also deeply influenced by Burke. What's needed, he suggests, quoting Empson, "is not to understand things, but to maintain one's defences and equilibrium and live as well as one can" (247).[8] In any articulate system of moral reasoning, Donoghue argues, terms inevitably become slogans which "disengage intelligence from the question in hand" and become exclusive, "designed to keep out rival claimants." Apparently innocent words "become ideologically charged, as if they wanted to turn themselves into manifestos or institutions: structure becomes Structuralism, form Formalism, existence Existentialism [. . .] and in each case disinterestedness gives way to a note of institutional arrogance. The only hope," Donoghue adds, "seems to me to remain in efforts of particularity, analysis, and irony. These efforts will not release us from the murky air of rhetoric, but there is no escaping that. Each of us wants to win" (*Adam's* 129).

It's worth noting how this essay ends. Rejecting MacIntyre's appeal to Aristotelian tradition, Donoghue offers no alternative solution to contemporary chaos. Instead he offers a statement of "what I think should be the case," a "school of criticism" that reflects his own views. "A school of criticism," he writes, "would be concerned with Poetics; that is, with the principles of language and form operative in works of literature. Locally, it would be concerned with methods of reading: how to read a poem, a work of fiction, a page. And it should act upon a number of related assumptions. Put with necessary brevity: it should ponder the relations among certain critical positions which I designate as Susanne K. Langer, Louise M. Rosenblatt, D. W. Harding, Geoffrey Hill, and Kenneth Burke" (129–30). Donoghue notes that he has already written at length about each of these worthies, but he outlines their contributions briefly, ending in this way: "Kenneth Burke, for his rhetoric, his sense of form and style as responsive to human desires and fulfillments."

In "The Force of Form," an essay that first appeared in *New Literary History* in 1999, Donoghue offers an extended consideration of literary form and provides a valuable context for his discussions of Burke. He draws from a range of poets and critics including Genette, Adorno, Bourdieu, advancing a series of interconnected definitions of "form": form is the conversion of matter "so far as possible" to spirit (*Speaking* 107); it is the "transposition of an objective reality to a subjective reality" [Wallace Stevens] (109); the deployment of energy to direct chaotic forces [Marshall Brown] (123); the particular form of a creative force bursting into being (125). It is, he writes, citing Bourdieu, "the value which allows writers to stand aside from political issues, even in the midst of public clamor, and to mind their own artistic business; the value that permits writers to take part in political conflict, but with weapons that 'are not those of politics'" (133). It is—and by now there is almost no need to cite Burke—"the creation of a desire and the adequate satisfaction of that desire" (134). Burke's understanding of form occupies a central and enduring place in Donoghue's thinking because on the one side, as counter-statement, it engages culture and the world of objects and on the other it traces the subtler and more mysterious trajectory of human feelings and experiences, the structures and sequences Burke calls "motives."

In focusing on the motives, experiences, and strategies at stake in poetic form, Donoghue's argument again stands in striking opposition to Nelson's. Forms involve acts of opposition, conversion, transformation, participation, creation. The symbolic animal is beset but undiminished. Though it does not serve the purposes of ideological critique, Donoghue's humanist reading moves to restore the aesthetic and the literary to full participation in an ongoing conversation about culture and human well being.

I want to end by advancing a more modest claim: that Donoghue describes with unusual clarity the terms of Burke's engagement with twentieth-century American poetry and the grounds for his influential, if sometimes fraught, friendships with American poets. Those associations extend far beyond the scope of the present essay, but I want to pause briefly over a moment of convergence that may help to illustrate this claim, a two-day conference at Seton Hall University in early December of 1986. The occasion, which anticipated Burke's 90th birthday, featured critics Harold Bloom, Paul Jay, J. Hillis Miller, William Rueckert, and Denis Donoghue as well as writers Ralph Ellison, Howard Nemerov, and A. R. Ammons. Donoghue spoke on "Kenneth Burke and the Status of Style," a talk that "greatly moved" Burke, according to a letter he wrote a few days after the event. But here I want to shift my attention to another participant at the Seton Hall conference, poet A. R. Ammons. Not a friend like Williams or Nemerov but a late acquaintance and, more to the point, a thoughtful reader of Burke over several decades,[9] Ammons read a poem called "Information Density." The poem, which later appeared in his volume *Sumerian Vistas* with a dedication to Burke, goes like this:

> Generalization scans the contours of terrain
> for the spot to take on concretion in,
> the way a squirrel, having floated through
> arches, zigzagged, digs for a nut, pear core,
> or pats one in: generalization acquaints us
> with the wider forms of disposition, airily
> leaves out a lot in order to be cursory and
> carries little substance so as to move big:
> the squirrel pops erect, checks out the boughs
> for dozing leapers, the bushes for stingers
> snapping approaches, and waits to see if in the
> chinks between branches a hawk's
> roving connects dots into nearing curvatures,
> then lets fall light forefeet and
> nuzzles into the ground again: the world,
> not everything, need not be less than
> it is—animals thrive and fail in similar
> problems of motion and risk, pull and haul:
> the jay lights squalling right into what he wants:
> the eagle wheels up into the rigorous quiet, higher
> and higher to find the right piece of ground.[10]

Like Donoghue's reading of Burke, Ammons's stresses the mind as it moves in the text. The poem hovers between desire and fulfillment in overlapping syllogistic progressions. Initially the poem is framed—in dramatistic terms—as a meditation on intellectual desire: generalization seeks its fulfillment in concretion; concrete detail pursues its satisfaction in larger schemes; scope and ground are suspended in mutual desire. At the same time, intellectual action is imagined as motion: the mind's desires are construed as creature needs—for food or safety, height or ground. Alternatively, animal instinct—non-symbolic motion—takes on the grander terms of symbolic action. The squirrel's cautious pounce, the jay's noisy landing are rendered as intellectual pursuit and fulfillment. In the first instance the chaos of the world submits to reason: the achieved balance, the warranted risk, the passionate logic of conversation or the cold logic of the food chain. In the second, orders of reason give way to chaos, noise, danger, joy. Fulfillment either way. The poem floats, zigzags, roves, nuzzles, wheels. The world is "not everything"—that's the poem's counter-statement. The mind moves among stories in unfolding (if also *prior*) forms of desire and fulfillment. The poem doesn't ask for a decision—which way to read, which thing to privilege; it doesn't seek action or to be obeyed, only to be inhabited in its moment.

"Form," Donoghue writes in "The Force of Form," "transfigures what otherwise merely exists, and by that transfiguration it maintains the validity of freedom" (*Speaking* 121). Against the density of information, the press of ideologies, and the severities of the natural order, Ammons's poem creates—in Burkean terms, by Burkean measures—a form in which the world is not everything. What the mind seeks, what the body demands, what the material world offers, what art makes possible—these things converge, not as knowledge or mastery but as vital play across the wide space words make.

NOTES

1. Letter dated January 1, 1980. A carbon copy is part of the Burke archive at Penn State University. Quoted with permission of both the Kenneth Burke Literary Trust and the Kenneth Burke Papers, Rare Books and Manuscripts, Special Collections, at the Pennsylvania State University Libraries.

2. Most notably in an obituary essay, "K.B.—In Memory."

3. In the same *Sewanee Review* essay Donoghue notes that *Towards a Better Life* is "one of my favorite books, one of the three books I would love to have written. [. . .] My *Towards a Better Life* is defaced with lines on every second or third page, marking sentences so luminously composed that I could easily be persuaded that style is everything" (444).

4. Donoghue draws heavily on Suzanne Langer's work in *Philosophy in a New Key* and *Feeling and Form*.

5. Donoghue begins this section of his Ellmann Lectures on Stevens by taking up Habermas's claim that the philosophy of consciousness is exhausted. Donoghue does not dispute this assertion but argues—citing Levinas—that even if it is so, "the validity of individual consciousness and introspection would in no respect be undermined." "It would be wicked," he adds, "to remove that possibility, or try to make people ashamed of themselves for resorting to it" (*Being* 71).

6. See *Connoisseurs of Chaos,* 178–81.

7. Quoted by Donoghue in *Adam's Curse,* 111.

8. Quoted by Donoghue in *Adam's Curse,* 128.

9. "Sometime—I think in the 60's—" Ammons wrote in a letter to me (July 29, 1997), "I found a paperback copy of *Counterstatement* [sic], in which I read enough to feel the power of oppositions, reconciliations, assimilations into category, etc. I recognized it as 'home.' [. . .] I feel that Emerson, Coleridge, Burke (not so much Thoreau) were already in my bones when I found them." Quoted with permission.

10. Permission to cite "Information Density" granted by W. W. Norton Company and John R. Ammons.

4 Burke's McKeon Side: Burke's Pentad and McKeon's Quartet

Robert Wess

Close friends from the time they met while attending Columbia, Kenneth Burke and Richard McKeon together form one of Burke's many circles, one that survives in their correspondence as well as in discernible affinities in their published work.[1] The overlap between McKeon's quartet—thing, thought, word, and action—and Burke's pentad arguably provides the best place for Burkeans to begin to look at Burke and McKeon together, and it will serve that purpose here.[2] In addition, we'll conclude our examination of the two together with a defense based on McKeon of the final part of "Terministic Screens," which Burke calls "Our Attempt to Avoid Mere Relativism." This famous essay, with its argument that terminologies are "selections" and therefore "deflections" as much as "reflections," seems to fit snuggly into the constructivist line of argument informing antifoundational theory and its rejection of naïve verbal realism. But then this final part seems to do an about face by making a foundational claim. Antifoundational purists no doubt see inconsistency in Burke's combination of the linguistic skepticism characteristic of postmodern antifoundationalism with a linguistic realism that seems often to have foundational status. McKeon provides a philosophical context within which it becomes apparent that the inconsistency is on the side of the purists rather than Burke.

Correspondence suggests that Burke associated his interests in theory, as distinct from his literary interests, with McKeon. In a 1974 letter, for example, Burke briefly recollects the beginning of their friendship (their "first communing when adolescent at Columbia"), and then relates an evening many years later when the Burkes, the Cowleys, and the McKeons partied together:

> I was so happy, I fell into compulsive sleepiness, with Dick lugging me by one arm, Malcolm by the other (we seemed to be on the road to somewhere), and me coming-to only now and then enough to call for another drink. [. . .] Somehow or other, Dick and Malcolm seemed to me like contrary loyalties within me—and in my plasterdom under such conditions all seemed resolved. (Letter to Howard Nemerov)

Burke repeats this recollection directly to McKeon in a 1979 letter, using the phrase "seemed resolved" to bring the letter to an end. Burke also depicts this same self-division much earlier, in a passage in a 1921 letter to Matthew Josephson, at which time Burke would have been 24, McKeon 21; only this time, while McKeon is again on one side, it's William Carlos Williams on the other (along with *Contact,* Williams's new journal at the time).[3] In this passage, however, unlike the later ones, there is no sense of resolution. Instead, the "contrary loyalties" dividing Burke are fleshed out a bit and Burke is resolute in affirming that he resides in a state of contradiction:

> Strangely enough, the one bright spot in my intellectual life is McKeon, whom I see once every couple of weeks, and who is a consolation to me because he *knows* things. True, this may wear off when he finally leaves school; but for the present, at least, it is still with him and is vitally operating. Christ! with all the wishy-wash of modern mouthing, it is positively invigorating to discuss what this man maintains and that man rebuts, wherein so-and-so is differentiated from so-and-so, how one thing can be divided and other things grouped. Williams and his damned Contact . . . who in the hell cares what the noumenon is? . . . the remarkable thing is the intricacy of the dance around it. Or, to borrow a point from a review I wrote of Williams's new book: Given a warm fire and the wind howling outside, Kant sits down and works out the categorical imperative; but Williams would never get over the delight in how warm he was and how ineffec-

tually the wind was raging outside. And I, personally, vote for the categorical imperative, although Williams is obviously right in his simplicity and Kant is obviously wrong in his intricacy.

While Burke divides himself into two in these letters, there are surely more than just two (see Rueckert, "Some"). I stress the existence of many Burkes to suggest not only that just one of these seems particularly prominent in his relationship with McKeon (Josephson was horrified to hear that Burke was consorting with McKeon [Selzer 215n59]), but also, and more importantly, to contrast Burke and McKeon on this score. Whereas there are many Burkes, there is, I believe, only one McKeon.

One way to get a sense of the identity of this one McKeon is through recollections of his teaching by former students. Of those I'll cite, Wayne Booth is the best known. The others are Thomas Farrell, author of the prize-winning *Norms of Rhetorical Culture,* and Dennis O'Brien, whose career includes service as president at Bucknell and the University of Rochester. Their essays appear together in a volume on McKeon that includes essays by other students as well as by a few colleagues.

Booth reports that he first encountered McKeon in 1943 when he took a few hours off each week from his Mormon missionary work to take a course on Plato's *Republic*. The experience convinced him that McKeon was a dogmatic Platonist, and he found the dogmatism particularly irksome. Booth was subsequently puzzled when he was told that McKeon was known as a dogmatic Aristotelian. Booth asks himself,

> What kind of mind was I then dealing with?
> Well, it was the same kind that I met in a later course with him after the war, that of an absolutely dogmatic Humeian, not just eager to defend Hume from every conceivable attack but brilliant at exposing the stupidities of any of us who raised what seemed to us obvious objections to Hume. It was the kind of mind that had earlier produced a "dogmatically Spinozist" book on Spinoza. [. . .] As any reader of McKeon might predict, I later met in him an equally persuasive dogmatic defender of Democritus, of Cicero, of Kant, of Dewey,

> and—somewhat peripherally from McKeon's point of view but highly important in my own thinking—of Anselm. ("Richard McKeon's Pluralism" 215)

The one downside for some students was that McKeon seemed to be without a doctrine of his own. Farrell concludes that McKeon never gets beyond showing the infinitely rich relationships among things, thoughts, words, and actions (192, 195). O'Brien similarly concludes, "If one wished to derive the truths of McKeon's work, they would not be truths of doctrine, but truths about what it means to have, hold, or discover a doctrine" (89). One sign of this emphasis, drawing from my own experience, is that in McKeon's classroom you never got very far by citing a passage in a text to answer one of his questions, even if it was exactly the right passage to cite to deal with the question he had asked. To get anywhere, you had to be able to address an array of questions: What steps in the argument lead to this passage? What problem arising from these steps does the passage address? How does the passage prepare for the next step in the argument? Etc.

The one and only one McKeon may thus be characterized at the very least as a master of philosophical argumentation. Whether he is more may depend on whether one is willing to ask a perhaps unfashionable question: if there are many truths that are nonetheless different, along the lines suggested by Booth's recollection, then what must the nature of world be for that to be the case?

While this one McKeon is very different from the many Burkes, in McKeon, Burke did have an invaluable friend whenever he wanted to develop his theoretical bent. Burke could always bounce his theoretical balls off a philosophical wall of considerable strength. Their correspondence gives evidence to suggest that such matters were the cornerstone of their long friendship.

This correspondence is located at the University of Chicago and at Pennsylvania State University. The first letter is dated October 24, 1934, shortly after McKeon left Columbia for the University of Chicago. If there was any correspondence prior to this date, I've never seen it. There would, of course, have been little need for correspondence while they were able to see one another in New York on a regular basis. McKeon did, however, study in Paris for a few years during the 1920s. Maybe there was correspondence from those years that didn't survive or has yet to surface.

In this first letter Burke writes to ask McKeon if he would read the manuscript that became *Permanence and Change* and respond, as Burke puts it, "with some erudite bleats." McKeon responds promptly, indicating he'll be happy to read it. This initial exchange leads to a few more letters spanning the time to get the manuscript to McKeon, with the last dated December 12th, a letter from McKeon to Burke. McKeon is reading the manuscript and plans to return to New Jersey later in the month. He proposes to Burke that they get together on the 20th to spend an evening talking about the book. Their main exchange about *Permanence and Change*, then, evidently occurred in their face-to-face meeting.

This exchange is a fairly representative anecdote insofar as the correspondence often amounts to a kind of "coming attractions" of the main event of a face-to-face meeting. Sometimes Burke anticipates McKeon's objections as he rehearses the argument he will present in detail when they meet. In a 1942 letter, prompted in part by the possibility of another McKeon visit to the east coast, Burke writes that he is working on his *Grammar*

> and would greatly appreciate a chance to discuss it with you under grovelike conditions. It all gets down to a "dramatist" approach to the category of substance—and an attempt to show that, if one begins by considering the relations among these five terms (as revealed in the contemplation of drama), one will best understand why philosophies (being theories of motivation, action, etc.) assume the forms they do. I hear you murmur "platonizing." But I think I can show you that it is, rather, "terministic." I.e., I take the five terms; consider their relations to one another; then show how different philosophic and rhetoric strategies take form from these ambiguities, resources, necessities.

Another exchange may offer a glimpse of what McKeon was like in their face-to-face discussions. Writing in June 1976 and expecting McKeon to visit soon, Burke issues a warning,

> Unless you write me, agreeing that there is a categorical distinction btw. (nonsymbolic) motion and (symbolic) action, I can't guaranty your safety. [. . .]

Frankilee, things would be best served if you wrote me a note saying, for instance, somethinks like "I do absolutely agree in principle that with regard to human motivation, there is a categorical distinction between motion and action, in their roles at least as terms."

McKeon replies, giving Burke what he demands, but doing so with qualifications couched in super-sophisticated philosophical refinements. My guess is that, rising to the bait of Burke's hyperbolic warning, he is trying to engage in a bit of self-parody, even though self-parody may be as much out of character for him as it is natural for Burke. Here is McKeon's reply:

> To add "with respect to human motivation" is a fudge, because categorical distinction[s] have no "with respect to." I like to think of language, ordinary and extraordinary, as composed of words which enlist an army of terms, infinite in number, drawn up in predicational ranks, finite in number, each headed by a category. I am willing to swear that there is a predicamental, i.e., categorical difference between motion and action if you mean a predicational difference based on differences of predicables and predicaments. [. . .] All actions are motions, but not all motions are actions. Therefore, if we spread your fudge, "with respect to human motivation," over these clear and distinct ideas and precise and meaningful expressions, I suppose I can take the oath—but I won't have words put in my mouth.

One record of a face-to-face encounter survives in the form of an unpublished transcript. At the University of Chicago in 1970, Burke and McKeon engaged in a debate, moderated by Wayne Booth, which centered mainly on how to draw a theoretical line between rhetorical and poetic analysis.[4]

Turning to the pentad and the quartet, one might argue that the quartet is more important to McKeon than the pentad is to Burke. To study the pentad, you can concentrate on *A Grammar of Motives*. Burke occasionally uses the pentad in other places but such uses are not extensive.[5] McKeon's use of his quartet, by contrast, increases as his thought develops from decade to decade, sometimes even appearing in the form of different terms. One McKeon scholar, Walter Watson, calls the quartet "the master topic of McKeon's philosophy" and compiles a long list of references to McKeon's uses of it to chart "three-stage cycles in the history of philosophy" (16, 234). Even this list, however, isn't exhaustive because McKeon's use of the quartet isn't limited to his charting of the history of philosophy. One essay not on this list that I consider particularly central in McKeon's work is "Being, Existence, and That Which Is"—which also just happens to be one of McKeon's most difficult essays. McKeon's difficulty is notorious. Burke himself, in correspondence, suggests that compared to McKeon his own "methodologic polysyllables are baby-talk, the billing and cooing of young love" (*Letters from Kenneth Burke to William H. Rueckert* 135).

The quartet is profitably considered from the standpoint of McKeon's discussion, in an autobiographical reflection, of the formation of two ideas seminal in his development: (1) "the true is sometimes false and sometimes true"; (2) "there is a sense in which truth, though one, has no single expression" ("Philosopher Meditates" 203, 204). Both address the unfashionable question posed above, but it's the second of these ideas that will be our main concern. Zahara McKeon, McKeon's widow, in writing the introduction to the first volume of the multi-volume series of McKeon's writings that the University of Chicago Press is publishing, cites this second idea in discussing the side of his work that she characterizes as "the metaphysical dimension he never discussed" (20). McKeon's quartet is the key both to the one truth and to the reason definitive expression of it is impossible. Burke's pentad is a variation of the same idea.

McKeon's quartet works on two levels of analysis: "historical semantics" and "philosophical semantics." In McKeon's words,

> The semantics I have practiced has two successive forms: "historical" semantics, in which terms are defined according to the assumptions, arguments, and conclusions of philosophical positions examined and differentiated historically, and "philosophical" semantics, in which terms are employed and related according to meanings adapted to a single set of assumptions and methods. ("Imitation" 207-08)

"Historical semantics" is the level where the quartet appears most obviously and is in my view the best place to begin a study of McKeon. We'll consider "philosophical semantics" only tangentially, mainly in connection with the problem of "principle." Philosophical semantics accounts for differences among thinkers who share a historical orientation. Both historical and philosophical semantics appear in the form of quartets.[6]

Familiarity with the pentad offers Burkeans unfamiliar with McKeon an initial sense in which there can be such a thing as one truth with no definitive expression. The key is that there is no limit to the number of discourses, with widely varying subject matters, that nonetheless all exemplify the pentad in one of its possible variations. Insofar as there is some kind of truth residing in the pentad, one would then have multiple expressions of this truth. Furthermore, insofar as no one of these expressions, in its particularity, could be cited as the paradigmatic or definitive expression that serves as a standard for all others, then one would have one truth—the pentad—with no expression that could be singled out as the standard by which to measure all others. One qualification that would have to be considered, however, would be the discourse of drama itself. Burke does single out drama as paradigmatic, so that perhaps the appearance of the pentad in drama is in some sense a more definitive expression of the pentad than its appearance elsewhere. To the extent that the drama plays this role, then, one would have to conclude that Burke's version of a truth with no definitive expression is a bit impure.

The pentad and the quartet are most alike in the way that for each there is no limit to the number of discourses, with widely varying subject matters, in which they can manifest themselves. The truth in the pentad or the quartet is not a doctrinal truth discovered in a subject matter but a relational truth discerned in the relationality among scene, agent, act, agency, and purpose, or thing, thought, language, and action. The truth of such relationality exhibits itself in the fashion in which it informs all the discourses one is considering.

Depending on how it's conceived, a truth that resides in such relationality may result in an empty formalism, that is, in the mere spinning of words in various combinations that are "apart from" rather than "a part of" the reality of the world. Such formalism is even encouraged by the above stress on the distinction between the quartet's and pentad's relationality on the one hand and the manifestation of this relationality in widely varying subject matters on the other hand. How can one avoid such formalism? An answer emerges as one considers two additional dimensions of the pentad/quartet overlap. It's essential to consider the two in combination, since the first, by itself, would be compatible with such formalism.

The first of these dimensions appears in the way that both Burke and McKeon derive different philosophical discourses from the privileging of different parts of their relational sets. Privileging different pentadic terms results in different philosophical -ism's (*GM* 128), while privileging different parts of the quartet results in different philosophical orientations characteristic of different historical periods.

"There is," McKeon observes, "no pre-established priority of being, cause, or rule among things, thoughts, actions, and statements; each in turn may be made fundamental [. . .]" ("Discourse" 45). Different parts of the quartet become fundamental in different historical periods that follow one another, as Watson notes, in "three-stage cycles." The first prioritizes thing (metaphysical periods), the second shifts the emphasis to thought (epistemological periods), and the third makes language and action together fundamental. One may emphasize language or action but both emphases appear together in one historical period because from a philosophical viewpoint they are equally important in making the concrete, situational level of what humans say and do the fundamental subject matter of philosophical inquiry.

This third orientation is our own period, for which the familiar phrase "the linguistic turn" sometimes serves as a shorthand designation. In this orientation, McKeon observes, "we test what is presented as that which is or as that which is thought by considering that which is said and that which is done, and by seeking in statement and action the marks and warrants by which to determine and certify being and thought in what is said and done and in consequences discerned in statement and occurrence" ("Philosophy of Communications" 101). An example of one effect of this orientation is the revival of rhetoric that the twentieth century witnessed. In such an orientation, rhetoric becomes "architectonic" in a world consisting of constructs:

> Rhetoric is an art of invention and disposition: it is an art of communication between a speaker and his audience, and it is therefore an art of construction of the subject-matter of communication, that is, of anything whatever that can be an object of attention. What is, is

> established by the convictions and agreements of men, and the rich potentialities of experience and existence are examined and developed by devices of discrimination and of opposition and adjustment in expression and communication. ("Philosophy of Communications" 108)

Each of the three orientations is vulnerable to critique from its successors ("Philosophy of Communications" 101–03). In the context of the "linguistic turn" of our time, for example, we've grown accustomed to the critique of any attempt to make thought or thing prior to and independent of language. Deconstruction of claims to such priority have focused particularly on thing. It's become commonplace to argue, as Burke does in "Terministic Screens," that languages mediates ("screens") our interaction with things beyond language.

The second of the two dimensions appears in the way that a good deal of the analytic richness in both Burke's pentad and McKeon's quartet resides in ambiguities arising from overlaps among their terms. In the *Grammar*'s introduction, for example, Burke uses the metaphor of the hand to liken "the [pentadic] terms to the fingers, which in their extremities are distinct from one another, but merge in the palm of the hand" (xxii). McKeon similarly puts particular stress on the way that there are senses in which each part of the quartet can be any of the others. In a lecture in one course, after developing this point, he concluded,

> It is this form of ambiguity—and I've gone through all this talk because experience has taught me that it is extremely difficult not only to get this point across but to keep it going in a conversation. [. . .]
>
> I am suggesting it is this ambiguity which is at the center of the philosophic problem, the philosophic enterprise, and therefore the relevance of philosophy to anything else. ("Subject Matter of Philosophy")

Consider the example so common in our time of work, like Burke's, that consists of language about language, words about words. It's easy to overlook that in such cases language is both language in the conventional sense and an existent reality, a thing, in another sense (McKeon, "Philosophy of Communications" 104, 105). The words in Burke's books are language in the conventional sense, but these words are used to identify language as a thing in reality that can be analyzed, as when, for example, Burke uses words to show how language selects, reflects, and deflects to produce "terministic screens" that are things that produce effects in the world. Similarly, when Burke remarks that "whenever we call something a *metaphor,* we mean it *literally*" (Burke, et al. 27), he is giving a simple example in which metaphor is functioning both as a "thing" and as a "word" used to refer to this "thing" in a literal sense. This ambiguity whereby words are in one sense words and in another sense things is crucial to the defense of Burke mentioned at the outset to which we'll return in concluding.

Another example in Burke of a sense in which language is a thing in the world prompts Samuel B. Southwell to suggest that Burke takes us to the "knife-edge border of a unifying metaphysics" (66). The passage prompting Southwell's remark appears in *A Rhetoric of Motives*: "nature must be more-than-verbal. For in its totality it encompasses verbal and nonverbal both; and its 'nonverbal' ground must have contained the 'potentiality' of the verbal, otherwise the verbal could not have emerged from it" (290). This dialectical argument for an ontological fusion of the verbal and the nonverbal not only places language firmly in the world but also places it in a teleological structure in which its emergence is nature's destiny, the actualization of a prior potentiality. Such a teleology is absent in other places, where Burke appears convinced that human beings (defined first as "symbol-using animals" and later as "bodies that learn language") are a contingency: a species that emerged, is staying around for awhile, but is likely one day to disappear and to take the verbal with it (e.g., "Sensation" 205; "Words" 160). But regardless of whether the verbal is a telos or a contingency, it's a thing in the world.

It's worth adding that Southwell is disappointed that Burke stops at this "knife-edge border": "Will not another small step or two carry us to a conception of God, the world, and man such as that proposed by Pierre Teilhard de Chardin, among others? In Burke there is hardly a hint of such questions. The argument stops where it begins [. . .]" (66). Southwell thus seems to reflect the common view that language is somehow relatively insubstantial, not something in the same league with "bigger" realities, even though it is certainly, when one considers all the human activities that would be impossible without it, among the most important phenomena on the planet. Southwell's orientation appears cosmocentric (god-centered) rather than geocentric (earth-centered).

We've emphasized the ambiguity in the quartet whereby a word can be a thing as well as a word because it is ambiguities of this sort, combined with the different historical orientations, that show why McKeon's quartet is substantive rather than a formalistic spinning of words. In "Being, Existence, and That Which Is," McKeon explicitly broadens the term "thing" to encompass the other components of his quartet (254–55), as he works out the three fundamental ways of conducting the philosophical enterprise corresponding to the three historical orientations. McKeon's point in broadening the notion of thing is that while there are senses in which thought, language, and action are apart from the reality of the thing in the conventional sense, there are also senses in which thought, language, and action are things in their own right. As things, they are different from thing in the conventional sense, so that the philosophical structures one builds on them are also different, but because there are senses in which they are things in the world they can serve as foundational realities for philosophical structures, in the way, for example, that language and action have served this function for the constructionist philosophies of our own historical period.

All philosophical structures require a foundation or principle, regardless of historical period, but it's the historical period that determines whether principles are to be found in things, thoughts, or language and action. The problem of principle, as noted earlier, is a part of McKeon's philosophical semantics. This problem arises from parts and wholes. Is the whole prior to the parts? Are the parts prior to the whole? Is there one or a plurality of wholes? Are such distinctions arbitrary? This problem is perennial, cutting across different historical periods, but it takes on a different character in the different historical periods, with their different subject matters or fundamental realities. Furthermore, as these questions suggest, this problem can be solved in different ways. Hence, philosophers who share a historical orientation, agreeing on the fundamental reality of philosophic inquiry (thing, thought, or language/action), may disagree among themselves over how best to solve the problem of principle, as well as the other problems that fall under the other parts of philosophical semantics. (See "Philosophic Semantics and Philosophic Inquiry," for McKeon's most complete statement of his philosophical semantics.)

McKeon's quartet, then, is best understood as demonstrating that what is "out there" is ambiguous to the core, an ambiguity in the nature of the world. A fundamental referent pervades philosophical controversy in each historical period (thing as thing, thought as thing, or language/action as thing), but no fundamental referent is fixed forever. McKeon thus refuses the temptation to see the truth of the present as disproving the truths of the past; no historical orientation can be absolutized over the others in theory, and history suggests that no orientation dominates forever. The different orientations produce different truths, each of which is sometimes false and sometimes true; historical periods typically see themselves not only disproving truths of earlier periods but also rediscovering past truths, as for example the revival of rhetoric in our time prompted a reevaluation of the sophists.

Together, the three historical orientations, along with the differences within historical periods charted by philosophical semantics, produce different expressions of the one truth that cannot be expressed definitively. This truth is not a truth limited to formal relationality but a truth about reality, albeit a reality that appears not as an unchanging fundamental referent but as different referents in different historical periods. The ambiguity in McKeon's quartet is in the nature of the world wherein intelligibility depends on aligning thought, language, and action with thing, without any way to determine absolutely and unambiguously the essence of a thing, a thought, a word, or an act.

The ambiguity in McKeon's quartet is thus metaphysical rather than verbal. Burke's pentad, by contrast, while it distinguishes different philosophies, does not have the historical dimension one finds in McKeon, whereby one gains access to different substantive realities in different historical periods. Neither dramatism nor logology contains the possibility a philosophical revolution whereby language and action would no longer be the fundamental starting point of philosophical speculation. In this sense, Burke absolutizes the language/action orientation, whereas McKeon's historical semantics does not.

Within the language/action orientation, Burke presents the pentad as suited to recover core "assertions" that might otherwise get lost in the intricacies of philosophical systems: "But with the pentad as a generating principle, we may extricate ourselves from these intricacies by discovering the kinds of *assertion* which the different schools would exemplify in a hypothetical state of purity" (*GM* 131). One approach to the pentad is to put all five terms on an equal level whereby one may privilege any one of the five in terminologically characterizing "substance." In this view, materialism (scene), idealism (agent), realism (act), pragmatism (agency), and mysticism (purpose) are different characterizations of substance, analogous to five people observing an accident and giving five different characterizations of what happened. This approach, however, runs the risk of conceptualizing language as "apart from" rather than "a part of" reality. A second approach is to privilege act in conceiving the hierarchizing of the pentadic terms involved in the five characterizations of substance as five equivalent instantiations of verbal action in the world.[7] This second approach combines the verbal ambiguity of the first with an unambiguous identification of verbal action as part of the reality of the world. There are many ways to verbalize a situation, constructing the situation in different ways, but each verbalization is nonetheless an action in the world. This second approach gets beyond formalism to a linguistic realism. As Burke remarks in the *Grammar,*

> So, one could, if he wished, maintain that all theology, metaphysics, philosophy, criticism, poetry, drama, fiction, political exhortation, historical interpretation and personal statements about the lovable and the hateful—one could if he wanted to be as drastically thorough as some of our positivists now seem to want to be—maintain that every bit of this is nonsense. Yet these words of nonsense would themselves be real words, involving real tactics, having real demonstrable relationships, and demonstrably affecting relationships. (57–58)

This second approach also offers a reading of Burke's hand metaphor, cited above in noting the ambiguity of the pentadic terms. The palm of the hand, where the terms merge, is verbal action conceived as a reality in the world. Different acts privilege different terms (fingers), as Burke illustrates in suggesting how scene, agent, act, agency, and purpose may be used to characterize war in varying ways (*GM* xx). Each characterization is as real a verbal action as any other, which explains the sense in which the different terms merge in the palm of the hand wherein they can substitute for one another in different acts. In this approach there are two acts in the sense that act is both a word (a pentadic term) and a reality (a thing). The relation between these two poses the same problem that Burke addresses in the final section of "Terministic Screens," to which we now turn.[8]

Prior to this final section, Burke shows how terminologies construct realities, that is, how the observations we make are implicit in the terms we use. Then, at the end, he steps back to examine the constructive process used in the earlier sections. Burke asks,

> Must we merely resign ourselves to an endless catalogue of terministic screens, each of which can be valued for the light it throws upon the human animal, yet none of which can be considered central? [. . .]
>
> Whether such proneness to symbolic activity be viewed as a privilege or a calamity (or as something of both), it is a distinguishing characteristic of the human animal in general. Hence it can properly serve as the basis of a general, or philosophic definition of this animal. From this terministic beginning, this intuitive grounding of a position, many observations "necessarily follow." But are we not here "necessarily" caught in our own net? Must we not concede that a screen built on this basis is just one more screen; and that it can at best be permitted to take its place along with all the others? Can we claim for it special favors? (52–53)

Burke's answer to this last question is, of course, "yes." The argument he uses to justify his foundational claim need not concern us. This McKeonesque defense of Burke is not directed against someone who objects only to Burke's justification, not to his attempt at a foundational claim itself. Rather, it's directed against the antifoundational purist who would object to any foundational claim whatsoever, arguing that Burke attempts to justify what cannot be justified in any way under any circumstances. This defense might prompt one to modify Burke's justification, but that's a secondary consideration.

It needs to be stressed, lest our contrast between Burke and antifoundational purists mislead some readers, that antifoundational constructionism is not necessarily a mere spinning of words, a la some readings (not mine) of Derrida's "there is nothing outside the text" (158). To speak of something such as gender as a construct is typically to claim that the biology of sexual difference is mediated by constructions of gender that inform activities and experiences in daily life. So conceived, gender is a part of life. What constructionism rejects is the rooting of gender absolutely in biology, as if the roles men and women play in society were biologically predetermined rather than mediated linguistically, culturally, and socially. Our focus is not on such constructs, but on the constructive process by virtue of which such mediating constructs take form. Is this process itself just another construct or is it something more?

Our focus, in other words, is the same as Burke's in the above passage. The principal reason for focusing on this particular passage resides precisely in the fashion in which in it Burke steps back to examine reflexively the constructive process he has been deploying to ask whether it too is a construction, before claiming it's more than that, that it's a universal foundation rather than a mere construct relative to the circumstances of its origin. This reflexivity is the crucial moment. The next time you encounter an antifoundational purist, ask yourself if he or she ever steps back to do what Burke does in this passage. Don't be surprised if such stepping back is resisted or dodged in some way. Look past the analysis of particular constructs such as a construct of gender; by definition, such particular constructs are contingent, emerging and disappearing in historic contexts. Look instead at the process by which the displacement of construct by construct is explained. Ask yourself if that process is subject to change or is immune to it. For the antifoundational absolutist should say that his or her version of the constructive process is itself just another construct, that it can't claim any "special favors," that it can come and go like any other construct. The absolutist should say that because according to antifoundationalism there is no such thing as a foundational reality, so that the constructive process can't be a foundational reality either. The difficulty is that this admission takes the air out of the absolutist's theoretical balloon because it opens the door to an infinite regress in which every process used to explain the formation of a construct becomes itself a construct, an effect of a constructive process. Constructing is thus endlessly asserted, but never grounded in principle: the beginning point of the constructive process is never reached.

Such a regress arises when one fails to recognize the sense in which language and action, as the resources from which one draws in devising a constructionist theory, are things in the world, as McKeon's quartet alerts us. The constructive process can construct endlessly, but it cannot construct the realities of language and action that make it possible and are in that sense prior to it. It's this priority that empowers these realities to serve as a beginning point, which is what a philosophical first principle is. These realities are what debates over which constructive theory is best are about. These realities are the location of the foundationalism beneath any antifoundational theory of the constructive process. Antifoundational purism results when one makes the familiar argument that things "out there" (in the usual sense) are not prior to discourse but are constructed by discourse, while forgetting that one's theory of the constructive process depends on a foundation that presupposes a particular sense in which language and action are things "out there." This forgetting allows one to fault a metaphysical antagonist for doing what one does oneself when it comes to language and action.

An antifoundational theory of constructs displacing constructs is intelligible if and only if the constructive process itself, however it's conceived, abides as a foundational reality to explain the displacement process. One can, for example, first distinguish abnormal and normal discourses and then invoke the conversation in which such discourses compete to explain how an abnormal discourse can become normal; but in turning such a conversation into an explanatory principle in this fashion, one elevates it above the level of the abnormal and the normal. This conversation can explain the shift from the abnormal to the normal if and only if it abides unchanged as the first principle of one's theory. The discourse theorizing this conversation would be neither normal nor abnormal but a representation of a foundational reality.

From McKeon's standpoint, then, Burke is perfectly consistent in his combination of antifoundational linguistic skepticism and foundational linguistic realism. One should look for inconsistency instead in claims of antifoundational purism. Burke's "linguistic skepticism" is consonant with what constructionist theory has taught us about the illusions of naïve verbal realism, but this has never kept Burke from seeing that constructivism doesn't construct the realities of language and action. For Burke these are realities rooted in human bodies, which are themselves embedded in the biological processes of life on planet earth. A Burkean construct can be subjected to the test of "recalcitrance" because it's "a part of" reality rather than "apart from" it, a synecdoche rather than a "prison house."

McKeon observes, "[M]etaphysics is not only a science of being qua being; it is also a science of first principles, and the arts of communication and construction must establish and use 'principles' which serve a function among the facts of discourse and occurrence not unlike the function of metaphysical principles ordering the structures of actuality and truth" ("Philosophy of Communications" 102). He adds, "[O]nce discourse has supplanted metaphysics and epistemology as architectonic methods [. . .] facts of existence take the place of principles of being and indubitable truths, [taking] on the characteristics of being and truth, and becom[ing] at once inclusive and the basis of discrimination" ("Discourse" 49).

One can ultimately only speculate about the extent to which Burke's sensitivity to the problem of philosophical first principles derives from his friendship with McKeon. But considering Burke and McKeon as forming a circle of two does help to contextualize one of the many Kenneth Burkes.

Notes

For permission to quote from Kenneth Burke's correspondence with Matthew Josephson, Richard McKeon, and Howard Nemerov, I wish to thank Michael Burke and the Kenneth Burke Literary Trust. For permission to quote from Richard McKeon's correspondence with Kenneth Burke, I wish to thank Alexandra Dorinson, step-daughter of Richard McKeon and daughter of Zahava McKeon, McKeon's second wife and widow, who died 19 February 2005. I wish also to thank Sandra Stelts, Curator, for permission to quote from Kenneth Burke and Richard McKeon letters in the Kenneth Burke Papers, Rare Books and Manuscripts, Special Collections, The Pennsylvania State University Libraries. Thanks also to Miriam Clark and Richard Thames for sharing unpublished correspondence cited in this essay.

[1] Signs of the closeness of their relationship include correspondence about family matters between Libbie (Burke's second wife) and Muriel (McKeon's first wife).

[2] The term "quartet" is mine, not McKeon's. McKeon doesn't refer to these terms as a "quartet" the way that Burke refers to his five dramatistic terms as a "pentad." In the interests of full disclosure, I should also add that the topic of McKeon takes me back to my initial classroom experience with him at the University of Chicago, which turned out to be one of those life-altering events that usually have a mix of positive and negative effects. Among the positive is my work on Burke. Were it not for McKeon, I probably never would have studied Burke seriously, which I started only after leaving graduate school, having read in all my years of schooling only the title essay in *The Philosophy of Literary Form*. After leaving Chicago, the continuing effects of the time I spent in McKeon's classroom, while writing a dissertation

on Henry Fielding and Jane Austen, turned me in a new direction that led me to Burke. This past experience may very well shape what I say in ways that elude me.

³ The first part of this passage may sound familiar, because Jack Selzer quotes it in his invaluable study of Burke and the 1920s (41).

⁴ They also once appeared together on a panel on the topic of "Communication and the Arts." Burke's paper: "Poetics and Communication." McKeon's: "Philosophy of Communications and the Arts." There is some inconclusive discussion in the correspondence prior to the event about how the two papers might relate to one another. In the end, specific references are limited to a few Burke references to McKeon that are tangential to Burke's main line of argument. In the later 1970 exchange at Chicago, which occurred not long after this event, McKeon takes issue on a minor point with one of Burke's references to him in "Poetics and Communication."

⁵ Burke's later suggestion that it might help to add the term "attitude" to make the pentad a hexad (e.g., *Dramatism and Development* 23) is also included as an "Addendum" in later editions of the *Grammar* (443).

⁶ The quartet in philosophical semantics consists of principle, method, interpretation, and selection, corresponding respectively in my view to thing, thought, language, and action. Watson also notes two other quartets: dialectic, logic, grammar, and rhetoric; and inquiry, arts, semantics, and topics (16). Relations among all these quartets would no doubt be a matter for debate among McKeon scholars.

⁷ See Wess 152–55 for an account of the relation in Burke's *Grammar* of action, substance, and the pentad.

⁸ In the *Grammar,* the theorizing of verbal action as a thing rather than a word appears in "The Dialectic of Constitutions."

5 Essentializing Temporality, Temporizing Essence: The Narrative Theory and Interpretive Practice of Kenneth Burke and Wayne Booth

Greig Henderson

The curious thing about narrative theory in the critical corpus of Kenneth Burke is its virtual non-existence. Though Burke repeatedly notes that story is a duplication of sensory experience and that narrative is what human beings add to speechless nature, his writings contain little if any sustained analysis of narrative technique, little if any discussion of narrative perspective and narrative voice, of the agent who is perceiving and the agent who is speaking. Indeed, Burke conspicuously ignores many of the defining features of narrative—temporality, focalization, narrators, narratees, and so forth. By contrast, narrative theory is a paramount topic in the critical corpus of Wayne Booth, and Booth not only has a deep sense of narrative's defining features but also develops a formidable rhetorical lexicon for its analysis. Though earlier works in the tradition of Anglo-American twentieth-century criticism, such as Percy Lubbock's 1921 *The Craft of Fiction* and E. M. Forster's 1927 *Aspects of the Novel,* began the process of codifying the rhetorical strategies and narrative techniques enshrined in modernist fiction, it is no exaggeration to say that Booth's 1961 masterpiece, *The Rhetoric of Fiction,* transformed the critical landscape by seeing fiction as the art of communicating with readers and by analyzing the rhetorical resources available to a writer as he or she tries, consciously or unconsciously, to impose a fictional world upon a reader. Anti-dogmatic and resolutely pluralistic, Booth demonstrates forcibly the radical inadequacy of the distinction between narrative telling and dramatic showing, along with the fallacy of embracing modernist dogmas exalting the latter over the former. He also bequeaths to us an equipment for criticism whose key terms have become part of our everyday vocabulary and have endured for almost fifty years, no mean feat given the vagaries of critical taste and the transience of theoretical fashion. Among those key terms are *dramatized narrator, unreliable narrator, implied author, narrator-observer, narrator-agent, self-conscious narrator, authorial intrusion, authorial absence, degree of privilege, degree of inside view, degree of distance,* and a host of others. Indeed, many of the so-called advances in narratology amount to putting abstrusely what Booth put plainly, substituting, say, heterodiegetic narrator for narrator-observer or homodiegetic narrator for narrator-agent.

What I want to focus on is the differing conceptions of narrative that underwrite the rhetorical projects of Burke and Booth, using their analyses of Joyce's modernist classic—*A Portrait of the Artist as a Young Man*—as a point of comparison. Though rhetoric is at the core of both these projects, what Burke offers is as much a grammar of fiction as a rhetoric, and what Booth offers is as much an ethics of fiction as a rhetoric. Whereas Burke sees terms as characters in his dramatistic analyses of philosophical systems, he sees characters as terms in his logological analyses of narrative systems, letting his formalist obsession with "labyrinthine internal consistency" ("Fact" 172) essentialize narrative into a logic of interrelating terms. That is to say, he essentializes temporality rather than temporizes essence, temporizing of essence being his phrase for spinning out into narrative a series of logical relationships. Booth, on the other hand, acknowledges the priority of temporality over essence but cannot help getting enmeshed in questions of moral judgment, letting ethical evaluation get in the way of narratological critique.

In making these distinctions between temporality and essence, narrative and logic, and technique and value, I do not mean to imply that the first term in each pairing is superior to the second or that either is dispensable, for both are necessary and there is no right mix between them. The key to a well-rounded position lies not in some ultimate metaphysical choice between the first and the second, but rather in a humble respect for the unending process whereby the one is ceaselessly modified and conditioned by the other. It is therefore futile to maintain that the supposed shift from dramatism to logology in Burke, and from rhetoric to ethics in Booth, represents anything like a final victory of the essential over the temporal in Burke, or the axiological over narratological in Booth. What we have instead is an ongoing dialectical exchange between temporality and essence, narrative and logic, and technique and value.

My suggestion that Burke is deficient in narrative thinking might at first blush seem scandalous, but a brief survey of his corpus, I believe, reveals its accuracy. The thematic discussion of Thomas Mann and Andre Gide in *Counter-Statement* centers on the conscientious and the corrupt, a distinction elaborated to be destroyed, and looks at irony and experimentalism as equipment for living in a capitalist society. The discussion of Flaubert, de Gourmont, and Pater as adepts of pure literature has nothing to do with narrative as narrative. *Permanence and Change* and *Attitudes Toward History,* appropriately enough, given their subject matter, do not deal with narrative fiction in any extended way; indeed, the poetic categories of *Attitudes toward History* do not even include the novel as a form. *The Philosophy of Literary Form* focuses on poetry and drama, briefly considering Erskine Caldwell as a maker of grotesques. *A Rhetoric of Motives* invokes various novelists (Kafka, Mann, James, and others) but again, appropriately enough, focuses on issues of hierarchy, bureaucracy, courtship, mystery, socio-anagogic criticism, and so forth, while *The Rhetoric of Religion,* as its title advertises, is not concerned with the novel *per se* and centers on reducing the temporality of mythic and religious narrative to an eternal logic of interrelated terms. This logological quest for essential definition is also reflected in occasional essays such as those on Joyce's *The Dead,* Woolf's *Mrs. Dalloway,* and Forster's *Passage to India,* along with the essay on *Portrait* we shall consider in some detail, "Fact, Inference, and Proof in the Analysis of Literary Symbolism." The essay on Forster is reproduced in *Language as Symbolic Action* and explores and defines Forster's liberal humanism and the "mood of ironically sympathetic contemplation" (*LSA* 225) that attends it, "throwing light thereby on the ways recurrent terms help establish the internal consistency of the novel" (*LSA* 232). In general, then, Burke takes a thematic and formalist approach to fiction.

The reason for this pervasive devaluation of narrative as a temporal form resides in Burke's entelechial mode of thinking and his deep-seated distrust of myth and archetype. For Burke, the overall title of a work, actual or imputed, "could be said to be the infolding of all the details, or the details could be treated as the exfoliation-in-time of the eternal now that was contained in the title" (*LSA* 370). "The title is in effect an 'essence.' And in the narrative expansion that comprises the drama, the 'essence' that is named in the title acquires in effect a kind of 'existential definition'" (*LSA* 381). What we should seek is not "some 'first' story from which the many versions and variants were derived, but rather a 'perfect' form towards which such a story would naturally gravitate" (*LSA* 384). To seek such perfection is to ask what would constitute a genre's entelechial fulfillment and to imitate what Aristotle does in his *Poetics,* a work in which he attempts to describe the essence of Greek tragedy by envisaging the perfection of the form.

Though the narrative expansion involved in temporizing essence would seem to be endemic to how human beings understand the world into which they are thrown, Burke treats it as an inferior mode of cognition if not as a debilitating genetic fallacy. Through such temporizing, "the logical idea of a thing's essence can be translated into a temporal or narrative equivalent by statement in terms of a thing's source or beginning" (*RM* 13). The biblical myth of Genesis, for example, has Eve created from Adam's rib, a beginning which narratively says that women in the logic of the social order are derivative of and inferior to men. Other examples are mythical concepts that tell the story of the emergence of order out of chaos, concepts such as Hobbes's state of nature or Freud's primal horde (*GM* 431–32). Whether one treats these concepts as heuristic models, ontological models, or genetic fallacies, they are narrative devices for explaining, justifying, and naturalizing the logic of a given social order. "The narrative style," Burke writes, "can spin out a simultaneity into a succession," and "we don't realize how often we are using the quasi-successiveness of narrative when actually we are but giving a synonym" (*RR* 225). What I call Burke's essentializing of temporality reverses the process, translating yesterday, today, tomorrow into major premise, minor premise, conclusion. In the analysis of narrative, it translates a sequence of events into a system of signs and symbols.

Frederic Jameson makes an analogous point about Burke's approach to narrative, when he remarks, with some justice, that Burke's rhetorical criticism "elaborately decoded the surface moves of the text, but in a non-narrative fashion, which failed to integrate the extraordinary intuitions of its conceptions of deep structure" ("Foreword" xi-xii).

Nevertheless, Jameson is willing to concede that "Burke's dramatism in hindsight has much in common with Greimassian 'actantial' or 'positional' analysis" ("Foreword" xii), A .J. Greimas being a major player in the Paris School of semiotics and a major influence on critics such as Roland Barthes, Julia Kristeva, and Tzvetan Todorov. Both Burke and Greimas assume that narrativity, our innate capacity to generate and comprehend stories, is at the core of human signification. And both, in Burke's words, recognize that discourse is inherently dramatistic, that "a character in fiction is as much a term as any definition in a scientific nomenclature" (*CS* 183) and, above all, that "terms are *characters* [and . . .] an essay is an *attenuated play*" (*ATH* 312). Both Burke's dramatism and Greimas's actantial analysis make the movement of an idea or philosophical term become intelligible as the procession of a character through multiple trials and perils, menaced by its conceptual adversaries and aided and abetted by its magical helpers.

Greimas uses the term "actant" to refer to an associative field of agents and ideas. In *King Lear,* for example, one actant would consist of Cordelia, the Fool, and intuitive innocence; another, of Lear, rational corruption, and punishable pride. A narrative sequence requires at least two actants in opposition or apposition, disjunction or conjunction. The quest sequence activates subject versus object, or, in Burkean language, agent versus purpose. A subject or agent desires an object or has a purpose, encounters an opponent or counter-agent, finds a helper or co-agent, gets the object from a sender or agency, and achieves his or her purpose. The pattern applies to novels and philosophical treatises alike. In *Lord Jim,* the agent is Jim, the object or purpose is heroism, the sender or agency is romantic literature, the receiver or patient is Jim, the helpers or co-agents are Stein and Marlow, and the opponents or counter-agents are Cornelius and Brown. In *A Grammar of Motives,* the purpose is a well-rounded vocabulary of motives with adequate scope and circumference so as to purify war, the agent is the actant that comprises dramatism and its pentadic terms, the counter-agent is the actant that comprises scientism and other essentialist, reductivist, and determinist vocabularies of motives, and the sender is the cultural situation surrounding the Second World War. Strangely enough, then, even though the *Grammar* deals mainly with philosophical systems, it is the most dialectical, anti-essentialist, and even novelistic of Burke's studies, for in it, terms truly are characters, characters on trial, characters in alliance and combat with other characters, characters in competitive cooperation moving toward a higher synthesis. The essays that deal with fiction, however, are the most essentialist, formalist, and logological of Burke's studies, for in them, characters are terms, mutually implicative terms in a self-enclosed universe of discourse.

Of course, as the Lord repeatedly says to Satan in "Prologue in Heaven" (*RR*), it is more complicated than that. But this bold oversimplification, I think, reveals a partial truth worth developing even if it makes a more categorical distinction between dramatism and logology in Burke and technique and value in Booth than a subtler critique would permit. Let us turn, then, to the interpretive practice of these two critics, and the method and theory that undergird it. The two essays to be examined are analyses of Joyce's *Portrait:* Burke's 1954 "Fact, Inference, and Proof" and Booth's 1961 "The Problem of Distance in *A Portrait of the Artist.*"

"Fact, Inference, and Proof" is part of a project called "Theory of the Index" and bases its methodology on "the principle of the concordance" (145). Burke starts out with the obvious proposition that the individual words of the work are the basic "facts" of that work, a proposition that only Stanley Fish and his fellow travelers would seek to confute.[1] The problem for the practical critic is "how to operate with these 'facts,' how to use them as a means for keeping one's inferences under control, yet how to go beyond them, for purposes of inference, when seeking to characterize the motives and 'salient traits' of the work, in its nature as a total symbolic structure" (145). Burke is quick to point out, however, that the literary work is "at least" words, not "nothing but" words (146). Nevertheless, his essay, like logology itself, is more infused with the spirit of "nothing but" than "at least."

The first step is to index the relevant terms into a rough concordance, a procedure that inevitably presupposes a "principle of selection" (150) and an eye for "key terms" (151).

> Such concordances are initially noted without inference or interpretation. For whereas purely terministic correlation can serve the ends of "analogical" or "symbolic" exegesis, it is far more tentative and empirical, with a constant demand for fresh inquiry. In fact, one may experimentally note many correlations of this sort without being able to fit them into an overall scheme of interpretation. (150)

But grounding our concordances in what Burke calls "terminal factuality" is by no means a solution to our problems, for the real question is how the associative clusters (what equals what), dramatic alignments (what versus what), and narrative progressions (what leads to what) interconnect. We must thus "inspect a work in its *unfoldings*. And we must keep on the move, watching for both static interrelationships and for principles of *transformation* whereby a motive may progress from one combination through another to a third, etc." (153). We must search for appositions, oppositions, progressions, transformations, sequences, consequences, synonymizings, desynonymizings, entelechial moments at which the work comes to fruition, and so forth. It is no easy process, for "any connection of synonyms should always be watched for lurking antithesis. That is, words on their face synonymous may really *function* as antitheses in a given symbol system" (158n). Burke makes the point imperatively: "Note all striking terms for acts, attitudes, ideas, images, relationships. [. . .] Note oppositions [. . .] Watch for shifts whereby oppositions become appositions [. . . .] Note beginnings and endings [. . .] breaks" (161).

It comes as no surprise to any reader of Burke that this eminently practical methodology is philosophically anchored in a theory of substance.

> That is, in contrast with those "semantic" theories which would banish from their vocabulary any terms for "substance," we must believe above all in the reasonableness of "entitling." Confronting a complexity of details, we do not confine ourselves merely to the detailed tracing of interrelationships among them, or among the ones that we consider outstanding. We must also keep prodding ourselves to attempt answering this question: "Suppose you were required to find an overall title for this entire batch of particulars. What would that be?" (153–54)

Thus it is assumed as a regulative maxim that "all the disparate details included under one head are infused with a common spirit, i.e., are consubstantial" (153). This organicist and formalist assumption, of course, has a built-in deductive aspect as well as an element of self-fulfilling prophecy. It goes a long way toward ensuring that we shall find what we are looking for; the limits are those of our ingenuity. Our process through a text is one of essentialization by entitlement, as we progressively essentialize the various parts until we arrive at the title of titles that inspirits the whole. One sees here in embryo ideas that are brought to fruition in *The Rhetoric of Religion.*

Given that *Portrait* is divided into five parts, Burke seeks to determine what their titles should be if one were to try to essentialize their contents. I propose neither to trace Burke's mapping out of the text's internal consistency nor to rehearse in detail his filling out of its stages. Rather, I shall give a skeletal outline of the stages he discovers in *Portrait* through his process of "essentializing by entitlement" (159).

Because *Portrait* "leads up to the explicit propounding of an Esthetic (a doctrine, catechism, or 'philosophy' of art)" (155), Burke feels that we should consider the parts from this point of view. The first chapter, he suggests, might be called "Childhood Sensibility" since it deals with "rudimentary sensory perception, primary sensations of smell, touch, sight, sound, taste (basic bodily feelings that, at a later stage in the story, will be methodically 'mortified')" (155). The aesthetic, then, "begins in simple *aisthesis.* [. . .] Family relations, religion, and even politics are thus 'esthetically' experienced in this opening part; experienced not as mature 'ideas,' or even as adolescent 'passions,' but as 'sensations,' 'images'" (155).

The second chapter, Burke suggests, might be called "The Fall" since its climactic episode is Stephen's succumbing to lust and falling into sexual experience. The sordid reality of his furtive encounters with prostitutes contrasts sharply with his idealized vision of Mercedes, a figure of virginal purity rather than libidinal desire.

The third chapter, he suggests, might be called "The Sermon," "for that ironic masterpiece of rhetorical amplification is clearly the turning point of the chapter" (160). The sermon exacerbates Stephen's sense of being in mortal sin and leads to his temporary repentance and regeneration.

The fourth chapter, Burke suggests, might be called either "The New Vocation" or "Epiphany."

> The partially involuntary fall through sexual passion at the end of Chapter II might be distinguished from the deliberate fall of Chapter IV (the choice of a new vocation) somewhat as "passive" is distinguished from "active." It is the latter Stephen equates with Luciferian pride, epitomized in his many variants of the for-

> mula, "I will not serve" [. . . .] By the time the book is finished, the theme of falling has been translated into the theme of ecstatic elevation. (169n)

According to Burke, the entelechial moment at which the work comes to fruition is Stephen's vision of the bird-girl, symbol of his new vocation and manifestation of "mortal beauty" and "profane joy," as opposed to the false allure of immortal beauty and sacred joy offered by the seductive call to the priesthood. However, "when the choice is between religion and art is finally made, it is a qualified choice, as art will be conceived in terms of theology secularized" (160).

The final chapter, Burke suggests, might be called "The New Doctrine," "for what we have here is a catechistic equivalent of the revelation that forms the ecstatic end of Chapter IV" (160).

"Fact, Inference, and Proof" does not lend itself to effective summary, for the details of Burke's indexings and concordances (his pursuit of such terms as swish, soutane, fly, flight, silence, and so forth) are what give solidity of specification to his remarkably thoroughgoing analysis of Joyce's text. As Burke's schematizing of *Portrait* attests, essentializing by entitlement makes for elegant architectonics, and, in conjunction with the principle of the concordance, turns the text into a total symbolic structure wherein every detail signifies. Nevertheless, "a way of seeing is also a way of not seeing" (*PC* 49), and Burke's focus on the symbolic runs the risk of viewing the work as *nothing but* "a circle of terminal relationships" ("Fact" 152). Whereas there is nothing necessarily anti-dramatistic about this sort of analysis, the context of situation is attenuated to the extent that formal self-sufficiency of the work is underscored. It is worth mentioning, however, by way of mitigation, that even within this unremittingly formalist and symbolic approach to Joyce's text, Burke keeps the dramatistic perspective in view. "The social and linguistic pyramids," he writes, "are naturally interwoven, we take it, as language is a social product [. . .] So our thoughts about hierarchical tension lead us to watch out for modes of *catharsis,* or of *transcendence,* that may offer a symbolic solution *within the given symbol-system of the particular work we are analyzing*" (165–66).

The formalist or symbolic approach to fiction has other shortcomings as well. It leads one to disregard aspects of narrative that many critics have found central to an understanding of *Portrait*. Burke asks no questions about narrative perspective, narrative voice, or authorial distance, and even more surprising, this master ironist is strangely insensitive to the possibilities of irony. He takes it for granted the doctrine of art is the consummation of the book, "the explicit propounding of an Esthetic" (155).

In general, the formalist or symbolic approach to fiction invites one to underemphasize the fact that fiction give us its *story* (the chronological and causal sequence of moments and events) in a particular *discourse* (the textual sequence of moments and events) from a particular angle of vision (narrative perspective) and in a particular language (narrative voice).² Crucial questions thus emerge, questions concerning the actual sequence of moments and events, the narrative sequence in which they are related to the reader, the agent who is perceiving, and the agent who is speaking, questions that the formalist or symbolic approach is likely to leave unposed. That is, given Joyce's rendering the verbal action primarily from Stephen's perspective though not always in Stephen's voice, is there an ironic distance between Stephen's perception of himself and the perception of him we construct from the symbolic action of the novel as a whole? Is Stephen an artificer, like his mythological namesake Dedalus, trying to escape the labyrinths of Irish society, or is he a rebellious son, like Icarus, doomed to fly too high and to plummet ingloriously down? Are the epiphanies authentic by definition or does their sometimes overblown diction indicate other possibilities? Is Stephen's philosophy of art aesthetic gospel or sterile aestheticism? Is his villanelle anticipatory of mature artistry or of barren formalism? Given that each of the four chapters ends with an epiphany of sorts and that each of the succeeding chapters begins with a depression of sorts, is the direction of the novel as a whole progressive, a gradual dialectical process toward a crowning synthesis (Stephen's doctrine of art and attainment of freedom) or is it cyclical, a repetitive pattern of rise and fall? Is Stephen's understanding of art and experience adequate? Are his apprenticeship and education successful? I am not suggesting that these alternatives are mutually exclusive or that Burke should be compelled to answer these questions. But these are the questions that a narratological approach to *Portrait* invites, questions that Wayne Booth explicitly formulates and confronts in the third and final part of *The Rhetoric of Fiction*, "Impersonal Narration." For Booth the questions are invidiously unanswerable because the impersonal narration Joyce deploys creates a problem of distance that makes definitive moral judgment impossible. As Booth puts it, "the deep plunges of modern inside views, the various streams-of-consciousness that attempt to give the reader an effect of living thought and sensation, are capable of blinding us to the possibility of our making judgments not shared by the narrator or reflector himself" (324). In an "authorless" work such as *Portrait*, Booth contends, we are so immersed in the *Lebenswelt* of the focal character, Stephen, that no other perspective is available, and the author's choice to efface himself from the narration elides his own evaluative stance toward the materials of his own novel. The third-person limited-omniscient style of narration is itself an impediment to moral judgment. Narrative technique obscures ethical value.

If no other perspective than Stephen's were available, then to understand and describe the relationship between the norms of the straight focal character and those of the possibly ironic implied author would be a task foredoomed to failure, for we would be unable to tell, as Booth points out, whether Stephen is "always to be viewed with the same deadly seriousness with which he views himself" (327). But, as I shall later try to show, other perspectives are available, and the novel is much more dialogical and dramatistic than either Burke or Booth acknowledges.

In making his argument that impersonal narration is the enemy of ethical clarity, Booth isolates "three crucial episodes, all from the final section: [Stephen's] rejection of the priesthood, his exposition of what he takes to be a Thomistic aesthetics, and his composition of a poem" (*Rhetoric of Fiction* 327).[3]

Booth cites critics who see Stephen's rejection of the priesthood as a choice of eternal damnation and critics who see it as an affirmation of artistic freedom. For Booth, the very existence of contradictory interpretations is an epistemic scandal. "Unless we are willing to retreat into babbling and incommunicable relativism," he writes, "we cannot believe that [the rejection of the priesthood episode] is *both* a portrait of the prisoner freed *and* a portrait of the soul placing itself in chains" (328). He applies the same logic to the other two episodes, maintaining that the aesthetic theory cannot be both serious gospel and immature ideation and that the villanelle cannot be both accomplished artistry and pompous precocity.

The problem for Booth resides in Joyce's rejection of traditional devices for controlling distance. Unlike in *Stephen Hero,* the forerunner of *Portrait,* wherein Joyce interpolated praise and blame through authorial commentary, Joyce writes himself out of *Portrait.* As a result,

Stephen is "ambiguously distant from the norms of the work," and the "complications of distance become incalculable" (332).

These complications would indeed be incalculable if the novel were as Booth describes it, but it is inaccurate to say that *Portrait* is an authorless and monological work that offers no other perspective than that of its focal character. The novel, in Mikhail Bakhtin's terms, is heteroglot and dialogical, containing different registers of language (heteroglot) and offering perspectives that counter and qualify Stephen's point of view (dialogical). A brief but inexhaustive survey reveals at least nine different registers:

1. a child's fragmented sensory impressions at the beginning of the novel
2. the schoolboy slang at Clongowes, the Jesuit school Stephen attends
3. the dramatic action and dialogue of the Christmas dinner scene with its informal rhetoric of invective, lamentation, and praise along with the pithy sarcasm, colorful language, and blasphemous ranting of Mr. Dedalus and Mr. Simon
4. the formal rhetoric of the majestic Jesuit sermon, beautiful though terrifying to a boy in a state of mortal sin
5. the language of epiphany, with its soaring and lyrical prose
6. the undergraduate bantering of Stephen's fellow students, intellectual talk along with profane and brutal colloquialisms mostly uttered at Stephen's expense
7. the magical language of folklore and Celtic legend in Gavin's evocative narrative
8. actual first-person stream-of consciousness in Stephen's diary fragments
9. the formal philosophic discourse of Stephen's aesthetic theory.

Such heteroglossia broadens the mimetic base considerably. One does not have to be told explicitly about the entanglements of politics, nationality, and religion when one hears Stephen's father say: "We are an unfortunate priestridden race and always were and always will be till the end of the chapter. [. . .] A priestridden Godforsaken race" (28). Nor does one have to guess what impact this dreadful row at Christmas dinner has on a sensitive, introverted young boy:

>   —God and religion before everything! Dante cried. God and religion before the world!
>
>   Mr. Casey raised his clenched fist and brought it down on the table with a crash.
>
>   —Very well, then, he shouted hoarsely, if it comes to that, no God for Ireland! [. . .]
>
>   —No God for Ireland! he cried. We have had too much God in Ireland. Away with God!
>
>   —Blasphemer! Devil! screamed Dante, starting to her feet and almost spitting in his face. [. . .]
>
>   Mr. Casey, freeing his arms from his holders, suddenly bowed his head on his hands with a sob of pain.
>
>   —Poor Parnell! He cried loudly. My dead king!
>
>   He sobbed loudly and bitterly.
>
>   Stephen, raising his terrorstricken face, saw that his father's eyes were full of tears. (29–30)

This is the end of a scene that goes on for ten pages, and Stephen's presence is infrequently and intermittently felt, his focal position being resumed only in the final sentence. There can be little doubt that the implied author is on the side of Irish nationalism with Mr. Dedalus and Mr. Casey, an allegiance which makes Stephen's rejection of the priesthood unambiguous. The call to the priesthood is a false call. The very terms in which it is couched, terms that stress power rather humility, make acquiescence akin to the sin of pride:

>   A strong note of pride reinforcing the gravity of the priest's voice made Stephen's heart quicken in response.
>
>   To receive that call, Stephen, said the priest, is the greatest honour that the almighty God can bestow upon a man. No king or emperor has the power of the priest of God. No angel or archangel in heaven, no saint, not even the Blessed Virgin herself has the power of a priest of God: the power of the keys, the power to bind and to loose from sin, the power of exorcism, the power to cast out from the creatures of God the evil spirits that have power over them, the power, the authority, to make the great God of Heaven come

> down upon the altar and take the form of bread and wine. What an awful power, Stephen!
>
> A flame began to flutter again on Stephen's cheek as he heard in the proud address an echo of his own proud musings. (134)

To my mind, this unequivocal appeal to power and pride makes morally clear the falsity of the priesthood's allure.

As for Stephen's Thomistic aesthetics, it is both impressive and pretentious. His capacity to unsheathe his dagger definitions shows that "Stephen has what Buck Mulligan in *Ulysses* calls 'the cursed jesuit strain . . . only it's injected the wrong way'" (qtd. in "Fact" 161). Cranly, too, later points out in *Portrait* that Stephen's "mind is supersaturated with the religion in which [he says he disbelieves]" (240). Anyone who starts a discourse by saying "Aristotle has not defined pity and I terror. I have" (175) is setting himself up for the ironic treatment. And the responses of his friends are telling. "Lynch halted and said bluntly:—Stop! I won't listen! I am sick. I was out last night on a yellow drunk with Horan and Goggins" (175). Throughout Stephen's attempt at monologue, there are many such interjections: "—You say that art must not excite desire, said Lynch. I told you that one day I wrote my name in pencil on the backside of Venus of Praxiteles in the Museum. Was not that desire?" (176). Clearly, Stephen's friends do not take him as seriously as he takes himself. Stephen has a brilliant mind, and his applied Aquinas is an intellectual *tour de force,* but it is not, as Burke would have it, the explicit propounding of an aesthetic shared by the novel as a whole. Again I see no ambiguity. Stephen is both a serious thinker and a pompous ass, hardly an unusual combination in academic circles.

The same goes for the villanelle. Stephen shows virtuoso technical mastery of a difficult form, but his erotic sentiments are those of an adolescent, and he expresses them, naturally enough, in the fin-de-siècle prose of decadent aestheticism, the prose he admires with all the passion of his youth as if its voluptuous rhythms were coursing through his veins:

> A glow of desire kindled again his soul and fired and fulfilled all his body. Conscious of his desire she was waking from odorous sleep, the temptress of his villanelle. Her eyes, dark and with a look of languor, were

> opening to his eyes. Her nakedness yielded to him, radiant, warm, odorous, and lavish-limbed, enfolded him like a shining cloud, enfolded him like water with a liquid life: and like a cloud of vapour or like waters circumfluent in space the liquid letters of speech, symbols of the element of mystery, flowed forth from his brain. (191)

It is hard not to see irony at work here, especially when his erotic desires get translated into the formally perfect but linguistically stilted style of the villanelle's patterned repetitions, the first two tercets of which read:

> Are you not weary of ardent ways,
> Lure of the fallen seraphim?
> Tell no more of enchanted days.
> Your eyes have set man's heart ablaze
> And you have had your will of him.
> Are you not weary of ardent ways? (191)

It seems to me that Booth gets it right when he sees the villanelle as a "sign of [Stephen's] genuine but amusingly pretentious artistry" (*Rhetoric of Fiction* 328). The entire episode makes it seem as if the creation of a competent but conventional verse form were the equivalent of the incarnation of Christ.

> Towards dawn he awoke. His soul was all dewy wet. Over his limbs in sleep pale cool waves of light had passed. He lay still, as if his soul lay amid cool waters, conscious of faint sweet music. His mind was waking slowly to a tremulous morning knowledge, a morning inspiration [. . .] O! In the virgin womb of the imagination the word was made flesh. Gabriel the seraph had come to the virgin's chamber [. . .] The verses passed from his mind to his lips and, murmuring them over, he felt the rhythmic movement of a villanelle pass through them. The roselike glow sent forth its rays of rhyme; ways, days, blaze, praise, raise. Its rays burned up the world, consumed the hearts of

men and angels: the rays from the rose that was her
willful heart. (186)

And so on for some six pages.

It is no surprise that hyperbole is the master trope of teenage love and that like most precocious young adults Stephen is a work in progress. It is enough that the novel has laid down the preconditions for successful artistry and that Stephen has found his salvation and vocation in choosing the aesthetic orientation over the social, nationalist, or religious orientation. He embodies both Dedalus and Icarus and bears within him the potential fate of either. Even if we cannot always distinguish absolutely between the focal character's viewpoint and that of the novel as a whole—the narrative perspective being almost entirely Stephen's but the narrative voice being a sometimes ambiguous admixture of Stephen's and the narrator's—it seems to me that ethical judgment is possible though, obviously, open to argument. In the three episodes Booth subjects to scrutiny, it seems clear that the call to the priesthood is false (Catholicism being the main cause of the stultifying paralysis that besets Irish society) and that the villanelle and the aesthetic theory are the products of an adolescent who is both a talented intellectual and a pompous ass. Whether the epiphanies are valid by definition or their sometimes overblown diction indicates other possibilities and whether the pattern of the novel as whole is progressive or cyclical: these issues are not so easily resolved. But once we see the novel as less essentialist and more dialogical than does either Burke or Booth, the novel's assumed internal consistency and putative problems of distance begin to recede as a more manageable ambiguity begins to emerge, an ambiguity which leaves intact our capacities both for close reading and for ethical judgment.

Notes

1. In *Doing What Comes Naturally*, Fish challenges absolutely the "the brute-fact status of the text" (75). For him, even at the most rudimentary level, the very grammar, syntax, and semantics of a text are created by the interpretive strategy of a reader. "There is no distinction between what the text gives and the reader supplies; he supplies *everything*" (77). In my view, a defensible claim that no priority can be ascribed to either the linguistic structure of the text or the interpretive strategy of the reader gets confused with a claim that is as unverifiable as it is irrefutable: namely, that the interpretive strategy of the reader entirely determines the intentionality of a text and its

formal realization. Although well aware that "'terministic screens' direct the *attention*" (*LSA* 45), Burke is also aware that "even if any given terminology is a *reflection* of reality, by its very nature as a terminology it must be a *selection* of reality; and to this extent it must function also as a *deflection* of reality" (45). That indexing has no absolute foundation in terminal factuality, that some principle of selection is unavoidable Burke readily admits. But this pragmatic admission need not be inflated into a metaphysical difficulty. For practical purposes one does treat words as linguistic facts, and in most contexts one does take grammar and syntax at face value. This is not to say that the nihilistic game cannot be played, for Fish plays it brilliantly, with panache, even genius. But, to my mind, when all is said and done, a nihilist is just a pragmatist with an attitude problem.

2. In what follows, I do not mean to chastise Burke for not doing what he had no intention of doing. The purpose of his essay is to illustrate a method. As he himself observes, however, "*every* insight contains its own special kind of blindness" (*ATH* 41), and indexing, like any other critical method, is a trained incapacity as well as a trained capacity. "Fact, Inference, and Proof" focuses on what modern narrative theory calls discourse at the expense of story, narration, and textuality. Such theory, as I have noted, is predicated on an enabling distinction between story (narrative content, what really happened, the actual chronological and causal sequence of moments and events) and discourse (narrative presentation, how what really happened is related to the reader, the textual sequence of moments and events). Story is an abstraction that can only be inferred and constructed by the listener or reader from the discourse(s) he or she must absorb and synthesize. Story is crucial to legal decision-making wherein the task of the jury or judge is to make a plausible and coherent story out of the disparate and chaotic particulars of a case that is often awash in a sea of conflicting evidence, contradictory versions of events, antithetical precedents, unclear controlling laws, incompatible expert reports, ambiguous legal documents, and, in general, at least two opposed and competing discourses. Unlike story, discourse (the sounds in the air, the words on the page) is a concrete reality whose existence is certain, but whose meaning is anything but. Along with story and discourse are two other levels of narrative: narration and textuality. Narration comprises focalization and verbalization, who is perceiving (narrative perspective) and who is speaking (narrative voice). Narration is the level of narrative Booth explores in "The Problem of Distance in *Portrait of the Artist*." Textuality comprises the interrelationships among what really happened, how what really happened is related to the listener or reader, and who does the telling and from what angle of vision. It also comprises intertextuality and metatextuality. Texts inevitably incorporate other texts (intertextuality) as well as presuppose generic foreknowledge, literary competence, and other kinds of prior knowledge. These presuppositions Burke calls conventional form, categorical expectations a

reader has anterior to the reading process. Other expectations arise from the reading process and are created, thwarted, and fulfilled as the reader tries to build consistency and make sense of the text (metatextuality). This process involves what Burke calls progressive and repetitive form. In "Psychology and Form," "Lexicon Rhetoricae," and "Applications of Terminology" (early essays from *Counter-Statement*) Burke has much to say about the metatextual building of form, "the creation of an appetite in the mind of the auditor, and the adequate satisfying of that appetite" (31). I discuss this topic in "A Rhetoric of Form: The Early Burke and Reader-Response Criticism."

3. The rejection of the priesthood episode is from the penultimate section, not the final one.

6 Style and the Defense of Rhetoric: Burke's and Aristotle's Competing Models of Mind

James Kastely

Kenneth Burke begins his essay "Semantic and Poetic Meaning" with a suggestive anecdote. With a casualness that often marks a Burke argument, he mentions that he had been told that the historian Arnold Toynbee argued for a pattern that recurred in moments of spiritual crisis and renewal. At the core of the crisis is a shift in the underlying situation faced by people when they find a prevailing value system no longer adequate for dealing with a substantive change in circumstances. During these times there is a necessary period of withdrawal that is marked by a falling apart—the old structure of values needs to collapse to make room for a new and more appropriate set of values. Burke characterizes this period as one of "hesitancy, brooding, or even rot" (138). The fact of withdrawal is central in this anecdote because Burke will take it up as the analogue to the activity of analytic abstraction, which he will argue is at the center of a project seeking to transcend the partisanship, be it intellectual or political, produced by contending perspectives within a given situation. Burke believes this project is governed by an impossible ideal embodied in the concept of "semantic meaning." In brief, he argues that the advocates for semantic meaning commit an error parallel to those spiritual leaders who, finding themselves in a state of crisis, misread the crisis, which is a historical moment through which we must pass, and treat it, instead, as our underlying condition. They thus mistakenly attempt to extend a moment into a lifetime. In a similar fashion, the advocates of semantic meaning take a necessary moment in our intellectual life—the moment when we seek analytic detachment—and then elevate this moment and treat it as the norm for the larger act that is human understanding.

For Burke, this more comprehensive act of human understanding is guided by an alternative ideal he labels "poetic meaning." He is quick to point out that semantic and poetic meaning are not inherently in opposition; rather, their relation is more like part to whole—although he acknowledges that there seems to be an ineluctable dialectic that ends up putting them in opposition. At the heart of this opposition are two approaches to understanding: those pursuing the ideal of semantic meaning seek a way to abstract from the particular content of a situation and to explore the dynamics of that situation in terms of its logical form; those committed to the ideal of poetic meaning seek the opposite—rather than emptying out the content of a situation they seek to bring all of the key elements into play, assuming that meaning depends on the fullest possible inclusion.

Burke offers this analysis on behalf of his "rhetorical defense of rhetoric" (138). His defense leads him to argue for the importance of rhetoric because he believes style to be an essential component of thought. In this, he contrasts sharply with those defenses of rhetoric, for which Aristotle can be considered as the chief spokesperson, in which style is not considered to make an intellectually significant contribution to rhetoric as an art. Aristotle, for example, relegates his discussion of style to Book 3 of his *Rhetoric,* where he seems to address style regretfully as a necessary evil, as a concession to human weakness. And although Burke's essay is more a suggestive than a developed defense of style, his difference with Aristotle provides a productive place to engage the question of the status of style within an artistic rhetoric. Is style in rhetoric primarily a strategic concern as to how best to move a particular audience, or is it a constitutive element that defines a way of being in the world?

The larger structure of Aristotle's *Rhetoric* reflects his understanding of the hierarchy of intellectual operations involved in an act of rhetoric and of the minor role that style should play in an artistic rhetoric. In Book 1, Aristotle lays out the conditions necessary for rhetoric to be an art rather than simply an instance of emotional manipulation. His reform of then current rhetorical practice starts from his recovery of the indeterminacy at the heart of rhetoric. According to Aristotle, those contemporary practitioners of a corrupt rhetoric failed to practice rhetoric artistically because they did not understand that the judgment at the core of any rhetorical act is open and that it is the skill or craft of the rhetor that allows for the temporary closure of this openness. The corrupt rhetors simply assumed that the materials of any case are given and that the only area of agency open to them lay in the emotional manipulation of the judge or audience. In contrast, Aristotle argues that the central and defining activity of rhetoric is providing guidance in those situations in which judgment is possible and in which technical knowledge is either insufficient or unhelpful in determining the judgment. The most important part of the rhetor's art is the invention or discovery of the best judgment in a particular situation and that is accomplished through the skillful use of inference from enthymemes and examples.

Once that judgment has been determined, it needs to be made effective for a particular audience. This becomes the tasks of Books 2 and 3. In Book 2 Aristotle discusses how to configure a judgment ethically and emotionally so that it is most likely to persuade a given audience. In Book 3 he takes up issues of style, arrangement, and delivery as the final and strategic concerns that, although playing no role in the determination of the content of the judgment, have consequences for the effectiveness of the speech. Aristotle seems to broach this area with some regret, with the feeling that if only humans were more fully and consistently rational, then matters of style, arrangement, and delivery would be irrelevant, as such matters are in arts that are more purely intellectual: "The subject of expression, however, has some small necessary place in all teaching: for to speak in one way rather than another does make some difference in regard to clarity, though not a great difference; but all these things are forms of outward show and intended to affect the audience. As a result, nobody teaches geometry this way" (218–19; 1404a6–7). For Aristotle, it follows that the chief virtues of a good style are clarity and appropriateness. The rhetor's language should be clear and appropriate because a language that embodies these qualities best serves the communication of the invented judgment. The force of the rhetor's argument should arise primarily from the uses of the pisteis (the persuasives), for it is the artful use of *logos, ethos* and *pathos* that justifies rhetoric's status as a *techne*. The rhetor's attention to style is, at best, a concession to the limitation of the human audience, and it is precisely this limitation that the inartistic practitioners and theorists made the center of their pseudo-art.

Accordingly, Aristotle defends rhetoric as an art by reforming it so that style is given only a minor supporting role to invention. It is the act of invention that makes rhetoric artistic, for invention is an intellectual practice in which an inferential reasoning process can discover judgments that can close indeterminate practical situations. Implied in this defense is a view of mind as an inferential agency whose primary operation is charting the logical entailment that occurs in enthymemic and paradigmatic structures. Mind, as a practical agency, is enacted through a process of logical or quasi-logical inference, and rhetoric, situated between logic and politics, becomes the civic art through which the practical mind acts.

Burke, who was a great admirer of Aristotle's *Rhetoric*, shares a concern with developing an effective political discourse, but he mounts a very different defense of rhetoric. For him, style is not simply a matter of accommodating human limitations but rather it is at the heart of any act of rhetorical understanding. He organizes his defense of rhetoric around the imperatives of style to challenge explicitly a model of thought that Burke saw as mistaken and, more often than not, pernicious. His guiding insight is that disciplined neutrality in language is itself a stylistic choice, and one with very limited application. At times, such neutrality may play an important analytic role and help one temporarily put an inherited frame of perception in abeyance, but even this important role is short-lived and unstable. Implicit in his argument is the point that such a view of mind offers a false security in politically difficult times by holding out the promise of a perspective that is not itself factional. The semantic ideal would be a way to stand outside or above the fray. But Burke questions both the possibility and desirability of such a stance. For him, meaning can only emerge through a participation in the symbolic agon that seeks to address the particular situation in which the speaker and audience find themselves, and, if meaning is to be possible, then it must be earned through an agonistic labor. The alternative is to empty language and thought of meaning.

In "Semantic and Poetic Meaning," Burke's particular target is the positivistic discourse prevalent at the time. Such discourse has only a historical interest for us now; however, we can broaden his discussion of the semantic ideal by focusing on certain features that need not be limited to the particular tenets of positivism. Burke's larger argument speaks to two possible conceptions of mind. The semantic ideal sees mind as an analytic instrument that works through abstraction. When mind reasons, it abstracts from the particulars in a situation, locates the key structural components, and defines their relationship to each other. Central to this process of abstraction—indeed the point of this process—is to cleanse the thinker's perception of the situation of the accidental coloring that it receives through the participants emotional involvement in that situation. The semantic ideal "would try to cut away, to abstract, all emotional factors that complicate the objective clarity of meaning" (148). The ideal would establish a perspective that has been emptied of particular identity; in effect, it would seek a perspective that has been purified of the partiality that marks all other perspectives. On this view, mind is ahistorical, and when it operates within the canons of logic, it can thus make a claim to be a superior perspective, escaping the bias of a particular faction and consequently offering the clearest view of the situation.

Burke has no quarrel with there being a perspective that is above all other perspectives; his only quarrel is over the way to achieve such a perspective. Where the semantic ideal would seek to achieve this perspective by freeing itself from the contamination and distortion produced by emotional involvement—a strategy Burke labels as "analgesic" (150)—Burke would seek this perspective by engaging the contending partial perspectives and structuring their contest as an agon or drama in which the conflict would seek to work through these partial perspectives to arrive at a more complete or comprehensive view. Such a strategy is "aesthetic," (150) in the sense that it seeks to compose feelings or find new and more adequate feelings by working through the conflicted feelings. For Burke, the act of working through the contending perspectives (which are not simply angles on a situation but emotional orientations within a situation) is absolutely necessary if knowledge is to be achieved. The last thing that serious participants should want is to remove themselves from the fray, achieve distance, and observe coolly what is going on. However appealing such a calm detachment appears to be, its appeal is deceptive because it cannot offer the one thing that it promises: knowledge. Knowledge must be earned, and that means that one needs to work through and not distance oneself from the conflicting attitudes within a situation. The goal of a poetically structured pursuit of meaning is not so much a universal truth as it is a more complex, mature, and appropriate feeling or attitude toward and within a situation.

Burke's claim that there is a necessary link between working through the various warring perspectives and obtaining knowledge has a close kinship to Jonathan Lear's reinterpretation of Freud. In explaining the nature of the talking cure, Lear argues:

> But the analysand's talking is not so much the formulation of a detached view *of* his subjectivity as it is an expression of a higher level of the very subjectivity he is trying to understand. The analysand's emerging, conscious theory of how he goes on is thus incestuously related to his archaic "theory." The conscious, verbal account grows out of an archaic attempt "to say the same thing." The analysand, then, is not the detached observer of his subjectivity; his talk is the growth of that subjectivity. And it is because talking stands in a developmental relation to its archaic forebears that it can exert some influence over them. Nothing less is at stake than the transformation of the mode in which a person's subjectivity is expressed. (38)

What Burke and Lear share is the assumption that knowledge is obtained by talking through the situation, and that knowledge is something that we can possess only if we are willing to participate in a dialectic or agon. This participation does not simply reveal a state of affairs but rather alters subjectivity (for Burke, the term would be "identity"), for as one engages in the symbolic struggle or undertakes the talking cure, that person is transforming an attitude by creating a more adequate view of the world and of the possibilities for action. To acquire knowledge is to transform nature, or at least it is to transform our nature, for, as Burke is always reminding us, action is creative. We are always in the process of making and remaking worlds that either serve or frustrate human intentions.

Since this rhetorical process is essentially contributory to the betterment or worsening of the human condition, it cannot be impartial and should not aspire to a condition of neutrality. The attempt to know is, for Burke, an inherently moral activity—it is propaedeutic to action. Such attempts to know are always attempts to take a position toward something or someone. Their goal is never what might be called mere knowledge—that acquisition of information either for the sake of such acquisition or for the sake of some future use—but rather, these attempts to know are always preparations for action: they are always the working through and towards an attitude. Burke argues that

> [a] fully moral act is basically an act *now*. It is not promissory, it is not "investment for future profit." It is not the learning of a technique in the hopes that this technique, when learned, will enable one to make wheels go or to add a few more metallurgical alloys to the 500,000 or so that "business" and "industry" have not yet found "use" for. A fully moral act is a total assertion at the time of assertion. Among other things, it has a *style*—and this style is an integral aspect of its meaning. (148)

Style is not something added to an already worked out idea that makes the idea more palatable or available to a given audience; on the contrary, it is an integral part of the larger moral act of coming to know. Since style designates the manner in which we make our assertions, it cannot be something imposed on a preexisting matter; rather, it must be something that evolves out of the on-going agon of contending perspectives. Style is an achievement; it is what results when one submits to the work demanded of us in those situations in which we seek understanding. As Burke puts it, "the style selected will mold the character of the selector" (148). This characterization can stand as long as we don't interpret selection as necessarily a conscious process; rather, what it marks is the fact of choices being made and those choices having consequences that cannot be confined simply to a particular action. In a language different from Lear's, Burke is making the same point: human subjectivity is an achievement tied to the skillful use of language. As we use our symbolicity, we continually remake ourselves and create and recreate our identities. One of our most important tasks is to earn a style that will, in the best of circumstances, allow for a human flourishing, and, in other circumstances, at least permit a humane stance toward others. For this reason, style is both a deeply individual matter and, at the same time, inescapably a political concern.

Burke's concern with the political importance of style, and hence of rhetoric, leads him to speculate on the benefits of a "strenuous cult of style" (161) and to raise in the same spirit the idea that no one should speak except on subjects on which one can become eloquent. What he seeks in this half-serious proposal is not a freedom of expression but a commitment to rigor, a commitment to search for a language adequate to our passions and situations. For him, the search would challenge a certain inertia that is produced by current political styles. The emergence of a genuine political style would equip us to deal with a situation that Burke characterizes as one of "political gloom ranging anywhere from a repellant aimlessness to an even more repellent aim (and if we get the latter, men will give blows with twice the furry of blows, striking with vengeance, and making him also the recipient of their rage against past uncertainties within themselves)" (161). I quote this because, although intended for the late 1930s and early 1940s, it seems to me to be a remarkable characterization of our current political situation, and it suggests that the reading of Burke should have consequences for our style and for our political scene. It should help us seek to discover or invent a democratic mind. Far from being considered an instrumental or utilitarian concern or an unmediated expression of a subjectivity, style should be seen as an occasion for moral responsibility within a political situation, and, when viewed in this way, it is especially crucial to a democracy with its commitment to government shaped, in part, by persuasion.

Style, then, as Burke conceives it registers the way in which symbolically motivated animals are invested in their symbolic actions, and style becomes a key component in a defense of rhetoric because rhetoric is the study and practice of stylized expression. If we are to understand ourselves and our worlds, then we need to find the styles that enable us to know and act in those worlds.

Let me close by extending this argument. Since the search for and discovery of style is a search for meaning, the on-going invention of style represents and embodies the development of mind. As we agonistically work through the contending perspectives that reside in a situation and invent a more complex and adequate perspective and attitude, we are creating our minds, we are forming and reforming our capacities to perceive. Again, as Burke puts it, we are learning not only what to look for but also what to look out for (164). Part of this ongoing drama will involve moments of analytic detachment, and these moments will be marked by a reasoning that seeks to abstract from the particulars of a situation in order to locate a ground that appears to not be limited by a particular history or perspective. Even if these attempts are inevitably doomed to failure, they can have beneficial effects. At the very least, they can have the important negative effect of inducing self-consciousness and reminding us of our own limited perspective. But these moments are not the paradigmatic moments of mind and we should not use them as our representative anecdotes to explore what mind is. Rather, we should look for mind by understanding it as act, as agon, as drama, and by recognizing that mind is not so much capacity as it is achievement.

It would be wrong to put Aristotle in simple opposition to Burke, for Aristotle was certainly not a proponent of the simplistic model of mind to which the positivists subscribed. Even in his *Rhetoric,* the role of *ethos* and *pathos* complicates that of *logos,* for all three are legitimate sources of persuasion. Nor is Aristotle naïve about the role of emotion in thought. His Book 2 is one of the most sophisticated discussions of the cognitive force of emotion (see Garver, 115–38) and it recognizes that emotions are not simply internal states but rather complex responses that in themselves register perceptions of reality. So I am not attempting to use Aristotle as representative of a naïve model of mind. Rather, I want to suggest that his defense of rhetoric gives place of preference to the logical act of inference and embodies a model of mind, which has little interest in style as a substantive component of thought. Geometry is his choice for the paradigm for a discourse that is not hampered by human limitations—it is an instance in which the mind is acting in an uncompromised way as mind. Because our practical discourses inescapably must deal with our emotional investments in a situation, he concedes a place for style as an important ancillary instrument for mind.

In his defense of rhetoric Burke challenges this account because he sees style not as something added to an already completed act of mind but as something integral to mind, for style is achieved only by participating in the agon of perspectives and attitudes. Style is what is earned when we seek to be adequate to our passions. To participate in these agons is to engage in the on-going creation of mind; it is to achieve a new perspective or attitude within and toward a situation. When we achieve this new perspective, we feel differently toward the situation, or perhaps because we feel differently toward a situation, we perceive it differently. Perspective, feeling, and style are mutually implicating. For Burke, to be a symbolic animal is to be fated to be passionately oriented in the world. Our minds are constituted by symbolic agons and this means that style is a central moral concern, for how we conduct these agons—our styles within and resulting from them—plays a central role in how we will act.

Burke's brief comments on the inanity of political style and its consequences for democracy can now be understood as pointing to a crisis in the democratic mind. The assumption that there can be an objective, impartial, or neutral language of information that is often an unreflective assumption behind mainstream journalism or the equally fallacious assumption that since no objectivity is possible, one is free simply and tenaciously to defend one's own privileged perspective: these are two extremes that threaten the growth of a democratic mind adequate to deal with the current world of significantly differing perspectives. Burke's playful proposal to hold oneself to the standard of only speaking on those topics on which one can be eloquent suggests a stylistic test that could have significant consequences for reinvigoration of a democratic style and the reinvention of a democratic mind. In such a defense of rhetoric, style would be both an inescapable component of any symbolic act and also it would be norm for any of these acts. And as we learned to be eloquent about our democratic passions, we would discover what it means to think democratically. By crediting our feelings, we would enable the growth of our minds as products of and resources for a creative democratic discourse that could challenge a political climate that veers between a "repellant aimlessness to an even more repellant aim." In seeking a genuinely democratic style, we would help transform ourselves into a democratic citizenry equipped to meet the challenge of a world in which the anxiety provoked by seriously conflicting perspectives has been met with a show of force that only threatens to transform the democratic mind into an imperial, monolithic, and static mindlessness.

7 Aesthetic Power and Rhetorical Experience

Gregory Clark

Music [. . .] would be the song above catastrophe.

—Kenneth Burke

Early in *The Varieties of Religious Experience*, William James defined religion this way: "Religion [. . .] shall mean for us the feelings, acts, and experiences of individual men in their solitude, so far as they apprehend themselves to stand in relation to whatever they may consider the divine." Out of this, James continues, "theologies, philosophies, and ecclesiastical organizations may secondarily grow," but James's primary interest is in those "immediately personal experiences" (29). That is because, as he puts it further on, "If religion is to mean anything definite for us, it seems to me that we ought to take it as meaning this added dimension of emotion, this enthusiastic temper of espousal, in regions where morality strictly so called can at best bow its head and acquiesce" (43).

This essay is an exploration of what we might learn about rhetoric if we set out to understand it in something of the same way that James understood religion: as, finally, the immediately personal experiences of individuals, experiences in the face of which—to adapt and paraphrase his words to the matter at hand—the "added dimension of emotion, this enthusiastic temper of espousal," renders the sort of critical rationality that we try to associate with rhetoric at best able to "bow its head and acquiesce." Put another way, I am exploring here what might follow if we understood the primary power of rhetoric to reside not in the logical process of deliberate persuasion but, rather, in the essentially felt experience that Kenneth Burke described as *identification*—an experience that is as aesthetic in its form and content as it is rhetorical in its effect. There the process of influencing people—of prompting them to change their beliefs, their attitudes, their aspirations, their actions, and even whom they understand themselves to be—operates in ways that reach well beyond our traditional and conventional assumptions about rhetorical reasoning. This essay is an exploration of that reach.

I find inherent in my own rhetorical experiences something very similar to what James was suggesting about the transformative power of religion when he located its power in "this added dimension of emotion, this enthusiastic temper of espousal." I am suggesting that much of the transformative power of rhetoric is encountered similarly, in an experience of an alternative kind of rationality—where emotion and cognition are not only inseparable, but are finally indistinguishable. Indeed, I think we might best understand the power of the rhetorical as it operates in the variety of ways we encounter it as an experience of—using James's interesting choice of term—"espousal." This term suggests a level of commitment to something, or to someone, beyond the self in which, at least for a time, our own sense of identity itself feels transformed. This sort kind of experience is often described as aesthetic. And it is this sort of aesthetic experience of personal transformation—of a transformation of self through feelings of intimate connection with something or someone other—that is central to Burke's conception of rhetorical power.

Burke's project of reconceiving rhetoric as something much more than the experience of mere persuasion—as the pervasive and essentially human experience of identification beyond the self—moves precisely in this direction. In my recent study of some of the implications of his expanded conception, *Rhetorical Landscapes in America*, I suggested that the idea that rhetoric does the work of identification extends the realm of the rhetorical well beyond words—and beyond what Aristotle called *logos*—to include a seeming infinity of experiences of the sort that prompt people to reconsider not only what they believe, but also what they want, and who they are, are not, and might become. These *rhetorical experiences* involve more than the mind—they involve, as well, the body, and they involve the heart. That book described encounters with landscape, both actual and vicarious, as rhetorical experiences with the power to change or at least intensify feelings as well as ideas of identity and affiliation.

My primary purpose in this essay, however, is not so much to apply Burke's rhetoric of identification as to further theorize it. To do so, I am looking at another place in Burke's work that is, I believe, as important to an understanding of rhetoric as his work on identification—and that is his work on aesthetics. Indeed, at this moment in my study of Burke I would say that the most significant contributions he made to our understanding of communicative interaction are his reconceptions of the nature of rhetoric and of the nature of the aesthetic, reconceptions that, in my reading, become interdependent and, indeed, inseparable in his work. For Burke, the aesthetic is essentially an experience, one that is immediate, individual, and—primarily—emotional. And it is in the intimate context of this kind of experience that the rhetorical power of identification is finally enacted. In effect, the rhetorical itself is experienced—and it is a felt experience, primarily, and its power to influence is located in, to use James' language about religious experience, that "enthusiastic temper." Burke's insight about the *end* of rhetoric, about its *purpose*—that it provides for individuals a transformative experience of identification—is revolutionary as it prompts us to recognize a much more expansive realm of the rhetorical than our traditional notion of persuasion allows. But to understand the true extent of that realm, as well as the extent of the power to influence that operates there, we must attend to Burke's equally important insight that the *means* of rhetoric—that its *function* as we experience it—is primarily aesthetic. I believe that a full understanding of the reach and power of this rhetoric of identification requires us to recognize that it is usually encountered as a personal experience of the aesthetic.

Burke's rhetorically resonant work on aesthetics begins in *Counter-Statement* where he articulates what amounts to a rhetorical concept of aesthetic form. Most of us are familiar with these particular counterstatements. Most familiar, perhaps is this one: "Form is the creation of an appetite in the mind of the auditor, and the adequate satisfying of that appetite. This satisfaction [. . .] at times involves a temporary set of frustrations, but in the end these frustrations prove to be simply a more involved kind of satisfaction, and furthermore serve to make the satisfaction of fulfillment more intense" (30). This was written as a direct counterstatement to what was the prevailing conception of art and the artist's project. That is because at that time, as Burke continued, the artist had come to "lay his emphasis on the giving of information—with the result that art tends more and more to substitute the psychology of the hero (the subject) for the psychology of the audience" (32). The fact he wished to assert, however, is that whatever the artist's *intention,* it is the *function,* the *effect,* of the art on others that prompts its creation and that determines its value. Burke put it bluntly: always, he said, "one aims at effects . . ." (211). Further along in a reading of *Counter-Statement,* here is another well-known description of the experience of the aesthetic: "*Form* in literature is an arousing and fulfillment of desires. A work has form in so far as one part of it leads a reader to anticipate another part, to be gratified by the sequence" (124). Indeed, Burke reiterated a few pages later, "A form is a way of experiencing; and such a form is made available in art when, by the use of specific subject matter, it enables us to experience in this way" (143).

Certainly in these statements Burke is talking about art—about what we conventionally categorize as the aesthetic. But more precisely, since he is talking so insistently about effects, I read these as statements that are also about rhetoric, as Burke himself suggests by using "Lexicon Rhetoricae" for the title of the chapter in this book that analyzes aesthetic effects most systematically. *Counter-Statement* is throughout a study of how the aesthetic functions rhetorically in its influence, in its effect. Although the Burke who wrote that book was still nurturing, at least half-heartedly, his own identity as an aesthete, Burke is in later work persistently adamant about his intention to challenge the distinction that divides the aesthetic and the rhetorical. As he tells the story in his essay "Rhetoric and Poetics": "I began in the aesthete tradition, with the stress upon self-expression. Things started moving for me in earnest when, as attested in *Counter-Statement,* I made the shift from 'self-expression' to 'communication.' The theory of form [. . .] centers in that distinction" (305). (I need to add that in a 1989 interview he told me that this shift in his interest from "self-expression to communication" occurred in the process of writing *Counter-Statement* and that he thought that fact should be evident to any attentive reader of the book.) In a recently published excerpt from his manuscript "Poetics, Dramatistically Considered," Burke described the experience of reading literary art in these terms: "the kind of 'learning' that goes with an audience's engrossed participation in the successive disclosures of a plot may be more directly explainable as a sympathetic delight in and perfect unfolding of a form" ("Watchful" 38). Consequently, he continued there, since the experience of that sort of engrossed participation clearly contains—and he put this in italics—"*more than can be discussed in terms of Poetics alone*" (60), we must understand what is happening as rhetorical—as "a guiding [of the] audience's expectations and responses." That is a rhetorical experience. And such experiences are located, as Burke continues, "in an area where Rhetoric and Poetic overlap" (61). Indeed, as he put it late in *Counter-Statement,* when he had completed his own transition in aspiration from self-expression to communication, an aesthetic form is "a way of experiencing." Identification—and the transformation of a sense of self that it accomplishes—occurs when our expectations and responses are guided, together with those of others, onto the common ground of affiliation that is created by an aesthetic experience that—while it is experienced personally, individually—is shared.

Again, in the context of such an experience the rhetorical and the aesthetic not only overlap, but merge. As Burke put it, "I am much more interested in bringing the full resources of Poetics and *Rhetorica docens* to bear upon the study of a text than in trying to draw a *strict* line of demarcation between Rhetoric and Poetics" ("Rhetoric and Poetics" 307). I share that interest. I share it because I am persuaded by my own experiences that, more often than not, people respond, first and perhaps foremost, emotionally to the offers of influence that surround them. They, or I should say *we,* do not rely upon the methods we usually consider rational to determine our responses to the many prompts to believe and to act that we constantly encounter. Simply put, I don't think we decide such things as our argumentation textbooks say we do. Rather, our cool reason is always interwoven with what James described as an "added dimension of emotion," that "enthusiastic temper of espousal," in the face of which logical thinking, systematic reasoning, must simply "bow its head and acquiesce." In my reading of Burke, much of his work acknowledges that, perhaps because of his life-long concern that his compatriots become more skillfully vigilant, more perceptively defensive, in response to the very wide variety of assertions of rhetorical power in the midst of which we all must live. While some of these assertions are more or less propositional in their form, most are not. Most prompts that we encounter to believe and to do differently—essentially, to identify ourselves anew—take the form of those "immediately personal experiences," in James's phrase, which we find ourselves inhabiting more than analyzing. These experiences rarely present us with orderly chains of reasoning; rather, they immerse us in patterns of experience that carry us through an "arousing and fulfillment of desires" that leave us feeling sufficiently, in Burke's term, "gratified," to consent to an identity transformed.

Perhaps it is time for an example.

It's the early evening of September 12, 2001. It's been a long day. We're working together in the kitchen on dinner. We're not talking. The radio is on. We're listening to journalists, consultants, and government officials trying to explain the events that began so abruptly the day before. Everything stopped for all of us the day before—stopped all day. But today we had to start again and now, as this day ends, we're trying to understand what comes next. But we don't. So we listen, separately, each with our own worries and fears, until seven when news coverage ends for the first time in thirty-six hours. We wait for the familiar voice of our local jazz host to come on to introduce his nightly show. We listen to him most every dinnertime, to his music that brings us a kind of calming energy to end of our complicated days. Tonight, though, we don't hear his voice, only a silence after the newscast ends and, then, the sound of a solo piano. It's hesitant, slow, almost painful, as phrases are slowly formed from the rich and firm chords of the gospel church and are simultaneously rendered uncertain by the bent inflections of the blues. We can hear a restless audience in the background—feet shuffling, chairs scraping, glasses clinking, unintelligible bits of idle conversation and, occasionally and gradually increasing, calls of encouragement and affirmation to the pianist. They quiet as the solo gathers momentum, the chords become more rhythmic, and we find ourselves straining with them to place and recognize the vaguely familiar form of their sequence. Pianist and audience seem joined in the effort. We're trying too. Then, suddenly, a bassist and drummer join the pianist and boost him into a jubilant groove. The audience cheers and applauds at precisely the same time we recognize a familiar melancholy melody that here has been given an entirely unexpected energy: "Glory, Glory, Hallelujah [. . .]" Nobody is singing, but the words are just behind everyone's lips. The audience on the recording is clapping and stamping together. The two of us are standing together in the kitchen, stopped in our chopping and stirring to listen as our somber national dirge is transformed into a song of defiant celebration.

The pianist chords twice through the chorus of "The Battle Hymn of the Republic," enriching it each time with increasingly ambivalent harmonies. But then, on the third, the right hand starts to embellish and transform the melody with all the confidence and control of a virtuoso. We can almost see his fingers blurring and the piano shaking with the energy of the trio's new invention. Another chorus, and another, and then a new voice—a tenor sax—sings out above the trio and reinvents the melody anew again. This is the sound of mastery, and on this night we hear mastery of more than a song—it is mastery of the situation that on this night this song has come to symbolize. This is a song about dire threat, about imminent loss, about the fragility of a social order. But it is, on this night, also a song about coming together to prevail, to carry on—individually as well as together. Then the sax, the piano, the bass, and the drums themselves come together to improvise their shared version of the "Battle Hymn" in four coequal and mutually supportive parts. They move together for a chorus or two—from intense to consolatory and back again. And that's how they end, slowing as one toward their four separate but simultaneous signatures in sound. Then it's quiet and we are standing in the kitchen looking at each other with the same grin. We turn off the radio, return to our chopping and stirring, and start to talk about tomorrow.

For us, this was an aesthetic experience of a profoundly rhetorical sort. And the jazz host knew it would be—he told me so later when I called to ask him the title and source of the track.[1] (It is, by the way, a 1985 recording titled *The Gene Harris Trio Plus One*, the extra one being Stanley Turrentine on tenor sax.) The jazz host thought his listeners might need that night what this performance could give them—on his part, a highly rational and deliberate rhetorical choice. And we did need that experience—a powerfully rhetorical one that was hardly rational and deliberate at all. Listening to that performance brought the two of us out of the isolation of our separate fears and back to the business of getting on with our life together. The experience this music provided us that night was emotional—it carried us together through a sequence of feelings—"an arousing and fulfillment of desires," in this case for people to come together in confident and joyous competence—that left us, using Kenneth Burke's term, "gratified." We were gratified because, without anyone speaking a word, we found ourselves now together when we had been apart and now sharing what we did not have before the music began—some hope.

Rhetorically, both the power and the limitations of this experience are clear. The power was inherent in that sequence of an "arousing and fulfillment of desires" that we shared. That sequence itself was an aesthetic experience that had the rhetorical power to constitute, for the two of us, on that night, a shareable sense of who we now were and what we might do in the aftermath of September 11. The limitations of that experience are those Burke ascribes to art in general and to music in particular. "The artist," he wrote in *Counter-Statement,* "as artist—is not generally concerned with specific political issues. He usually deals with the attitudes, the emphases, in which the choice of some one political or economic policy is implicit, but he need not, as artist, follow the matter through to the full extent" (113). Indeed, often the artist cannot do that. An aesthetic experience such as this one works rhetorically by carrying an audience through what Burke called a "qualitative progression": "Instead of one incident in the plot preparing us for some other possible incident of plot [. . .], the presence of one quality prepares us for the introduction of another" (124–25). This evokes something Aristotle wrote in his *Politics* about the rhetorical function of music: it functions to "induce a certain character of soul" (466: 1340b10). And that inducing of a certain character of soul is the office of epideictic rhetoric, the Aristotelian category about which Perelman and Olbrechts-Tyteca observed that it is at once the "foundation" upon which a pragmatic deliberation is built (52) and too general most of the time, too "poetic" as Burke would use that term, to direct any deliberate outcome.

Burke used that term in the second essay of *The Philosophy of Literary Form,* an essay titled "Semantic and Poetic Meaning" that he introduced as his "rhetorical defense of rhetoric" (138). As I find with many of his most concise statements, this one is quite opaque. But here is what I think it means: we conventionally think of rhetoric as the application of what he called here "semantic meaning" to the more or less cognitive project of influence. Taking as his example of semantic meaning the street address of a building, he described the assumption that governs much of our deliberate rhetorical interaction as the "semantic ideal": it is "aim[ing] to evolve a vocabulary that gives the name and address of every event in the universe" (141). His advice to us about our reliance on that semantic ideal is blunt: "The best thing to be said in favor of the semantic ideal is that it is a fraud" (159). It is a fraud because it denies feelings, and in doing so it denies the fact that feelings are a primary element of all of our usable meanings. A street address tells us nothing more about a building than its physical location. It becomes meaningful beyond that project of location only when we associate with that address our experiences with it, with the events that have occurred or might occur there, with the people who are there, the relationships that reside there, or that might. And that, for Burke, is the sort of meaning—he calls it "poetic"—that is finally the stuff of rhetoric. If this essay defending the primacy of poetic meaning is Burke's rhetorical defense of rhetoric, its point is that what we call rhetoric can wield rhetorical power only when its content expresses and asserts meanings that people feel—or, in his preferred term in this essay, when it expresses and asserts their *attitudes*. These attitudes—emotional things that they are—convey the sort of usable meanings we experience as rhetorical. He did offer another example, one immediately familiar to most of us: it is not particularly rhetorical to identify a stranger to another by name. It is, however, eminently rhetorical to identify that stranger by expressing an attitude. As Burke put it, "To call a man a son-of-a-bitch is symbolically to make a complete assertion of attitude towards him now; it is itself a culmination" (149)—it is a culmination of meaning.

So Burke suggests to us that we accept the fact that the meanings that are the most rhetorically powerful are the poetic ones. These meanings are inherently metaphorical (144), dense with morality (146), and bound up with "emotional weightings" (138). That is necessarily so. As he put it, "Semantic ideals of meaning could not possibly provide a proper vocabulary in which to consider the complexities of moral growth" (147), and it is, after all, moral growth—or its opposite—that, finally, it is the function of the rhetorical to address. Indeed, Burke wrote, "It is the moral impulse that motivates perception, giving it both intensity and direction, suggesting *what to look for* and *what to look out for*. Only by wanting very profoundly to make improvement, can we get a glimpse into the devious personal and impersonal factors that operate to balk improvement" (164). And this, for him, is the whole project of the rhetorical.

All through that day, September 12, we had been listening to the news. And at the end of the day were as confused, as frightened, as stupefied in attitude and action as we had been when it began. At the end of that day it was not the news, it was not even words, which helped us understand how to move on—it was the music. Our experience of the news was semantic—it informed us of the facts, but it told us nothing about how we might live with those facts. Our experience of the music was, by contrast, poetic. As Burke explained it, "The poetic ideal being obviously aesthetic, we could in contrast call the semantic ideal 'anesthetic'; for though *aesthetic* [. . .] derives from a word meaning 'to perceive,' it has come to include the idea of emotionality in the perception, whereas the semantic ideal would aim at perception without feeling" (150). And it was the aesthetic, not the anesthetic, that we needed in order to proceed. We were, in effect, already anesthetized by the data of the day. What the aesthetic experience of this particular musical performance did was something that the news could not do: it reached us each in a place where we did not know we could be reached—a place deep inside ourselves where we were living in anxiety, in confusion and fear—and brought us to another place, a shared place where we were not alone. After the music ended we were still confused about the semantic meanings of September 11, still anxious about the events that would follow, but we were now in it together. And it was not just the two of us together. It had been just the two of us and a radio in that kitchen, but it *was* radio and so we were able to imagine thousands of others listening too—people who had been, like us, hailed together by that music of jubilant collaboration to identify themselves, along with us, with a certain shared character of soul—and that is hope.

That is why for us the experience of listening to the Gene Harris Trio perform the "Battle Hymn of the Republic" on the night after the September 11 terrorist attacks was powerfully rhetorical but not particularly political. Rather, it was an aesthetic experience that worked on us rhetorically in ways that are prior to and more important than the political. That night, in that situation, this musical performance presented us with an immediate solution to a problem—what had been for each of us a very private and personal problem—that is inherent and persistent within American political culture. In his great analysis of the political culture of the new United States, *Democracy in America,* Alexis de Tocqueville identified this private problem as the new nation's greatest public liability. It is this: "Not only does democracy make every man forget his ancestors, but it hides his descendents and separates his contemporaries from him. It throws him back forever upon himself alone and threatens in the end to confine him entirely within the solitude of his own heart" (2: 99). That is precisely where we separately stood as we listened together to the news in our kitchen on the evening of September 12, 2001. This is a lonely and, for most of us, a familiar place. With the possible exception of those who are physically present and immediately needed at an actual ground zero, this place of solitude is precisely where we tend to go in a crisis. And it was to help each of us out of that place that the jazz host chose this particular musical performance to share with his listeners as soon as the network news programming ended that night. He seemed to know intuitively that night the lesson that Burke tried to teach as he worked out his reconception of the rhetorical. What Burke was teaching was that—and I'll use Terry Eagleton's formulation from *The Ideology of the Aesthetic* here because he articulates what I take to be Burke's belief more precisely and concisely than Burke ever did—"[a]t the very root of social relations lies the aesthetic source of all human bonding. If bourgeois society releases its individuals into lonely autonomy, then only by such an imaginative exchange or appropriation of each other's identities can they be deeply enough united" (24). And so the jazz host played for his listeners a version of an American anthem that exemplified in its very performance that imaginative unity of emotional identity that characterizes improvised jazz at its best—and it is the sort of identity that, in the throes of a crisis, people seem to long for.

We did not go on after that concert in our kitchen to support many of our nation's actions in response to the September 11 attacks. Indeed, the rhetorical function of this sort of aesthetic experience is not to direct anyone toward particular political attitudes or actions. That is the office of another, more familiar, and more practically contentious sort of rhetoric. And my purpose here is not to dismiss or devalue that. Rather, it is to remind us that the experience of the rhetorical is much more pervasive and penetrating in our lives than we think it is—and *that,* I believe, is the primary lesson that Burke's work on rhetoric has to teach. His is not like, say, the work of Perelman and Olbrechts-Tyteca—a revisionist theory of argumentation. Rather, it is a revisionist description of the nature of the *rhetorical* that points to the myriad of ways we don't readily recognize that rhetoric shapes our experience through the means and method of the aesthetic. In doing so it continually reshapes our sense of identity as well, and more often than not, *not* in a way that directs anyone toward what we might call "semantic" action. Indeed, as he put it in some of his early music criticism for *The Dial,* "In the aesthetic as a category, there is implicit a wholesome skepticism towards the practical. Not the least service of art lies in its ability to make action more difficult" ("Musical," Dec. 1928, 530).

Nonetheless, as Burke wrote in that same 1928 review, "music would be the song above catastrophe" (529). That is because music is, for him, a kind of representative anecdote for the essential power of eloquence. Eloquence, as he defined it in *Counter-Statement,* is the rendering of a particular emotion into the shared experience of a transformed identity—an essentially aesthetic process that Burke named "transcendence." Eloquence is—paraphrasing him—that rhetorical "exercise of human propriety" that occurs through the aesthetic means of presenting to others "symbols which rigidify"—rigidify by rendering sharable—"our sense of poise and rhythm" (42). Put another way, eloquence is a vivid aesthetic assertion of a rhetorical vision of common identity and aspiration. It is in this sense that, as he suggested in another *Dial* review, music "[is] a substitute for religion, a secular mysticism, a belief without theology" ("Musical," Dec. 1927, 535). The rhetorical experience afforded by the aesthetic, then, is an assertion of, in that resonant phrase of William James, "an enthusiastic temper of espousal," and it works on us with a power of influence that extends well beyond the reach of the "semantic"—the realm of practical rationality—to encompass the "poetic" realm of feeling that is the foundation upon which shared meanings and practices that enact them *might,* through subsequent deliberation, be built.

Here, since we are talking about music, is Burke's own example of this sort of a rhetorical experience. Covering in one of his reviews a concert sponsored by the League of Composers and a performance in Harlem, Burke contrasted a piano sonata at the concert, which he faulted as "stunt writing," to the Harlem performance he saw later the same evening:

> Fifteen minutes afterwards, we found ourselves translated—listening now to the Hall Johnson Jubilee Singers at the Embassy Club. Perhaps our difficulties

at the League of Composers figured somewhat in the blossoming of our delight; but in any event the zest, the unction, the physical undulations, the naïve Epicureanism of these singers overwhelmed us, like a revelation. ("Musical," Apr. 1928, 357, 358)

This was a rhetorical experience, and quite a powerful one, apparently. It seems to have been—absent perhaps the immediate national crisis—an experience of the same sort that we shared in our kitchen on the night of September 12, 2001. After a long evening of hard deliberation, this was an encounter with an aesthetic experience that hailed a man out of his own thoughts and into the intimate company of the emotion of others in a way that did the profound rhetorical work of reminding him he was not, after all, alone and in doing so gave him hope.

Notes

I am grateful to Carolyn Miller and Michael Halloran for their helpful comments on an earlier version of this essay. I am particularly grateful to James Kasteley for offering a related argument that directed me to Burke's essay, "Semantic and Poetic Meaning."

1. The jazz host Steve Williams broadcast the *Gene Harris Trio Plus One* recording on the evening of September 12, 2001, on Salt Lake City's NPR affiliate, KUER.

8 The Romantic in the Attic: William Blake's Place in Kenneth Burke's Intellectual Circle

Laura E. Rutland

The title of this essay, "The Romantic in the Attic," of course alludes to the title of Sandra L. Gilbert and Susan Gubar's classic work of feminist literary criticism, *The Madwoman in the Attic*. The madwoman in question is Bertha Rochester, the first wife of Jane Eyre's employer, who, because she is insane, is kept hidden away in the attic, so that her ravings will not interfere with daily life, nor, perhaps, with Rochester's courtship of more respectable women. This essay will explore the notion that a shade of William Blake lives in Kenneth Burke's intellectual attic, like a bothersome mad cousin, perhaps, hidden away, but finally acknowledged in the end. The attic metaphor is suggested by the fact that Blake plays an important role in Burke's 1932 novel, *Towards a Better Life,* then virtually disappears for twenty-nine years, except for a handful of mentions.[1] Finally, however, in 1961, Burke again turns to Blake, offering him a tip of the hat in *The Rhetoric of Religion.*

This final gesture takes its most obvious form when Burke describes The Lord in "The Prologue in Heaven," as a "Blakean bearded patriarch" (276). Yet this seemingly casual mention is only one of several subtle Blakean links in the book. When Burke mentions a "Blakean bearded patriarch," he is highlighting Urizen, a very specific character in Blake's mythology. Urizen appears in some of Blake's earliest mythological texts but comes into his own in *The Book of Urizen,* one of three books that together comprise a parody on the book of Genesis, and, through Genesis, on the rest of the Bible. In older Blake criticism, Urizen is usually seen as a representation of reason, but his role is really far more complicated. Urizen is the one who creates the world by separating himself from the unity of the Eternal whole. He is also the source of language, religion, mathematics, science, architecture, and law. That is, he is responsible for most forms of symbolic order. In addition, he is the creator of a rigidly structured world of "iron laws" that no one can obey and that finally lead, both in the *Book of Urizen* and in its companion text, *The Book of Ahania*, to sacrificial behavior on Urizen's own part and on the part of all his "children" or followers. For the rest of his life, Blake continues to struggle with Urizen. Must he be simply thrown out? Can he be? And finally, can he be changed, and become something more flexible and malleable?[2]

Certainly, there are major differences between Burke's Lord and Blake's Urizen. Burke's Lord advocates a flexible order that Urizen eschews entirely. But there are also clear parallels between Blake's Urizen texts and *The Rhetoric of Religion*. First, in the beginning of *The Rhetoric of Religion*, Burke also talks about an iron law, "the Iron Law of History," by which the creation of Order leads to sacrifice (3). Second, Burke and Blake both treat the first three chapters of Genesis as a focus for analyzing the relationship between order and sacrifice. Finally, Burke asks us to see his own ordering principle, the Lord, in the form of Blake's ordering principle, Urizen. Clearly, Burke's Lord is not Urizen; generally, he is the opposite of Urizen as Blake portrays him in the early, most commonly known prophecies. But the reference does point to an acknowledgement of a common set of concerns and themes. Both Burke and Blake treat order and sacrifice as deeply related.

So, if there are concerns and themes in common, and if Burke shows a conscious awareness of them, why then does the elder Burke make this playful, but still distinct, tip of the hat towards Blake almost thirty years after his initial appropriation of Blake's voice in *Towards a Better Life?* Why is Blake mentioned so rarely in all that time? What does this mean, and what can it tell us about Kenneth Burke and his thought?

Certainly, there are a number of reasons, the most obvious one being rhetorical. References to Blake fit readily into a novel, but in Burke's critical works, systematic thinkers like Aristotle and Samuel Taylor Coleridge are better suited to his purposes. Yet close examination of Burke's allusions to Blake in *Towards a Better Life* and his comments about the novel reveal another explanation, one that lies close to the center of Burke's thinking. Arguably, Blake's appearance at the beginning and near the end of Burke's book-writing career has something to do with the antinomianism that Burke shares with Blake, an antinomianism with which Burke felt more or less comfortable at different points in his career.

Stephen Bygrave, who endeavors to persuade an English audience of Burke's importance, introduces Burke as a creator of "a Bible of Hell, an antinomian rhetoric" (9), and connects him to Blake (19, 63), seeing them both as thinkers who respond to their suspicions about symbolic order by creating highly developed systems of their own. Certainly, the term "antinomianism" has considerable importance in the study of both Blake and Burke. This term has been hugely important in Blake studies for the past decade. In his case, it applies primarily to a Christian heresy that puts excessive emphasis on mercy and forgiveness and ignores or even totally rejects the concept of law. Ever since E. P. Thompson identified Blake with working-class antinomian sects in *Witness Against the Beast: William Blake and the Moral Law,* Blake's religious antinomianism has become one of the working assumptions of historically based Blake criticism. While Burke's use of the term is secular, he happily applies the adjective "antinomian" both to John Neal, his novel's anti-heroic protagonist (3), and to his own work in *Counter-Statement,* published in 1931, the year before his novel, where he says that his essays are "antinomian, as regards everything but art" but only because "art is naturally antinomian" (viii).

Yet, in Neal, Burke satirizes an antinomian approach to life. In other words, Burke calls himself antinomian in *Counter-Statement,* then only a year later, severely satirizes antinomianism in *Towards a Better Life.* One can hardly avoid the conclusion that in the early 1930s, Burke's attitude toward antinomianism is ambivalent. Indeed, at around the same time, Burke states that he is not entirely comfortable with some aspects of himself. In a letter to Malcolm Cowley dated August 9, 1931, Burke writes: "I rely upon the Declamations [in *Towards a Better Life*] to burn away certain very uncomfortable parts of me. If I could by a ritual, like the old Jews, load my sins upon a goat, I should beat it mercilessly and drive it into the wilderness to die" (qtd. in Selzer 168).[3] It is very possible that the antinomian aspects of his nature are part of what is troubling him.

But of course, Burke does not burn away his antinomianism, as is evident when in *The Rhetoric of Religion* he tips his hat to that great antinomian William Blake. Rather than eliminate his antinomianism,

Burke works out a way to place it into a dialectical relationship with order as a necessary aspect of language, and less directly, as a necessary element of social life. But he does not do this all at once. This task requires years, and in *Towards a Better Life* one can see Burke beginning to deal with the intellectual problem of how to use antinomian thinking, and, perhaps more importantly, how not to use it.

This beginning appears in the way Burke uses Blake quotations in the novel. Extensive references to Blake appear and are often seriously misused in *Towards a Better Life,* but they come not directly from Burke nor even from Burke's first-person narrator John Neal. Instead they come from the narrator of a short story by John Neal that takes up one chapter late in the novel. By distancing himself from the Blake quotations in this way, Burke creates a space in which the problems with extreme antinomianism can be explored without a complete rejection of the entire antinomian position. He is also able to make a distinction between Blake's use of antinomianism language and its misuse by John Neal's fictional character.

Neal's narrator, who refers incessantly to William Blake, treats antinomianism as a "thoroughgoing" system.[4] He employs the Blakean opus as his antinomian Bible from Hell. Thus, he associates Blake with his own personal style of antinomianism, and, as was mentioned earlier, regularly distorts Blake's meaning. But his adaptation of Blake is buried within layers of ironic distance from Burke. Thus, the reader can discern two separate appropriations of Blake within the text—the narrator's, which simultaneously adulates and distorts Blake's thought, and Burke's, which deploys Blake in his ironic critique of extreme antinomianism.

All of this takes place within John Neal's epistolary short story, found in chapter four of the third section of *Towards a Better Life.* The narrator, a novelist like Neal, writes to a woman friend with whom he shares, at the beginning of the story, a romantic relationship and an impassioned interest in the poetry of William Blake. As long as the relationship continues, the narrator refers constantly to Blake, citing no less than twenty references from seven different Blake texts over the course of approximately fourteen pages. These texts are used and misused in various ways, but their main purpose is to allow the epistolary voice to describe and justify his passionate but irresponsible desire as part of a deliberately antinomian mode of life. Yet his antinomianism is grounded in a kind of manipulative self-involvement that is antithetical to Blakean antinomianism. Whether it is because his attitudes are different from his master's, or because he is so devoted to antinomianism that he must defy and transmogrify even an antinomian mentor's words, he dismantles Blake even as he fawns upon him. Two specific examples will demonstrate both the importance of Blake to the narrator's antinomian philosophy and the extent to which the narrator distorts Blake in the process of emulating him.

In the first example, a clear misapplication of Blake, the epistolary speaker implores his lover to come to him. This plea occurs after the speaker realizes that he is not writing effectively, although he has left his lover behind solely to concentrate on his work. Still he is unable to promise his beloved either successful work or much in the way of relationship: "For if an occasional quick breath of hope raises this burden of dismalness that is upon me, it is because I dare expect you. Yet I can promise you nothing, nothing but the abject tributes of one who loves you 'like the little bird that picks up crumbs around the door,' if I may quote again a passage from Blake which you have heard me quote so often" (172). Here Blake is being used to describe and to justify the speaker's inability to offer commitment, or anything but his own emotional and sexual hunger, to his beloved. In other words, the speaker is using Blake's words to support sexual self-involvement in the guise of antinomian philosophy. Indeed only a few paragraphs later, the speaker describes the lonely character in his own novel, saying that he has "made himself a Mole to learn what Eagles cannot imagine" (173).[5] The speaker explains that both he and his character are destroying themselves in their mole-like quest for wisdom, but he asks his lover to accept him by using words from an entirely different context. These words, in their original placement, express an entirely different brand of antinomian thought.

Originally, the passage about the "little bird" appears in "Little Boy Lost," from *Songs of Experience*. The words belong to a child who speaks, not to a lover, but to his father God, whose commandments and dogmas he does not understand:

> Nought loves another as itself
> Or venerates another so.
> Nor is it possible to thought
> A greater than itself to know:
> And Father how can I love you,

> Or any of my brothers more?
> I love you like the little bird
> That picks up crumbs around the door. (E 28, ll. 1–8)[6]

The poem concludes with the speaker being burned to death by a priest defending orthodoxy against the "attack" of this child.

Certainly the poem contains an antinomian philosophy, as does the narrator's misuse of it. But the tone is vastly different. The child rejects a religious dogma he does not understand, he asks questions, and he expresses a naturally childish, and thus self-centered, love for a parental figure. The poem's antinomianism is not really found in the child's words, but in the words of the poem's adult speaker, who attacks the church for scapegoating the child to preserve its system. "Are such things done on Albion's shore?" Blake's speaker asks at the end of the poem. Burke's speaker, on the other hand, asks a sexual partner to treat him as an innocent, incapable of anything but a childish self-centered affection, even as he acknowledges that his unpredictable behavior is part of a self-chosen pose, a deliberately unstable lifestyle by which he seeks wisdom through unconventional means. Despite his protests of devotion, the speaker's manipulations shine through in his misuse of Blake.

An antinomian rejection of mores, particularly sexual mores, marks several of the speaker's appropriations of Blake in *Towards a Better Life*. Unlike the passage about the little bird, some of these quotations almost match Blake's antinomian philosophy, insofar as they celebrate sexual liberation. Yet they usually take on a flavor of deceit and manipulation that is not present in Blake's original. For example, when the narrator speaks of his delight in his beloved's ability to meet his every need, he quotes a love scene between Mary and Joseph taken from Blake's late prophecy *Jerusalem*:

> Then Mary burst into a Song: she flowed like a River of
> Many Streams in the arms of Joseph & gave forth her tears of joy
> Like many waters, and Emanating into gardens and palaces upon
> Euphrates, & to forests & floods & animals, wild & tame from
> Gihon to Hiddekel, & to corn fields & villages & inhabitants
> Upon Pison & Arnon & Jordan . . . (Burke 176–77; E 212, ll. 28–33)

The speaker describes how his lover had laughed when he had insisted, as they enjoyed reading the passage together, that he was like Mary in the story.

At first glance, Blake's passage appears to be a truly shocking and antinomian text. There is plenty to shock the orthodox in Blake's characterization of Mary as a sexual being, but, in fact, in this passage, Blake is aiming at something even more threatening to the concept of law than the raw celebration of sexual rather than divine love. In its original context, this passage is part of a larger scene, in which Jerusalem, a female character, is weeping because she has been withheld from Jesus, her true groom, and has become a blasphemer as a result. Jesus, to comfort her, shows her the story of his parents. Mary had conceived Jesus out of wedlock, not through a virgin birth, but through a sexual act, and Joseph, her betrothed, had forgiven her. The speaker's use of the quotation above, where Mary sings with joy at her forgiveness, implies not only the fulfillment of the speaker's usual emotional and sexual needs, but the need to be forgiven for sexual infidelity: "if I were pure, never could I taste the sweets / Of the Forgive[ne]ss of Sins! (E 111, ll. 11–12).

The antinomianism is parallel, but again, the tone is not. For one thing, in Blake's prophecy, Mary openly acknowledges her infidelities. The speaker's infidelities are implied only by the reference to the Blake text. Secondly, Blake states that forgiveness is always mutual: "The Continual Forgiveness of sins / In the Perpetual Mutual Sacrifice in Great Eternity" (E 212, ll. 22–23). In *Towards a Better Life*, we see no mutual exchanges of forgiveness between the speaker and his woman friend. Nor do we see an outpouring of generous love on the part of the speaker, who admits to the barrenness of his own affection: "I felt this expansiveness of Mary. I felt as though I were pouring forth bounty—is that not funny, when I was silent even, had not even one sentence to offer, could show nothing more serious than my gratitude to you?" (177). The speaker's gift of gratitude is not accompanied by the productive activity which erupts from Mary's gratitude. In fact, the speaker does not even speak his gratitude at all. Nor does the speaker develop the joy in the intimacy of his beloved that both Mary and Jerusalem experience in the prophecy, because we know that he eventually feels he must leave his beloved in order to be fruitful in his writing.

It seems a small wonder that, finally, the speaker's lover writes to tell him that, however great Blake's talent may be, she has "found [her] interest in Blake waning" and that, although she can still "*perceive* his excellence [. . .] it no longer matters whether he is excellent or not" (177). At this point, it becomes clear to what extent the speaker sees his relationship with her as an experiment in what he believes to be Blakean philosophy. Their mutual enjoyment of Blake was not simply an exercise in aesthetics: "If his excellence has ceased to matter, then you have ceased to perceive it—and where am I to turn, who realize only too well that the very foundations of our union rest upon Blake?" (178).

For a time, after the loss of his girlfriend, the speaker tries to continue his interest in Blake. He describes himself as one who has lost his Emanation (his female counterpart) and is trapped in Selfhood, as a result of her departure.[7] But eventually the narrator also loses interest in Blake, turning his obsessions instead upon a "wooden policeman" whom he thinks about constantly and whose constancy is intolerable: "And I can assure you: he is so unchangeable, that to think of him repeatedly is to feel the mind inexorably rigid" (184, 187). The speaker finds himself gazing at people on the streets, hoping for some kind of relatedness or connection, but instead, finds himself trapped in his compulsive ruminations on the wooden policeman.

Considering the thoroughgoing antinomianism of this character, his obsession with the wooden policeman in the end is both ironic and predictable. Before he became obsessed with the policeman, he was rigidly antinomian, ironically treating a defiance of traditional standards, including the demands of reciprocity in relationship, as an absolute law, twisting and distorting his own antinomian mentor in his attempts to pursue his philosophy to its final conclusion. His own rigidity becomes associated with the wooden figure that he imagines law, or order, must be. In fact, a living breathing flexible order is precisely what he needs if he is to be restored into any kind of relationship with his fellow human beings. No such order appears anywhere in the text. At the end of *Towards a Better Life* John Neal, the creator of this fictional narrator, is himself lapsing into a fragmented condition, even losing control of the complex and rich prose style that he has maintained throughout the text.

Undoubtedly, the young Burke who called his own work antinomian and then launched his satirical attack on antinomianism in *Towards a Better Life,* was not yet able to deliver the fully articulated dialectic between antinomianism and the hierarchy of values that his characters needed. Developing the dialectic between skeptical resistance to order and the absolute necessity for order becomes the heart of Burke's later critique of language and, for that matter, of all symbolic systems. Indeed, some years after both *Counter-Statement* and *Towards a Better Life,* Burke articulates his appreciation for his early antinomianism precisely because it leads him to something fuller. Reflecting on *Counter-Statement* in 1953, Burke remarks that the development of a complex dialectic comes after this book, growing out of the individualistic antinomianism of the early work (*CS* 214–15).

So what does all this say about Blake, the mad romantic in Burke's attic? Clearly the Blake of Neal's narrator is not the real Blake, and Burke knew it. It is the narrator who has misread and misapplied Blake's antinomian philosophy, not Burke. Finally, it is the narrator who goes mad, desperately seeking company with a rigid wooden cop in order to counter his own rigid antinomianism, supposedly Blakean, but in fact devoid of the sense of relationship and compassion that motivates Blake's antinomianism and prevents it, at its best, from becoming rigid. The brunt of Burke's irony is leveled at Neal's narrator, not at Blake, whose words the narrator twists and distorts.

Yet the issue of whether Blake ever attains in his poetry or prophecies the dialectical tension between system and anti-system that Burke develops is arguable, and beyond the scope of this essay. It is also impossible to determine, simply by looking at the two Burke texts examined in this essay, what Burke really thought of Blake, or how fully he embraced any similarity in their aims or insights. Certainly Blake is capable of moments of harsh recrimination and violent partisanship that are alien to Burke's model of irony. Thus, it could be argued that Burke more or less rejects Blake in his association of the romantic with the mad antinomianism of Neal's short story. Certainly Burke identifies a tendency in Blake that could be dangerous to those who are frustrated by the moral inconsistencies of society or obsessed with enacting avant-garde bohemianism in everyday life. A close look at *Towards a Better Life* and Blake's place within it does make it clear that, in the late 1920s and early 1930s, the young Burke saw fit to remind himself and his readers that the "road to excess," recommended by Blake in *The Marriage of Heaven and Hell,* can lead not only to "the palace of wisdom" (E 35, 1.3) but also to madness.

Nevertheless, it is important to remember that in 1965, after his own antinomianism is securely placed within a dialectical order, Burke can praise the "purification by excess" (*TBL* vii) that his younger self has enacted in *Towards a Better Life,* echoing Blake's recommendation that one should follow the "road to excess" in order to find wisdom. Furthermore, in 1961, Burke can tip his hat to a poet who shares his antinomian concerns about "iron laws" and the dangers of rigid systems of order. It is after all, The Lord, a Blakean bearded patriarch, who represents the ordering function of language, while stating, as clearly as Burke ever stated it, the dialectical relationship between order and antinomian skepticism:

> Empirically, I sanction dialectic. [. . .] And the dialectic, in its fullness, is never without such a principle of transcendence, an Upward Way that, when reversed, interprets all incidental things in terms of the overall fulfillment towards which the entire development is said to be striving. So far, so good. But where the Earth-People are concerned, any terminology is suspect to the extent that it does not allow for the progressive criticism of itself. (*RR* 303)

In the end, Burke's subtle nod towards Blake may turn out to be a fairly grand gesture after all.

Notes

1. To the best of my knowledge, these mentions are limited to *Attitudes toward History* 61, "Ideology and Myth" 201, and *Rhetoric of Motives* 82. Most relevant to the argument in this essay is the one in *Attitudes,* where Burke, in his chapter on poetic categories, categorizes Blake as "grotesque." Burke groups the "grotesque" and the "didactic" as, respectively, the "mystical" and "propagandistic" sides of "transition," midway between the categories that gravitate toward "acceptance" of reigning symbols of authoritative order (epic, tragedy, comedy) and those that gravitate toward "rejection" of such symbols (elegy, satire, burlesque) (57).

2. For a full analysis of *The Book of Urizen* and *The Book of Ahania* from a Burkean perspective, see my *Hindrance, Act, and the Scapegoat: William Blake, Kenneth Burke, and the Rhetoric of Order.* See also Robert Essick's *William Blake and the Language of Adam* for an earlier note on the kinship between Burke's view of the negative in *The Rhetoric of Religion* and Blake's *Book of Urizen* (149).

3. In quoting this passage, I do not mean to enter into the debate about whether or not *Towards a Better Life* is an autobiographical text. Burke's re-

marks to Cowley seem to indicate a link, at least at the level of ideas and emotions. Such a link does not necessarily imply a biographical connection. See Jack Selzer's *Kenneth Burke in Greenwich Village* 167–74 for a full discussion of this issue.

4. The word "thoroughgoing" is placed in quotation marks because it refers to Burke's phrase, "thoroughgoing modes of persuasion." This term is used in *The Rhetoric of Religion* to explain that religious language can function as an analogy for language in general (v), because religion is a symbolic order that sets out to describe the absolute. It is the thoroughgoing quality of religious language that concerns Burke, because he sees this quality as one primary cause of scapegoating. Thus, thoroughgoing systems, even antinomian ones, are problematic whether or not they are religious.

5. This refers to Blake's *The Book of Thel*, a text that describes a young woman's quest for meaning and her first terrifying encounter with the power of sexual desire. While the meaning of this passage has been widely debated, this passage bears an arguably rational relationship with the speaker and his interests. The descent into the earth with the mole can be understood as a retreat from the spiritual heights of the eagle into the body. Thus, it has some applicability to the narrator's antinomian project and to his sexual interests.

6. All Blake quotations are from Erdman's revised edition. References all include "E" (for Erdman), followed by page numbers and line numbers.

7. The narrator is again seriously distorting Blake when he sees the Selfhood as something that developed because he loses his lover. A typical definition of selfhood is this one by S. Foster Damon in *A Blake Dictionary:* "The SELF or SELFHOOD is the innate selfishness with which we are born; yet it is not the central Humanity, but is opposed to it" (363). Selfhood is not caused by any other person's action, or by abandonment; rather, it is that which must be overcome in order to overcome our aloneness. This concept of Selfhood is illustrated by the use of the term in Blake's *Milton,* in which the poet Milton must voluntarily descend from his isolated heaven if he is to be reunited with his Emanations (or feminine counterparts, his wives and daughters) (E 110, pl. 15, ll. 51–52 and pl. 17, ll. 1–3). Burke, incidentally, knew Damon from his early days at *The Dial.* See Selzer 116, 119.

9 Leveraging a Career with Kenneth Burke: The Politics of Theory in Literary Studies

Cary Nelson

I must begin by saying unequivocally why Kenneth Burke has been at my side throughout my career. I studied with Bill Rueckert at the University of Rochester. I am among his many students who wonder what would have become of us if he hadn't been there, for Bill was indeed the only "theory person" in the Rochester department in the 1960s; luckily he was a very good one. Unlike so many of his peers, Bill could see both continuities and discontinuities in the history of criticism. Thus there wasn't much chance of his believing Burke could easily become irrelevant. I saw Bill not long ago, just before his health took a turn for the worse. Ed Folsom, Dianne Sadoff, and I had made a visit to Bill's home to reconfirm a commitment and a history that still meant a great deal to us. While there, I convinced him he could make a great contribution to the conference where this essay was first presented just by talking through the new old Burke, the Parlor Press edition of Burke's *Essays Toward a Symbolic of Motives, 1950-1955*. It was not as if Bill needed to write a formal essay to tell us why this book would matter. He agreed, but it was not to be. So I want to dedicate my essay to this great, cranky, courageous, bloody-minded, and always brilliant Burkean who guided so many of us through the sometimes anti-intellectual waters of a 1960s English department.

There is at least one other reason to invoke Bill's name at the outset of this piece. I would never have imagined I could tell Bill Rueckert anything he didn't already know about Kenneth Burke. And I'm sure I'm not alone in feeling the same way about the contributors to this volume or its most easily anticipated Burkean readers. But perhaps I can put some of what you already know in a somewhat different context.

Some years ago, Stanley Fish remarked that a book of literary criticism, if it had a life at all, might last five years. After that, you need not forget it; it would already be forgotten. Fish was thinking of the discipline as an ongoing conversation in which individual contributions would inevitably be superseded and replaced. The ongoing analysis of individual texts certainly often works that way. Of course a great many scholarly books never really make even that long a mark. They are above all lines on a vita, not active participants in a dialogue. Not that any of us likes to hear this, but unpleasant truths are not less true for that. The character of theory's interventions are more variable. Unlike many readings of individual works, few major theoretical texts can be modestly and incrementally superseded. They aim for significant paradigm shifts and are not inherently disposable. Histories of theory and even works of theoretical recapitulation and synthesis, however, can fade fairly rapidly. How many copies, say, of Jonathan Culler's *Structuralist Poetics* now sell in an average fortnight?

With Burke, to be sure, there is no single decisive book to enter into the contest for influence. Roland Barthes continually reinvented himself; many of his individual books represent quite different theoretical models. It would be equally difficult to name the one key book by Michel Foucault, for his early and late concerns mix continuity with radical difference. Northrop Frye, however, is above all the author of *Anatomy of Criticism*. Jacques Derrida, on the other hand, kept traversing the same terrain in different ways. His career comprises one project repeatedly revisited and recast. That is much closer to Burke's pattern, though Burke's habit of recycling essays and chapters makes his record still more complex. There is a certain arbitrariness to picking a Burke volume to recommend to colleagues and students.

Within English studies Burke's reception has been notably idiosyncratic. Despite the great power and inventiveness of his work—and his propensity for taking up issues of permanent interest—he has been intermittently and inconsistently remembered and forgotten. Fish's model clearly does not apply to Burke, whose work passed the half-century of vitality some time ago and certainly shows no sign of dropping out of all conversations. In rhetoric and speech communication Burke has had an unbroken career that is, however, structured by the warring wings of the discipline. Classical rhetoric and its heirs, long peopled in part by students of Burke, is on the wane in Speech Communication programs at some schools, including my own, which prefer product research funded by corporations. Recent heads of Speech Communication at Illinois admire faculty who get funding to interview shoppers at the local mall, rather than those who deconstruct the rhetoric of contemporary politicians. Casting a cold eye on political rhetoric is no longer popular in a discipline looking for ways of profiting from either serving business or serving the military-industrial complex. Yet progressive politics is more deeply rooted in English than in Speech Communication, so the discontinuities of Burkean investments require other explanations.

As we all know, Burke has been rediscovered by some of the more notable literary theorists of the last several decades, among them Fredric Jameson and Frank Lentricchia, although some may say Jameson rediscovered him only to dismiss him once again. A much larger number of people in theory have probably never read much of his work and certainly have never thought deeply about it. As with Speech Communication there are necessarily two dimensions to this history—the nature of Burke's work and the character of the discipline. That Burke's fundamental work has been—even if only intermittently—repeatedly taken up by literary scholars says something good about the discipline's occasional openness to rereading what, in Fish's model, it might otherwise have easily persuaded itself it had passed by. On the other hand, those convinced that only the latest, hottest thing matters are less likely to pause long enough to reconsider anyone who does not seem a mass intellectual phenomenon. English can be alternately thoughtful and fickle, and Burke does not fare well when the discipline's intellectual horizons are so fleeting, when celebrity sets the terms of intellectual devotion.

In my decades in the discipline I have seen what I assumed were discourses that would remain permanently on the cutting edge fall relatively or entirely out of favor. Of course earlier generations have witnessed the same phenomenon repeatedly. When I was in graduate school in the 1960s Northrop Frye was still a critical figure in literary theory. Now there are graduate students who have never heard his name. For me in the 1960s and 1970s it was Barthes, Derrida, and Burke, among others, who were at the fulcrum of my intellectual life. First Barthes, now Derrida, seem to be falling out of favor.

Also largely gone are the phenomenologically derived literary critics and theorists who still offered powerful inspiration in the late 1960s. When I was in graduate school, the Yale School critics were in their phenomenological phase. Geoffrey Hartman's *The Unmediated Vision* was still a relevant book, and J. Hillis Miller was writing in the wake of French critics like Georges Poulet, whose *The Metamorphoses of the Circle* remained influential to many. A cluster of these writers—including Gaston Bachelard, whose *The Poetics of Space* had more staying power than his phenomenologies of the four elements—remained inspirational until they fell out of favor. Their loss, in my view, is to be regretted not because they offer fundamental models of linguisticality or even of literary meaning but rather because they foreground the persistently mimetic and expressive content of literary analyses. Having convinced ourselves we have moved beyond phenomenology, we continue in part to practice it unawares. It returns, to be sure, under the sign of poststructuralist plurality in Roland Barthes's late work, but then we get cultural warrant to credit it to an entirely different philosophical tradition. This is what it means to be aware of both continuities and discontinuities in interpretive traditions, something Burke's prodigiously anticipatory work leads us to be.

The half-life of theorists may frequently be shorter than it was a generation or two ago. No doubt the vicious job system in higher education bears some of the blame. Graduate students are led to believe that wagering who will be the next hot theoretical voice—and proving themselves modestly skeptical acolytes—is one of the few ways to increase their odds of getting a job. Burke's only contribution to this pattern might be to urge hesitance in our devotion to terministic screens, the very hesitance many suspect they must abandon. Yet if Burke is not likely to produce masses of converts, he does appear in his own way to have many more than nine lives, though some of them are very short indeed.

In teaching theory courses over a series of decades, I have placed Burke alongside structuralists and poststructuralists repeatedly. It's not just a question of seeing how Burke anticipated later work; it's a matter of opening a perspective of incongruity on the contemporary and of thereby potentially distinguishing between what is new and what is not, what is part of recognizable intellectual continuity and what breaks with the past. One is otherwise likely to claim newness when it is unmerited and—more importantly—to disable philosophical inquiry into the foundations of current interests.

On the other hand, Burke's presence within the contemporary animates a mix of similarity and difference that precisely enables reflection about core assumptions and aims. More than anything else, it is probably Burke's relentless linguisticality that places him in productive dialogue with interpretive theory of the last forty years. From "The Rhetoric of Hitler's 'Battle'" to *The Rhetoric of Religion,* Burke sees culture as fundamentally linguistic—constructed, manipulative, and systematic. Into language are channeled all the most base and most ethereal of human motives.

Yet unlike classical structuralism Burke makes no pretense for his method to a supremely rational scientificity. Nor, perhaps more importantly, does he dehumanize linguistic efficacy. Characterized at times in classical structuralism as an independent system impervious to human agency, language acquired an absolute power over us that many found both offensive and implausible. Burke's model is more complex. Language seeks to do to us what we have historically sought to do to ourselves and to one another. It is at once a repository of human motives and a source of motivation. It is susceptible to modification and enhancement. It can be manipulated but not wholly mastered.

A network of historically accumulated impulses and connotations, the language system is a portrait of human wishes and fears. For Burke, then, detailing its impact within a given text or textual tradition means keeping a wry eye on its source and destination—the human animal. This double focus—on language systems and on their impact on human behavior—means that it is especially easy for Burke to move between his own version of structuralism and psychoanalytic reflection. In fact Burke makes it clear that the study of systematic meaning has led to inquiry into how meaning goads us to feel and act. Otherwise one remains blind to linguisticality's human and historical consequences. But academics have been widely unwilling to admit any pervasive purchase for psychoanalytic theory, let alone to hear its call for personal and collective reflexivity. Some faculty prefer to believe they do not possess an unconscious. Psychoanalysis in the academy has thus been consistently cordoned off and contained, treated as a specialization, an object of choice, rather than a theory to which we are all subject. If the psychoanalytic component of Burke's were not alone distasteful for those in English who choose to think of themselves as exclusively rational beings, the fact that Burke fuses psychoanalysis with an incipient structuralism makes things still worse.

Burke's conviction that language systems are sources for personal, national, and subcultural aims and values requires that we reject any independent status for a whole range of verbal and ontological categories that various communities have preferred to imagine existing outside linguisticality—among them the demonic, the angelic, the patriotic, and the aesthetic. What we idolize as transcendent, what we reject as subhuman, Burke locates well within human culture. Many are psychologically unprepared to take this step, one that is itself doubly empowered by Burke's fusion of language theory and psychoanalysis.

Burke's notion of the rhetorical has thus always been an affront to those who would believe certain discourses operate outside ordinary persuasive mechanisms. Early on, to deconstruct the rhetoric of Hitler's prose was to place it within the range of possible human verbal strategies, not outside it in a realm of unfathomable negativity. Later in his career, to deconstruct the rhetoric of religion was to suggest that religious texts speak to us not from the whirlwind but from the resources of human history. Burke deflates all claims for the extra-human, reducing all extraordinary efforts to hail us to strategies embedded in language's connotative web.

Unlike most who have since pursued similar claims for the centrality of linguistic influence in human culture, Burke does not try to treat language as a neutrally constructive force. Nor does he use the linguistic turn to dehumanize or mechanically instrumentalize culture. Replete with extreme implications we cannot control, a thoroughgoing agenda for human action and belief, language for Burke is a kind of puppet master. Part of what is distinctive about Burke, however, is that he keeps his eye on the puppet when he makes such claims. In other words, Burke repeatedly asks what it is like to live in a world where we derive our purposes from language, where we are separated from our natural condition, where we goaded by a spirit of hierarchy that is textually derived.

While most of us have little difficulty admitting that the consequences might be tragic if we are terminologically manipulated into storming the gates of heaven, far fewer of us are prepared to see the consequences as fundamentally comic. One of the more notable features of Burke's work is that he sees the comedy of our constitutive linguisticality. That puppets might be amusing is not surprising. That not only individual critics but also whole scholarly communities might be reluctant to make that a fundamental tenet is equally unsurprising. Criticism for Burke, however, is as a result partly a form of wit. It deflates conviction by turning it into systematicity. Belief is a structural product of linguisticality, and its acolytes are thus more than a little absurd. Discomfort with Burke's humor is almost certainly one of the other things that has made his reception discontinuous.

Yet Burke's insistence on the comic character of our terminologically driven compulsions is also part of a cultural and political project. He aims to maximize our reflexive capacity, to insert critical awareness into our construction as agents of linguistic patterns. If actual freedom from terministic determinism is impossible, a degree of reflexive distance is achievable, and a certain comic reductiveness can facilitate that distance. Burke's sense that criticism seeks to lift the veil from our eyes was forged in the midst of 1930s Marxism, and while Burke was anything but doctrinaire he retained a strong sense that criticism should aim not simply for neutral description but rather for maximizing human freedom. Once again, through the long night of the New Criticism Burke's commitment to interpretation as a socially and politically reflexive vocation met with little sympathy. It was the last thing most academics wanted to hear in the wake of McCarthyism.

When the omnivorous linguisticality of Burke's oeuvre is combined with its ethical and political mission, its clearest contemporary analogue may be cultural studies. Discourse analysis was central to all the founding figures of British cultural studies—Raymond Williams, Richard Hoggart, Stuart Hall—and to all the coauthored books to come out of the Birmingham school. In the classic *Policing the Crisis,* which analyzes a moral panic over mugging, discourse is at once the primary evidence, the focus of interpretation, and the means to mass persuasion. As cultural studies extended its terrain to cover other social practices, discourse and the techniques of discourse analysis remained a constant. The same is true of Burke's work from the beginning to the end of his career. British cultural studies has also been methodologically reflexive in a way that, though not inspired by Burke, is in sync with his practice.

The Americanization of cultural studies, notably, has seen not only a partial break with the principles of discourse analysis but also a break with the social and political mission of cultural studies. Unsurprisingly, Burke is once again not an imperative part of the American cultural studies tradition. That he should be seems quite clear, for his reach and his methods range from political speech to poetry's pure persuasion. His career models what it can mean to study contemporaneity as a whole, to reject disciplinary specialization and address the current condition of the world. He would be a healing and unifying figure for American cultural studies to embrace. But then American cultural studies would have to accept a level of political responsibility, a commitment to methodological reflexivity, and a capacity to laugh at itself, all in all a tall order for sometimes short attention spans.

In a country and a world increasingly beholden to religious fundamentalisms, in a country and a world with increasingly unforgiving political agendas, one could use Burke's example and his help. As Tariq Ali has argued, we are facing a clash of fundamentalisms on the world stage, not, as some Americans would have it, a simple opposition between fundamentalism and freedom. How Burke himself would have responded we cannot know, but we can see how he responded to the last epistemic political configuration. As the Cold War replaced the more morally stark conflicts of the 1930s and 1940s Burke's view of the world adapted to changing circumstances. He saw not good and evil arrayed against one another—simplifications anyone can be forgiven for adopting amidst 1930s and 1940s fascist assaults on democracy and humanity—but rather two equal superpowers in competition with one another. It was a somewhat European view, one that people lacking superpower citizenship were more likely to adopt. Once again the cold warriors seated in chairs of American criticism were unlikely to find Burke's views comprehensible, let alone appealing.

We are still paying a price for the very unBurkean absolutism of the Cold War, as our leaders once again adopt the model of Manichean conflict for circumstances that do not merit it. How much more we now need Burke showing us that the emperor has no clothes it is difficult to say. But our public rhetorics propel us toward multiple disasters and toward risks we show little inclination to admit. We need Burke's methods turned on every discourse of public life. Academics, journalists, students, opposition politicians, ordinary citizens—all need to become Burkeans exposing and debunking not just the ultimate agendas permeating public life but also the extreme implications of a transformed ordinariness. As Burke argued repeatedly, even apparently trivial uses of terms have systematic and ultimate implications.

Since my own rhetoric here is drifting toward an apocalyptic conclusion, I will counter it by saying that I have no objection toward more modest uses of Burke. Adapting Foucault, I acknowledge that Burke has served minor pedagogies before and will do so again. And in any case those determined to fiddle with Burke will surely suppress the knowledge that Rome is burning. All I can do is to call on those deploying minor pedagogies—doing modest Burkean readings of individual objects and seemingly localized practices—to interrogate all objects of interpretation about ultimate aims and implications. Since the press does not, for the most part, seem to be writing pieces about "The Rhetoric of Bush's Battle," it is up to us to do so.

The culture desperately needs reflexivity about all that seems contained or naturalized. For our freedom as academics to mock and critique and contradict the power of the nation state is at risk. All the experts—if that's what they are, and Burke would surely have his doubts—say one apocalyptic future is merely a matter of time: repeated terrorist attacks on American soil. Tolerance for oppositional discourse on campus would decline rapidly thereafter. And rhetorics about national purity and national destiny, casting out the other in our midst and demonizing the other elsewhere, would immediately escalate. We need rigorous Burkean doubt and incongruity now to deal with such possible futures.

Disciplinarity, in any case, will not suffice—neither as a world view nor as a talisman to ward off disaster. We need to reconceive academic identities within national and global citizenship and to take on the risks and responsibilities that that entails. We will need to do so in part to protect the humanities, increasingly marginalized within global capitalism, increasingly instrumentalized within the academy, just when they are most needed as sites of political critique. What does it mean, then, to be a Burkean citizen now? What might it mean to be a Burkean citizen in the months and years ahead? These are some of the absurd and unsettling questions we might frame as we ask ourselves what Burke's legacy should be now and in the future. Events, to be sure, will surprise us. For now, I am only suggesting that we would be better off facing them with Burke at our side.

10 Kenneth Burke and the Claims of a Rhetorical Poetry

Melissa Girard

In 1974, Kenneth Burke published the short essay "William Carlos Williams: A Critical Appreciation." The then recent re-issuing of Williams's writings in the volume *Imaginations* had inspired Burke to revisit his close friend's poetry. As he rereads Williams's early work more than a half-century after its initial publication, Burke realizes that its essence lies in an "ebullient leaping from word to word," a formal poetic practice of disjunction and dissociation that houses the potential to destabilize habitual social and linguistic linkages (16). Burke claims to borrow this reading of Williams's poetry from Williams himself. In a 1932 essay on Marianne Moore, Williams had characterized Moore's similarly disjunctive poetics as a "thrilling" progression of ideas that proceed "without connectives unless it be poetry, the inevitable connective, if you will" (qtd. in "William" 17). Burke finds Williams's characterization of poetry as the "inevitable connective" to be an extremely suggestive one. Meditating on Williams's poetry, Burke speculates that it is like "traffic": "a constant succession of momentary fragments" bound exclusively by the poem (16). This insight leads Burke to re-consider poetry's connective properties more broadly. By throwing together previously disparate and even incompatible discourses, poetry enables the possibility of new meanings. "Out of such disjunction," Burke writes, "new junctures would be formed" (18). Unfortunately, Burke's brief, whimsical reading does little to illuminate Williams's poetry. His comments seem—ironically—disconnected, as if he might not have had Williams's poetry in mind at all. Yet, in the context of Burke's own writing, the idea of poetry as the "inevitable connective" develops into a fully realized aesthetic and political method. While Burke's thoughts may seem tangential to Williams's poetry, they point toward the very essence of his own complex work with poetry and poetic form.

For Burke, poetry is a "bridge" that moves off the page and into the social realm, "constantly pressing about the edges of the area specifically confined to poetics" ("Unburned Bridges" 396). Unlike theories that isolate the poetic object from the social and cultural fields, Burke's poetic repeatedly emphasizes principles of "social and material cooperation," "categorical joining," and "fusion" (*PC* liii, 267). Historically and presently, Burke's theories distinguish themselves through their fundamental insistence that poetry must connect—and thus communicate—with its audience and its world. In the wake of literary modernism, amid the growing social, political, and economic upheaval of the Great Depression and, later, World War II, Burke feared that poetry was being positioned as a "secondary matter," one which threatened to divert writers from "really fundamental forces": "It never occurred to a person until a few years ago that each time he goes to eat, or to shave, he must formally renounce all poetry. When an invader came upon a peaceful people, and the call went forth to lay down hoes and take up muskets, this was not construed as a renunciation of hoes. They took up muskets that they might return to hoes" (*ACR* 55).

Throughout his criticism and poetry Burke attempts to suture this growing breach between literature and the social. Against literary models that construct poetry as a purely technical, specialized, and, hence, artifactual cultural endeavor, Burke posits a poetic form that engages in an organic, even symbiotic, exchange with the social. "Literature," he continues, "must always have its 'gravitational pull,' by which I mean that it must always be directed towards some worldly situation" (55). By placing a connective, relational impulse at the forefront of poetry's formal operations, Burke departed significantly from most of his critical contemporaries and provides a provocative rejoinder to the field of literary studies even today. My essay begins by outlining in more detail Burke's conception of a "connective" poetry. I situate Burke's ideas within emerging critical discussions of poetry to demonstrate the continuing relevance of his ideas to the contemporary and historical fields of poetry studies. My reading draws equally from Burke's poetry and his more established critical corpus. While Burke remains highly regarded as a literary critic, his poetry continues to be neglected. In an attempt to press "the edges of the area specifically confined to poetics," the main part of my essay revisits Burke's body of poetry to examine his conception of poetic form as a communicative act.

The Poem as "Bulwark": Locating Burke's Connective Poetics

Unlike the New Critics, Burke never conceived poetry as a linguistic hallowed ground, cordoned off from non-poetic discourse and speech. As Burke writes in an early letter to Malcolm Cowley, "The idea of escape or flight to poetry will change to the idea of poetry as bulwark. Not poetry as retreat—but poetry as basis of protest" (8 September 1933). According to Burke, poetry and propaganda—while certainly not identical, or perhaps even equivalent, cultural forms—share a similar structural relation to the social and political sphere. Poetry is not conflated with propaganda in Burke's model, but it ceases to derive its cultural and linguistic value from a definitional opposition with "low" discursive forms. As Burke argues, both high ("pure") and low ("applied") forms rely upon the "manipulation of vocabulary," "images," "motions," and "emotions" to relate to the world that surrounds them (*ACR* 55). By emphasizing poetry's rhetorical properties, Burke re-connects it with the social, cultural, and political contexts that surround it.

While Burke's distinction from other literary critics may at first glance seem subtle or inconsequential, his re-orientation of poetic form as a rhetorical structure represents a radical departure from the New Criticism dominant in the middle of the 20th century and even from some contemporary critics. In fact, Burke's ability to re-connect the literary text to its context is the distinct value Frederic Jameson attributed to Burke's writing more than twenty-five years ago. As Jameson explains in his 1978 study, Burke's theory of the symbolic does much more than merely anticipate the linguistic-oriented focus of literary theory in the academy. Residing at a crucial nexus in the history of literary studies, "Burke's conception of the symbolic as act or *praxis* may equally well be said to constitute a critique of the more mindless forms of the fetishism of language" ("The Symbolic Inference" 508). For Jameson, Burke's writing offers an advantage over many forms of poststructural and postmodern theory because it embeds its conception of literary form so radically within the social: "Burke's stress on language, far from reinforcing as it does today the ideologies of the intrinsic and of the anti-referential text, had on the contrary the function of restoring to the literary text its value as activity and its meaning as gesture and a response to a determinate situation" (509). Rather than an opposition between form and context, poetry and rhetoric, Burke's philosophy connects the ideological critique of the 1930s and 1940s with the formalism of the New Critics to produce a unique dialectic between form and context. Jameson argues that Burke's writing can thus help to correct "the unavoidable historical reality of a breach between text and context," which has necessarily resulted from the perceived historical opposition between literary objects and critical or theoretical discourse ("The Symbolic Inference" 513). Within Burke's writing, Jameson proposes, "the false antitheses of an intrinsic and extrinsic criticism are dispelled" (513).[1]

Though written more than twenty-five years ago, Jameson's assessment of the field of literary studies and the perceived value of Burke's work to alter its foundational presumptions remain remarkably current.[2] In one of his most effective metaphors, Burke claims, "Critical and imaginative works are answers to questions posed by the situation in which they arose" (*PLF* 1). Yet, Burke goes on to explain, "They are not merely answers, they are strategic answers, stylized answers" (1). Unlike most of his critical contemporaries, Burke argues that literary objects derive their meaning from a complex dialectic between their "inner" form and their "external" contexts:

> Words are aspects of a much wider communicative context, most of which is not verbal at all. Yet words also have a nature peculiarly their own. And when discussing them as modes of action, we must consider *both* this nature as words in themselves *and* the nature they get from the non-verbal scenes that support their acts. (*PLF* xvii)

Like the New Critics, Burke retains a solid commitment to the "peculiar" nature of the word and its inability to ever be fully known by or interpreted through an external, "non-verbal" context, but unlike them, he doesn't disconnect text from context . Even though the meaning of a literary object is not determined by its social, cultural, and economic fields of production, it nonetheless provides an "answer" to questions arising in these external circumstances.

It is in this sense that he identifies himself, in *Attitudes Toward History,* as a "revolutionary" critic, one tasked with breaking down historically and ideologically entrenched oppositions:

> Our own program, as literary critic, is to integrate technical criticism with social criticism (propaganda, the didactic) by taking the allegiance to the symbol of authority as our subject. [. . .] And since the whole purpose of a "revolutionary" critic is to contribute to a change in allegiance to the symbols of authority, we maintain our role as "propagandist" by keeping this subject forever uppermost in our concerns. The approach, incidentally, gives one an "organic" view of literature, sparing him the discomforts of discussing the "social" and the "technical" as though they were on two different levels. [The revolutionary critic] spontaneously avoids a dualism of "form" and "content," "beauty" and "use," the "practical" vs. the "esthetic," etc. He gets a unitary approach to the matter of "dialectical interaction." (2: 234–35; 331 in later editions, in revised form)

Following Jameson, I would suggest that this "organic" and "revolutionary" dialectic between form and context, the "technical" and the "social," represents Burke's most significant contribution to the historical and present fields of literary studies. Consistent with his revolutionary project as a critic, moreover, as the rest of my essay tries to show, is the manner in which Burke re-articulates the relationship between literary form and its social and political contexts both (1) in his systematic re-invention of the lyric poem as "connective" and rhetorically structured, and (2) in his most unique poetic invention, namely, his "Flowerishes." Both of these poetic achievements have yet to be fully appreciated by the field of literary studies.

Making the Lyric "Do Something": Burke's Dramatistic Form

Despite Burke's characterization of poetry as "the inevitable connective," his own poetry dwells in a state of considerable isolation. For years, critics have studied Burke's theories of poetry, but ignored and sometimes even mocked the poems themselves. In an early review of

Burke's first collection of poetry, *Book of Moments: Poems 1915–1954,* Donald Davies establishes what would become a paradigm for approaching Burke's poetry. Davies implies that the poems are hardly noteworthy on their own, and, instead, "remind us that Burke is an idiosyncratic and influential critic" (95). Simultaneous to this construction of Burke's poetry as inferior, there is a related move on the part of critics to voice dissatisfaction with his prose on the grounds that it is too "poetic." As early as 1948, Bernard I. Duffey claims to speak for many critics when he suggests that Burke's method of thought "caused not only philosophers but ordinary readers to cry out in pain and frustration." Rather than the "coherence and consistency" that philosophers typically strive to achieve, Burke is accused of providing "acute, isolated insights, the relation and larger purport of which are very difficult to perceive" (139). Perhaps unintentionally, Duffey's critique of Burke's method of "acute, isolated insights" points not to a failure on Burke's part, but the extent to which his philosophy and poetry are deeply connected. Burke's method, long considered philosophically idiosyncratic, is actually a perfect embodiment of the characteristic traits of the lyric. These two tendencies on the part of critics—to ignore or devalue Burke's poetry and to mourn the more "poetic" aspects of his prose—both reveal the foundational level at which Burke theorized the lyric as a mode of thought and a mode of being.

The lyric, like so many of Burke's isolated moments of philosophical insight, strives not for coherence and consistency over a duration of time, but to crystallize an emotion or idea that arises in an instant. In fact, the lyric distinguishes itself from other literary forms, like drama or narrative, because of this unique relationship to time and space, as Sharon Cameron observes in *Lyric Time:* "Unlike the drama, whose province is conflict, and unlike the novel or narrative, which connects isolated moments of time to create a story multiply peopled and framed by a social context, the lyric voice is solitary and generally speaks out of a single moment in time" (22–23).

The traditional lyric voice thus imagines itself as asocial, and, in a sense, out of time. Even the title of Burke's first collection of poetry, *Book of Moments,* indicates his investment in the momentary quality of the lyric. In his "Foreword," he emphasizes that lyrics are "moments insofar as they pause to sum up a motive" (viii). While Burke retains this momentary aspect of the lyric, his other sentiments toward the form are far from conventional. He tells his reader, "The ideal lyricist would probably speak through as many shifting personalities as the ideal dramatist" (vii). Burke was undoubtedly aware that the lyric traces its very definition to a distinction from drama. By welding a bit of the dramatist to his model of the lyricist, he fundamentally undercuts the poetic theories that prevailed in the American academy of the 1950s. Most importantly, his strategic conflation of the lyrical and the dramatic serves the specific purpose of calling into question the most vexed aspect of the lyric tradition: its formal insistence upon autonomy and socially isolated privacy. Just as the dramatist produces an art that exists in a moment of connection with its audience, so too does Burke re-interpret the typically asocial lyric as a form structured upon a moment of communication with its readers.

Here is Burke's most significant departure from New Critical formalism and the culmination of his own socially or culturally embedded formal vision. As Northrop Frye declares, there is "no word for the audience of the lyric" (31). Frye, like many traditional critics of the lyric, borrows from John Stuart Mill's classic 1833 essay, which still remains an influential paradigm for approaching the lyric. Whereas "eloquence is *heard*," Mill claims, "poetry is *overheard*." Readers sneak up on the lyric, capturing an intimate moment to which they should never have been privy. "Eloquence supposes an audience," Mill continues, "the peculiarity of poetry appears to us to lie in the poet's utter unconsciousness of a listener" (12). Mill's theory of lyric privacy isolates poetic discourse from other forms of speech, constructing the lyric as a special act of utterance with the purported power to deny its own communicativeness. In a letter to Burke, Allen Tate echoes Mill when he quips, "A great poem is great whether anyone reads it or not" (qtd. in Selzer 156). In binding lyric poetry to drama, Burke destroys Mill's opposition between "eloquence" (as oral utterance) and "poetry" (as written text). "There are no forms of art," Burke claims, "which are not forms of experience outside art" (*CS* 143). Furthermore, "That work would be most eloquent in which each line had some image or statement relying strongly upon our experience outside the work of art" (*CS* 165). Burke's privileging of eloquence as a formal feature returns the lyric to its roots in drama, foregrounds the lyric's communicative action, and ends the lyric's critically imposed exile from its social audience. Rather than accepting Mill's categorical opposition between poetry and other forms of discourse, Burke sees poetry and rhetoric as structurally similar in that both "use weighted vocabulary" and "exploit attitudes and form attitudes" ("Study of Symbolic" 9).

Burke's poem, "The Conspirators," perfectly captures the aesthetic and political significance of his dramatistic reformulation of the lyric. Although "The Conspirators" has received very little critical attention, it is one of Burke's stronger lyric poems (*CP* 27). The first of the poem's three stanzas opens with a man and a woman "furtively" exchanging romantic endearments, "You best" and "You above all," in a space "Beyond earshot of others." Perhaps the most basic "conspiracy" at work in the poem is the reader's own eavesdropping upon the couple's escapades. By foregrounding the reader's presence, "The Conspirators" humorously confirms Burke's repeated claim throughout his critical work that poetry—and, in fact, all literature—is intimately bound to its audience.[3] In the poem, the presence of an audience redoubles, as we voyeuristically witness the conspirators' futile attempts to escape the prying eyes that haunt their hyper-scrutinized world. Burke deploys the trope of lyric isolation for the strategic effect of mocking the presumption that anyone can exist "Beyond earshot of others." "The Conspirators" thus conjures and denounces an entire lyric tradition that defies its own socialization, suggesting, instead, that lyric subjectivity is always already audience-oriented.

The "Conspirators" first appeared in *Furioso* in 1950 and was later collected in *Book of Moments* in 1955. Considering the poem's historical context—published as it was at the height of McCarthyism—it is not surprising that it reveals a struggle over cultural definitions of privacy. At a moment of intense public scrutiny toward Communists and the Left, the poem satirically transforms an ordinary, middle-class couple into conspirators by criminalizing their desire for private property, dramatized in the poem's middle stanza by their "[g]oing into the market" to get things such as tables and chairs from the "public stock-pile." In the poem's imagined collectivist economy, the couple must secretly, in the final stanza, play out their desire for commodities "behind drawn blinds," a politically charged reversal of McCarthy era surveillance.

One of the most interesting aspects of the poem is its reference to the "public stock-pile." The phrase is most likely an oblique allusion to the Collectives that briefly took hold in some Spanish villages under Communist control during the Spanish revolution. Many of these Collectives went so far as to abolish money entirely, organizing experimental, communal farms and removing all private goods to a public stock-pile at the center of the village (Leval 74–75). Burke was no stranger to the politics of the Spanish Civil War, as his poem "An Old Liberal Looks to the New Year, 1953" clearly indicates (*CP* 18). At the height of the House Un-American Activities Committee (HUAC) investigations, the poem takes as its starting point the revelation by a friend that "activities legal in 1935 lead to one's being regarded as a criminal in 1952" (ll. 2–3). "An Old Liberal" underscores the irony of HUAC's persecution of Spanish Civil War veterans who fought Franco's fascist armies:

> You said, "Let's help Democracy in Spain."
> Well, lad, I think you'd better say again.
> Such attitudes are now deemed vile and ranko,
> To be quite Franco. (ll. 16–19)

As Cary Nelson reminds us, "Spain was the first great confrontation between democracy and fascism" (*Revolutionary Memory* 54). Yet, even after WWII, HUAC refused to recognize that the veterans had fought for a noble cause. Rather than celebrating those who fought against fascism in Spain, HUAC labeled them "premature anti-fascists," a new category invented for the sole purpose of persecuting and prosecuting these liberal sympathizers (*Revolutionary Memory* 54). Looking back longingly on the overtly political climate of the 1930s, Burke concludes his poem

> Recant! Recant!
> What you did then, to be elect,
> Is now a crime in retrospect.
> The realm of charity grows scant.
> Recant. (ll. 39–43)

The quiet force and implicit resignation of Burke's final "Recant" add a new dimension to "The Conspirators" and its struggle to find privacy.

In the "Author's Note" that accompanied the first edition of *Book of Moments,* Burke comments on the social and political role he hopes his poetry might play. He suggests that his book of poems might serve a "documentary purpose," and help "put into proper perspective some of the past public and private motives that have become obscured by the sociopolitical overemphases of the immediate 'global' moment."[4] While Burke's language, here, is intentionally cryptic, he strongly hints at the poetry's political agenda, and implies that he means to address and even correct the skewed perspective brought on by the "global" imperative of the Cold War. Additionally, poems like "The Conspirators" and "An Old Liberal" are meant to "document" a revolutionary political history that was being increasingly forgotten by the American public. Around the time of the publication of *Book of Moments*, Burke writes to Malcolm Cowley claiming that he had recently found himself "essentially Thirty-minded," because the *Book of Moments* "leads up to and away from the things I did in the Thirties" (Letter to Cowley 1955).[5] Read in light of this political nostalgia, the *Book of Moments* marks an important statement concerning political action and the necessity of making political poetry public in the HUAC dominated landscape of the 1950s.

The few critical mentions of "The Conspirators" that do exist tend to read the poem, and subsequently the entire collection, with politics almost exactly the opposite to those that I have discussed. In his 1956 review of *Book of Moments*, W. C. Blum describes the poem as "a satire about a young married couple that makes collectivist cant and finance matrimony appear equally hilarious" (364). By constructing the poem as a transparent satire, Blum entirely evades Burke's consistently Leftist sentiments throughout his poetry. The poem, for Blum, simply celebrates the conspirators' desire for privacy and argues for a world where their love would not need to be contaminated by economic necessities. The sentiment is out of sync with Burke's other poetry, his critical theories, and even the poem itself. The comment seems a symptom of Blum's larger claim that the *Book of Moments* should be "recognized for the high comedy it largely is," a gesture that dismisses with a chuckle Burke's entire poetic project (366).[6]

Unfortunately, as Burke's writing was filtered through the increasingly zealous conservatism of the Cold War academy, comments like Blum's became far more common.[7] In 1955, for example, Donald Davies strips the politics entirely from Burke's poetry to find merely "horsing around" and "childish" language play (95). More than three decades later, in 1986, Robert L. Heath mimics Davies's sentiments, labeling Burke's theory of poetry "the purest enjoyment of words as words" and "the desire to use language not for some ulterior utilitarian end but for sheer joy" (230, 235). Heath's casual disavowal of poetry's "ulterior utilitarian end" obliterates in one sentence Burke's lifelong commitment to the social and political value of poetry. In his reliance on Davies, Heath is duped by what Cary Nelson has called "our discipline's testimony before HUAC": the critical project of systematically de-politicizing many modernist works in order to make them ideologically palatable to a McCarthy era audience. Nelson warns contemporary critics not "to repeat that testimony," not to accept at face value the frightened formalism that was valorized throughout much Cold War criticism (*Revolutionary Memory* 68). My reading of *Book of Moments* demonstrates that Burke viewed his poetry as a crucial vehicle for moving beyond formalist and aesthetic theories toward social and political action.

Nonetheless, the issues of humor and linguistic play in Burke's writing deserve more sustained treatment, since they are each crucial to the function of his dramatism. By co-opting a mode of linguistic experimentation from the New Critics, Burke was seeking to rearticulate their methodology through the lens of Leftist politics. More recently, Timothy W. Crusius has argued that comedy and humor in Burke's poetry are tied to his formal method of "perspective by incongruity." "The method is comic," Crusius emphasizes, but "subversively comic, the intent to liberate from the bondage of received ideas, habitual linkages forged and jealously guarded by tradition, cultural authority" (18). I will amend Crusius's framework only slightly, to move away from satire to focus more specifically upon the pun as a formalist strategy. Burke's poetry, I would argue, less than satire, uses the pun as its primary trope of moving from the poetic to the social. The pun uses wordplay to shift between disparate levels of meaning and experience. Burke's "family jewels," for example, is a classic, Shakespearian example of the pun, simultaneously registering in both economic and sexual terms, leaving the reader utterly uncertain as to where the intention of the joke resides. The disorienting power of the pun is precisely why "The Conspirators" comes across as such an ambivalent poem, leaving the reader to wonder what precisely is being called into question. A focus on the pun reveals the extent to which Burke's poetry experiments with language in all of its slippery imprecision. In "The Conspirators," the pun fuses both sexual and economic meanings within the term "playing treasure"—not to advocate one sense of meaning over the other but to demonstrate the inextricability of the two discourses, and, ultimately, to alter the connections between the two. This linguistic operation is a key strategy for Burke, as he argues in *Permanence and Change:* "The poem is a sudden *fusion,* a *falling together of many things formerly apart*" (158). This juxtaposition, or fusing, of ideologically incompatible discourses through the use of the pun perfectly captures the radical possibilities Burke imagined for a rhetorical poetry.

Burke's Rhetorical "Irruptions": The Poem as "Planned Incongruity"

In discussing the potential for his poetry to "put into proper perspective" the contemporary political scene, Burke's "Author's Note" explicitly references his "Flowerishes," which he describes as "prose epigrams on the Human Scramble." Burke claims to have adopted this experimental, "topsy-turvy" style because of "a feeling that realistic observations can emerge these days only somewhat dizzily, as from a muddle." A "flowerish" is, to borrow Paul Jay's phrase, "a peculiarly Burkean poetic form" that combines "prose epigrams" in a distinctly ornate "flourishing" pattern meant to resemble "the shape of a flower" (327). In his "Foreword" to the *Book of Moments,* Burke comments on the "Flowerishes" only to say that "having let down the bars" and having admitted a few other bits of prose, "we added a few prose epigrams ("Flowerishes"), since that form also is a variant of the 'momentarily summarizing'" (ix). Burke's comments do little to prepare the reader for the "Flowerishes" that follow. "Flowerishes" are visually detailed documents that are unique within the history of modern poetry and certainly among Burke's most complex realizations of his poetic method. Critics, however, seem to have taken Burke's comment about "letting down the bars" a bit too literally, and, as such, the "Flowerishes" have received no sustained critical treatment. Blum calls them "so baffling that a magnifying glass is needed to unscramble them" (366), and one can most likely speculate that for Davies they would fall under the category of "childish" and "playful" nonsense.

The "Flowerishes" belong more properly, I would suggest, within a tradition of political and formal poetic experiments reaching back to Guillaume Apollinaire's "Horse Calligram," Tristan Tzara or Francis Picabia's Dada works, and Ezra Pound's Imagist and Vorticist manifestoes, and looking forward to the visual and linguistic experiments of Concrete Poetry.[8] Some of the statements contained in "Flowerishes" provide overt political critique, such as the Gothic-styled "Crime: next to defense our biggest industry" or "they would fight dirty wars with clean bombs?" and the biting but brief "her progress from socialist to socialite" (*CP* 299, 300, 89). The second and more common category of flowerish represents statements that are explicitly trite, as in "The next time they want something. They'll remember to thank you for the former time" or "DOWN with sedition UP with sedation" (90, 297). The "Flowerishes" are part avant-garde experimentation and part street graffiti. In their specific attention to the clichéd, they also provide an interesting precursor to the Language Poetry experiments of the 1970s, where poets like Charles Bernstein and Bruce Andrews would similarly subvert the poetic by deploying borrowed or randomly selected, banal language. As a means of concretizing his strategy of collapsing the boundary between the poetic and the rhetorical, Burke's "Flowerishes" achieve a perfect discursive welding of poetry's "weighted words" and rhetoric's over-determined circulations.

As Paul Jay also notes, the Latin root of flourish, *florere*, means "to blossom" (327). This action points to the essence of "Flowerishes": to force open or expand the boundaries of poetry and, specifically, the boundaries of metaphor. Traditional metaphor traces its roots back to the Greek word for "transference" and denotes a trope or expression in which a word or phrase "shifts" from its typical context to a new context where it will expose unexpected meanings (*New Princeton Encyclopedia* 760). In the operations of traditional metaphor, however, the new context into which the word or image shifts is always stabilized by the sense of a primary or originary context. For example, in the phrase "the sky wept," rain may momentarily take on the characteristics of human tears, but it is an ephemeral linkage that does little to challenge the pre-existing boundaries between the human and the not human. The sky resembles a human crying, but it is not actually a human crying. Traditional metaphor "transfers" meaning, but does not disrupt it.

Metaphor, however, is a broad term that has been interpreted differently by critics for generations. Burke's own slippery use of the term even extended to his creation of the verb "metaphored": "the informative experience with familiar roles may be carried over, or 'metaphored,' into the experience with extra-familiar roles, giving these latter, in so far as they are, or are felt to be, analogous with the former, a structure of interpretations and attitudes borrowed from the former" (*PLF*

285). The broadness of Burke's understanding of metaphor is perhaps responsible for its innovative uses in the "Flowerishes." For a word or sound image to be "metaphored" means not just that the connotations of one will blur into the other momentarily, as in the traditional sense of metaphoric operations, but that the entire "structure of interpretations and attitudes" of one will be at play simultaneous to the other. As Debra Hawhee argues, Burke borrows his understanding of metaphor and his subsequent metaphoric experiments from Nietzsche, whose claim that all language is metaphoric still remains one of the most innovative treatments of the poetic trope: "For Nietzsche, then, language is mobile, tumbling toward accurate representation, willing to truth. Language moves the will to truth, and though 'it leads nowhere to the truth, language still produces effects by forcing an encounter with the world'" (136). Burke's "Flowerishes" similarly enact a "mobile," destabilized metaphor where sign is not privileged over signified as it is traditionally conceived to do. Burke's metaphors, like Nietzsche's, question the possibility that language is ever bound to literalness or truth. Thus, the combined work of the "Flowerishes" is to leave the reader not only amidst the clichés and aphorisms within which he or she started, but with the sense that no language is ever originary, that all phrases are "flowerishes," that all language tropes language.

Burke's "Flowerishes," then, are undoubtedly playful—but strategically so. They suggest that the free play of poetic language has the possibility to disrupt—or "irrupt" to borrow Burke's term (*CP viii*)—the ideological blindnesses that incapacitate individuals (*CP* viii). Burke's "Flowerishes" are each unique, with different type-settings and designs, but they are similar in their collage-like assemblage of aphoristic witticisms and small bits of seemingly found language. Much of the impact of the "Flowerishes" is in their deceptive sense of familiarity; like Freud's "uncanny," the "Flowerishes" appear to be messages the reader has heard somewhere before. Yet in their subtle rewritings of conventional speech and clichés, they simultaneously evoke a sense of strangeness or distance. This is the sense, too, in which Burke expands metaphor into the realm of pun. Unlike traditional metaphor's stabilized transference of associations, pun requires the free play of multiple meanings simultaneously. For example, Burke's "They never reign but they pore" conjures the familiar "when it rains, it pours," but alters the meanings of that proverb to a truly incomprehensible extent (*CP* 92). The pun remains "meaningful" through its play of associations, but its exact alterations no longer actually "mean" anything; that "They" will "pore" is little more than non-sense. The reader is left to chart meaning through the lingering associations that once made sense of the expression. This action of disrupting previously stable linguistic and social connections, what Burke terms "planned incongruity," is his prime theoretical means for the poetic to move off the page and into the social and ethical realm. As Burke writes,

> Day after day, year after year, [a person] may have a fairly fixed attitude towards something, and may in fact build the whole logic of his life in accordance with this attitude—yet of a sudden, for a spell, he may be invaded by some quite different attitude, and this irruption may be that element that, for him, falls into the pattern of a momentary poem. (*CP* vii-viii)

Burke's reference to a "fixed attitude" suggests his discussion of "trained incapacity" in *Permanence and Change*. Borrowing from Thorstein Veblen, Burke establishes trained incapacity as ideological blindness, our own inability to resist or even recognize our condition of social and cultural confinement. The "irruption" of the lyric form then, in challenging one's "fixed attitude" and patterns of daily life, has the potential to refigure the relationship between the self and the social. Borrowing from Veblen's theory of "trained incapacity," Burke suggests that the very schemas we use to know and organize our worlds can limit our range of perspectives:

> By trained incapacity [Veblen] meant that state of affairs whereby one's very abilities can function as blindnesses. [. . .] Veblen generally restricts the concept to the case of business men who, through long training in competitive finance, have so built their scheme of orientation about this kind of effort and ambition that they cannot see serious possibilities in any other system of production and distribution. (*PC* 7)

As Burke develops his theories in *Permanence and Change*, he will make the important shift from "trained incapacity" in the social register to the systemic blindnesses that are a condition of language: "[T. S. Eliot] offered a casual moral revaluation or perspective by putting the wrong words together ["decadent athleticism"]. Veblen's term, 'trained incapacity,' is of the same order" (*PC* 91). The poetic possibility of juxtaposing incongruous images or discourses is equated, for Burke, with the social and political act of re-orienting an individual's schema of orientation: "We may say that an entire cultural movement is like a sentence" (*PC* 182). The social "grammar" that prohibits individuals from even recognizing the confines of their "scheme of orientation" is mirrored in the linguistic grammar of the sentence, which, through logical or conventional language and metaphors, reifies one of the possibilities of language to the exclusion of others.

Burke's "Flowerishes," then, function to subvert stale, clichéd, and conventional language by using stale, clichéd, and conventional language. As one of the flowerishes states, "better when business becomes a ritual than when ritual becomes a business" (*CP* 90). More than just a weird proverb, Burke's message here is clear: the function of poetry is to destabilize the pre-existing connections between language and images (ritualized connections) by communicating in new and incongruous ways. "Flowerishes" may actually, in this sense, be the fullest and most radical realization of Burke's poetic theories. Similar to Pop Art, Burke's poetry disrupts ideology through a strategy of kitsch that saturates meaning to its breaking point. By crafting poetry out of overdetermined, rhetorical circulations, Burke playfully undermines "the categorical opposition between poetry and rhetoric" ("Study of Symbolic Action" 16). In fact, the "Flowerishes" cut to the very heart of Burke's beliefs regarding poetry and poetic form: flowerishes subvert ideology through a process of communication.

While many literary critics in the last half century have emphasized literature's social and political embeddedness, none have been as bold as Burke in demonstrating poetry's communicative possibilities. More commonly, models of politically and linguistically innovative poetry are indebted to the work of Theodor Adorno. In his now classic essay, "On Lyric Poetry and Society," Adorno, like Burke, shatters the conventional view of the lyric poem as "the most delicate, the most fragile thing that exists" (37). Offering an important linguistic and ideological analysis, Adorno counters that the lyric form is fundamentally bound to the social, since "language mediates lyric poetry and society in their innermost core" (43). Adorno's socialization of the lyric relies upon a notion of "protest" that is inherent to poetry's formal negotiation with culture. He defines protest as the extent to which a work of art can "give voice to what ideology hides" and move "beyond false consciousness" (39). Adorno's theorization of "protest," here, points toward what has now become a defining feature of many Marxist and neo-Marxist conceptions of radical poetry. For these critics, the value of radical poetry is founded in its unique ability to perform a negative dialectic with the social—to expose, in other words, the inherent falseness of ideology. Barrett Watten's recent study, *The Constructivist Moment: From Material Text to Cultural Poetics,* works squarely within this tradition incited by Adorno's theories, attempting to assemble a kind of genealogy of such "negativity" in poetry. The "constructivist moment," for Watten, is precisely this poetic possibility of "unveiling what eludes representation" or "a confrontation of aesthetic form with social negativity" (xxii).

While acknowledging the tremendous value and influence of such criticism, as a reader of Burke I am also made aware of the limits of these theorizations of poetry. Namely, Burke's innovative understanding of rhetorical poetry challenges the fundamental anti-communicativeness upon which these theories are built. As Adorno asserts, "[T]he lyric reveals itself to be most deeply grounded in society when it does not chime in with society, when it communicates nothing, when, instead, the subject whose expression is successful reaches an accord with language itself, with the inherent tendency of language" ("On Lyric Poetry" 43). At its core, Adorno's attempt to implicate the lyric in the framework of the social demands a transcendence of the social. To deny its own communicativeness, the lyric must imagine itself as a "utopian site [. . .], a tiny post-revolutionary or predictive spot in a pre-revolutionary situation" (DuPlessis 9). Adorno's theories undoubtedly provide a compelling structural analysis of the function of many radical and avant-garde works of literature. Yet he leaves untheorized and homogenized an entire tradition of "communicative" art that has historically contributed to progressive political and social aims.

In his "Flowerishes" and throughout his poetry, Burke deploys a poetic form that no longer resists communication, but provides a bridge into the social. Rather than grounding poetry in opposition to culture—text as divided from context—Burke demands cooperation between the poem and its audience. Against Adorno's "negative" conception of political poetry, Burke's "positive" poetic, in the "Flowerishes" and more broadly, communicates entirely within the framework of capitalism. Unlike Adorno who envisions vision of protest as a turning "critically against the sphere of individualism," Burke "assumes that the poem is designed to 'do something' for the poet and his readers, and that we can make the most relevant observations about its design by considering the poem as the embodiment of this act" (Adorno, "On Lyric Poetry" 40; *PLF* 89). As I have suggested throughout my essay, the radical connection and social cooperation posed by this poetic methodology remains unique within the last century of poetry and poetic criticism.

By focusing on Burke's "connective" impulse in his poetry and poetic theory, my essay has thus attempted to piece together many diverse aspects of his life and work in order to point toward the facets of his thinking that may prove useful to the contemporary field of literary criticism. While I have merely outlined Burke's notion of a rhetorical poetry in broad strokes, I believe that his attempt to fuse the poem with other non-specialized forms of discourse and his foundational belief in poetic form as a communicative act intersect productively with current critical models. Perhaps most importantly, I have tried to demonstrate the ways that Burke's methodology for literary criticism extends into his own poetry; in fact, his poetry might even produce a more radical political vision than his criticism. As Cowley writes in a 1924 letter to Burke, "The function of poetry is to make the world inhabitable, a process which must be repeated for every generation" (156). Illustrating this tenet, Burke produced poetry for his time that demands a fresh look on the part of literary critics.

Notes

1. As many readers of Burke are probably already aware, Burke responded rather harshly to Jameson's assessment of his work in *Critical Inquiry*. In Burke's published response, "Methodological Repression and/or Strategies of Containment," he reacts especially strongly to Jameson's use of the term "ideology." However, Burke never disagrees with the points I have drawn from Jameson's reading, namely his suggestion that Burke restores a sense of the "organic whole" of literary history ("The Symbolic Inference" 513). Nonetheless, it is worth pointing out that Burke himself distrusted Jameson's theoretically inflected reading of his work.

2. The journal *American Literary History* recently hosted a debate concerning poetry and its fraught relationship to social and historical methods. The debate surrounding poetry and new historicist scholarship is especially relevant to my discussion regarding Burke. See, in particular, the essays by Robert von Hallberg, Barbara L. Packer, Shira Wolosky, and Andrew DuBois, all found in *ALH* 15.1 (Spring 2003).

3. See, especially, *Counter-Statement*, where Burke first reconstitutes literary form as "the psychology of the audience" rather than the psychology of the artist. In what has become *Counter-Statement*'s most famous edict, he proclaims, "Form is the creation of an appetite in the mind of the auditor, and the adequate satisfying of that appetite" (31). Later, Burke lays out an entire program for literary criticism that moves away "from a stress upon self-expression to a stress upon communication" (223). Burke's shift to "communication" over self-expression explicitly foregrounds the role of the audience in affecting the form and function of a literary work.

4. I am grateful to David Blakesley and Julie Whitaker for a research exhibit, which first alerted me to the existence of this "Author's Note." The exhibit occurred as part of "Kenneth Burke and His Circles: The 19th Penn State Conference on Rhetoric and Composition and the Triennial Conference of the Kenneth Burke Society," 10–12 July 2005, Penn State University. Blakesley's and Whitaker's exhibit was the culmination of their research into Burke's uncollected poetry for the recently published *Late Poems, 1968–1993: Attitudinizings Verse-wise, While Fending for One's Own Selph, and in a Style Somewhat Artificially Colloquial*. I wish to thank the Kenneth Burke Literary Trust for permission to quote from unpublished letters that Kenneth Burke wrote to Malcolm Cowley.

5. Ned O'Gorman first made me aware of this remarkable letter. My reading here is indebted to his paper, "Reading Kenneth Burke's 'Marxism' in *Permanence and Change* with Lewis Mumford."

6. W. C. Blum is the pen name of J. Sibley Watson, one of the co-founders, along with Scofield Thayer, of the influential literary magazine, the *Dial*. Burke, who was associated with the *Dial* in a variety of capacities from 1921 through 1929, counted Watson among his closest friends and colleagues. For a detailed treatment of Burke's experiences at the *Dial* and his association with Watson, see Armin Paul Frank's *Kenneth Burke*. In his discussion of Burke's poetry, Frank relies heavily on Watson/Blum's assessment, noting that he "accurately sums up Burke's poetic achievement" (129). While I acknowledge that Watson was generally one of Burke's more sensitive readers, I tend to part company with his overall interpretation of the meaning and values that are espoused within Burke's poetry.

7. Marius Bewley's "Kenneth Burke as Literary Critic" is an excellent marker of the critical attempts to de-radicalize Burke's legacy. While Bewley himself can never get past Burke's Marxism, finding that it contaminates his work too fully, he references other critics of his time, like Stanley Edgar Hyman, who ignore Burke's politics and see him solely as an idiosyncratically styled "Burkologist" (214–16). This shift in reception from viewing Burke as a literary critic, as he was typically labeled in the 1930s and 1940s, to fashioning him as a "semanticist" or "Burkologist" had the effect of de-

politicizing his theories and making them more palatable to politically wary, Cold War era critics.

8. Apollinaire's "Horse Calligram" is an especially apt precursor to Burke's "Flowerishes." With text shaped to resemble a rough outline of a horse, the poem opens with the statement, "You will find here a new representation of the universe. The most poetic and the most modern" (119). As a forerunner to the "Flowerishes," Apollinaire demonstrates the potential for antiquated, "shaped poems" to take on a new, more modern charge through manifesto-like declarations. Burke's "Flowerishes" similarly innovate old, clichéd language and form, announcing a distinctly modern sensibility.

11 The "Logological Organizing" of Corporate Discourse: A Burkean Case-Study Analysis

Peter M. Smudde

Kenneth Burke once said of himself and the critical enterprise: "I think that there has to be a lot of leeway in this business. I see no reason for being authoritarian. . . . The fundamental notion of choice in my scheme is difference" (qtd. in Chesebro 365).[1] The fact that Burke created an open system, welcoming views of others that are different, allows it to grow beyond what he originally set forth. As James Chesebro argues, "To remain viable, a system of analysis must be an 'open system,' responding to changing human conditions and adapting to shifting attitudes, beliefs, and actions. In this regard, even Burke's system of analysis must undergo transformation if it is to remain receptive to ever-changing human dynamics" (364). During the seventy-plus years of Burke's writings, he, other critics, and surrounding circumstances helped to reshape and extend his system. The breadth of application and appeal to those in many fields demonstrates the importance that critics have placed on Burke's ideas and critical method. This circle of Burke's influence extends to organizational discourse, particularly corporate discourse (e.g., public relations, technical communications, financial reporting, managerial writing, etc.).[2] Burke links himself to this area when he suggests that *Attitudes Toward History* might have been entitled "Manual of Terms for a Public Relations Counsel with a Heart (we shouldn't overlook the cardiac touch) " ("Introduction" i).

By far the most used Burkean concept in scholarship about organizational communication is identification, and the leading scholar of rhetorical identification in this area is without question George Cheney

149

(and his varying coauthors). Cheney's *Rhetoric in an Organizational Society*, based on the premise that "organizations are fundamentally rhetorical in nature" (ix), employs an in-depth analysis of a single case (i.e., the U. S. Catholic bishops' 1983 pastoral letter, *The Challenge of Peace*) to account fully for the organizational, rhetorical, and identity-related aspects of a series of events: the development of a historic 'corporate' document" (164). For organizational rhetoric, as Cheney puts it, "[t]he coordination of identities in expression becomes complicated in proportion to the multiplicity of identities for which and to which a collectivity such as a corporation must speak, including both members and outsiders" (17). In studying the coordinated identification of multiple identities in the production of a "corporate" document, Cheney thus studies one of the distinctive features of organizational or corporate discourse, namely, the extent to which its production is typically the coordinated product of many hands.

A related feature, also distinctive, is the organizational structuring, usually defined in advance, of such coordinated activity. In the case of something such as an annual report, for example, the document's production process includes writers, editors, photographers, graphic designers, management, and legal counsel, all following recipes to produce one discourse type to induce identification between the organization and its publics, such as stockholders and new investors (cf. Smudde, "Practical"). All the individuals involved in such a process must govern themselves by the overarching rhetorical aim of the organization.

Less scholarly attention, however, has been given to cases in which an organization finds itself in a situation in which it must act to sustain its identification with its publics but it must do so in the absence of any such prior organizational structuring. In such situations, organization emerges in the process of acting, but it's not there in advance to coordinate multiple actions over time, as in the production of documents like annual reports. What generalizations, if any, might one venture about organizational structuring in such situations? It's a situation of this kind that one finds in the General Motors (GM) case to be examined here.

On August 14, 1992, the Center for Automotive Safety, a Washington consumer group, and Public Citizen, a nonprofit public interest law group, filed a petition with the National Highway Traffic Safety Administration (NHTSA) to recall GM's full-size C/K pickups (9.6

million of them) built and sold between 1973 and 1987, alleging a defect in their fuel-system design ("Feds Want"). The issue was whether the pickups' "side-saddle" fuel tanks, which are mounted on the outside of the truck's frame rails (i.e., the structure that supports the mass of the vehicle) and just behind the outer body panels, are more vulnerable to puncture and fire in a crash than fuel tanks that are mounted between the frame rails (Weiser 1).

GM's response to this recall petition, also on August 14, stated simply:

> GM believes, [sic] that its full-size pickups, both current and former models, meet the safety needs of GM's customers. All GM vehicles including our full-size pickups continue to meet or exceed all Federal Motor Vehicle Safety Standards, including the specific requirement applicable to fuel system integrity. (General Motors, *Abbreviated Chronology* 1)

The ensuing debate lasted six years, from 1992 to 1998, encompassing a multitude of events too complex to trace here, but with the help of Burke it will be possible to see the forest that organized all these trees.

With the filing of this recall petition, GM found itself in a situation described as "ill-defined" by Ed Lechtzin, then director of GM's legal and safety issues, in that no established crisis plan could help company officials manage the issue. As Lechtzin explains, GM does have plans for certain crises such as

> a fire in a plant, a worker gets killed—who do you notify, what do you do, how do you handle it, et cetera. That's a purely defined [. . .] situation. This [the C/K pickup issue] was an ill-defined situation where you never knew who the players were, where they were coming from, and what you could even begin to control. [. . .] Those are real textbook cases [i.e. Pepsi and Tylenol] on how to handle product tampering—how to be prepared for product tampering. They don't know exactly where it's going to happen, when it's going to happen, or exactly how it's going to happen, but you have all the material and all the people ready

to go to talk about your process and how it's impossible. (Personal interview)

Lechtzin explains GM's internal response: "The multi-pronged attack on the trucks' safety prompted something that now seems so simple but is not practiced in many organizations: We formed a 'swat' team that eliminated traditional bureaucratic boundaries so we could react quickly and without constant direction from management" ("One Year" 4). This team consisted of the director for public affairs for GM's North American Operations, three attorneys, two engineers, and one public relations person. This "swat" team's job, of course, was to do what's best for GM, but the team had to do this in the absence of a predefined organizational structure. Instead, this team had to monitor, on a daily basis, a highly equivocal environment in which new challenges could arise from any direction at any time. In deliberating about whether or how to respond to these challenges, the "swat" team was in effect deciding whether or how to engage in "symbolic action"—that is, to enact a "strategic" response to a "situation" (Burke, *PLF* 1-3)—designed to structure people's thinking about the issue, induce identification between targeted publics and the automaker, and, ultimately, to achieve vindication for the pickups.[3]

This process no doubt seemed chaotic to the "swat" team in the absence of the kind of organizational structure typically in place to coordinate most corporate activities. Nonetheless, an organizational structure did emerge over time to contextualize the multiple discourses produced along the way. Retrospectively, one can reconstruct the organization that did dictate the rhetorical purposes of the discourses GM produced, but it's not the kind of organization one can map out in advance. It's an organization that Burke's dramatism in general and logology in particular can help one to discern, and in turn, the example of this organization in this particular case can deepen our understanding of Burke's logology.

The structure organizing the seeming chaos was the structure of a drama in which GM found itself in conflict with its accusers, and surrounded by arbiters of the conflict: law courts, NHTSA, media, and ultimately the public. This drama became the organizational structure framing the whole episode. "In a nutshell, a methodology for a public relations counsel with a heart would be a dramatistic one" (Smudde, "Implications" 424). Taking its lead from drama, this was a structure with different possible conclusions. While various aspects of Burke's dramatistic analysis could be used to analyze this particular drama, the one that proves most useful is the logological progression analyzed in *The Rhetoric of Religion:* order, guilt, purification, and redemption. This evolution from order to redemption enables one to see the forest encompassing all the trees in the six years it took for the drama to play itself out.

Logology defines, as it were, the conditions GM had to meet to restore the order in place prior to the recall filing on August 14, 1992. This order consisted of the public trust in the safety of this particular product. Restoration of this "order" was GM's ultimate aim. The conflict between GM and its accusers in this case was one of competing dramas about how order became disordered and what steps needed to be taken and by whom to achieve redemption.

The accusers claimed that a defective fuel-tank design for GM's 1973–1987 C/K pickup trucks (GM's guilt) undermined their designation as safe vehicles (the order of things). These accusers wanted GM to be held accountable for the defect and stand up and publicly proclaim its responsibility for the defects (purify itself through mortification). Then GM would have to fix every 1973–1987 C/K pickup on the road (achieve redemption).

For GM, however, the accusers falsely asserting that a defect existed were the ones guilty of polluting the order of things for its safe pickups. To make things right again for the automaker and its customers (purification), the opposing groups would receive the blame for the false claim (victimage), and the C/K pickup designs would be vindicated (achieving redemption for GM).

In this dramatic struggle, GM eventually succeeded. NHTSA agreed that no recall was needed. From a traditional public relations standpoint, keys to that success were at least three things:

1. Consistent and aggressive adherence to and evidential support for a core set of messages about the trucks' safety, GM's conduct, and opponents' suspect motives against the company and its vehicles.
2. A high level of support from prominent, influential people (i.e. safety experts, industry analysts, publication editors, independent auto industry writers, other auto industry leaders, and key federal legislators) who actively and publicly voiced their support for GM.

3. The marked reduction in the importance the news media placed on the issue, including falling public awareness of it after the agreement between GM and NHTSA and the settlement of class-actions brought against the company.

A study by the Public Relations Society of America Foundation singled out in particular GM's success in leveraging the credibility of outside sources in support of its key messages. This study shows that the public's most-trusted sources of information about a company come from respected third parties, including "experts" and "print news sources" (12).

No doubt such factors were important. For example, in late 1992, not long after the August 1992 petition filing for a recall, while NHTSA's own investigation was already underway, NHTSA requested additional information from GM. In response, GM created a lengthy statement supplying the information requested, including empirical data about the safety of the pickups as gathered by a third-party research firm, Failure Analysis Associates, whose credentials were also summarized (General Motors, *Statement on Data*).

Such third-party evidence obviously enhanced GM's credibility. But however important and essential, such credibility operates on a more or less legalistic level that leaves untouched the deeper level disclosed by Burke's logological perspective. It's this deeper level that one needs to examine to find the "organization" that ultimately determined whether GM could restore order, that is, the public trust in the safety of its vehicles that existed prior to August 1992.

The two main turning points in GM's favor were highly dramatic, especially the first. GM had to struggle against the public attitude that, as a monolithic enterprise, it is uncaring and impersonal. Indeed, "the mainstream press seemingly views every statement by the government or big business as half-truth or bald-face lie. [. . .] [T]he press has a pervasive feeling that they are being manipulated by spokespeople, spinmeisters and public relations professionals" (Bailey 20). In this struggle, the cornerstone discourse that turned this attitude around for GM was a press conference featuring a GM senior executive.

The events leading to this press conference began when media coverage of this recall debate peaked with an NBC *Dateline* show, "Waiting to Explode," which aired on November 17, 1992.[4] As Lechtzin explains, "[the issue] didn't really catch public attention until *Dateline* in

November of '92" (Personal interview). The program segment about the C/K trucks was described by an independent report on NBC's conduct in producing it:

> The GM truck segment was called "Waiting to Explode?" It reported on allegations about the safety of certain GM C/K pick-up trucks manufactured between 1973 and 1987. The allegations were that the trucks were prone to catch fire in side-impact collisions because their gas tanks—which were mounted side-saddle outside the frame of the truck—had a tendency to rupture on impact. The segment lasted fifteen minutes and included interviews with families who had lost children in truck fires, plaintiffs' lawyers, auto safety consultants, and GM representatives. The segment also included videotape of accident scenes, television commercials for GM trucks, crash tests of trucks by GM and NHTSA, and "unscientific crash demonstrations" conducted for *Dateline*. (Warren and Kaden 15–16)

Although the segment ran for a total of 15 minutes and addressed much of the controversy about the pickups, the most important part were the 56 seconds devoted to crash tests of two C/K pickups.

As indicated earlier, deciding whether and how to respond to such attacks was daily business for the GM "swat" team. According to Lechtzin, the team recognized three levels of confrontation:

> One was the peer, almost behind the scenes confrontation and maneuvering (that's as good a word as any) between us and the government, and that was going on. Then you had the plaintiff bar coming at us constantly. And then you had the PR side, the public, and [. . .] the media, and our job was to control that piece of it so that it did not overwhelm or cause politicians to do something that we didn't want them to do. Basically, we were working to keep as much heat off NHTSA and the regulators as possible. And they can say all they want that there's nothing wrong with these trucks and there's no reason to recall them, but if public pressure becomes high enough, that's the way

government works, that's the way government agencies work. And our job was not so much corporate reputation as to keep the heat off the government. (Personal interview)

The *Dateline* report threatened to increase public pressure on NHTSA. A challenge to the report would help if it succeeded, but it could make things worse if it failed.

The decision, finally, was to investigate the *Dateline* report. For nearly three months after the report, GM sought to obtain the trucks NBC used, but the show's producer wrote in a letter that the vehicles were destroyed. Through a tip from a journalist that the tests were rigged, from the help and depositions of witnesses to *Dateline's* crash test, and from GM's own investigation of the surrounding area of the crash-test site in Indiana to collect evidence and the very vehicles used in the tests, GM built a case that the *Dateline* report was based on purposely rigged crash tests and, on February 8, 1993, filed a defamation lawsuit against NBC for fraud. That suit stated specifically that "NBC knowingly and purposely rigged two car-truck crashed [sic] with remotely detonated incendiary devices to attempt to cause vehicle fires to fraudulently characterize GM's 1973–87 full-size pickup trucks as being prone to post-collision fuel-fed fires" (General Motors, *Abbreviated Chronology* 3).

GM reinforced this lawsuit's claim in what proved to be the cornerstone discourse in the whole drama, a press conference held on February 8, 1993 by GM Executive Vice President and General Counsel Harry J. Pearce (Lechtzin, "One Year"). This event was attended by almost 200 representatives of the news media. Pearce conducted the session that included exhibits of the trucks used in *Dateline's* report, video excerpts of the program, enhanced photographs of parts of the report to show how the tests were rigged, results of analyses about the pickups' safety, and a complete kit of information, including copies of photographs and statistical analyses and statements about the program. Copies of that kit were sent to all GM communications offices to help manage the issue for employees.

As a result of the work of GM's "swat" team, including Pearce's presentation of the enacted environment surrounding the *Dateline NBC* story, NBC management recanted the story and apologized on the air the next evening, February 9, 1993. On the logological level, in the dramatic conflict between GM and its accusers, guilt was in the eye of the beholder unless and until it could be definitely placed on one side or the other. With NBC's recantation, guilt was definitively placed on the side of at least one accuser and to that extent GM was purified and redeemed.

News reports for days and weeks to follow covered the redemptive strategy GM officials enacted to bolster the company's image and reputation. The broad response in GM's favor—from NBC's recanting of the story, to articles placing GM and the public as victims of journalistic misconduct, to reports reframing the pickups' safety—indicate successful restructuring of people's thinking on the issue.

A second turning point over a year later was less dramatic but more important insofar as it for all intents and purposes decided things in GM's favor. From April 1993 through December 1994, GM and the NHTSA wrangled over recalling the allegedly defective C/K pickups. Even though NHTSA'S own investigators concluded that no recall was warranted, given that real-world performance of the trucks "does not suggest any significant increased risk of fires" (*Detroit News,* April 28, 1993), NHTSA asked GM to voluntarily recall the vehicles. GM rejected the request, providing the agency with a 1–1/2-inch thick document to that effect (General Motors, *Abbreviated Chronology* 4). On October 17, 1994, Frederico Peña, U.S. Department of Transportation secretary, acted on his own and announced that a safety defect existed in GM 1973–1984 C/K pickups and that a "final decision on whether to proceed with a government-ordered recall or to close the investigation would be made after a public meeting scheduled for December 6" (General Motors, *Abbreviated Chronology* 8). GM countered the announcement by saying Peña's decision was unjustified, citing the data from independent researchers and "real-world" surveys of the trucks' performance. At this point, according to Lechtzin, the GM strategy shifted from a reactive mode:

> From *Dateline* until October 17, '94, we were in maintenance, figuring that the government was actually going to drop the case. Three or four times we had good information that they were going to dropt it. [. . .] October 17 he [Peña] says recall them for no reason—has no right to do it. He steps completely out of bounds, at which point, from a public relations standpoint, we went very active. (Personal interview)

Media reports about Peña's action asserted that Peña was motivated by political concerns, not the facts as demonstrated by the agency's own and independent investigations. On November 3, 1994, members of the U.S. Congress—Representative Bob Carr (Michigan), who was then chairman of the House Appropriations Subcommittee on Transportation, and Representative John Dingell (Michigan), who was then chairman of the House Committee on Energy and Commerce—led the call for and launched investigations into these claims about Peña. The chief executives of the Big Three—Chrysler Chairman and CEO Robert Eaton, Ford Chairman and CEO Alex Trotman, and GM President and CEO John Smith—signed a letter to U.S. President Bill Clinton to "address the intolerable state of regulatory uncertainty that will otherwise result from Secretary Peña's decision" (Eaton, et al.). GM also filed suit in U.S. District Court in Detroit challenging Peña's legal authority to order a recall of the pickups.

An investigation of Secretary Peña's actions surrounding his personal decision to recall the pickups revealed in late November 1994 that, although he acted "within the scope of his authority and discretion," the Secretary had a pattern of continually overruling NHTSA technical staff that had in this case recommended closing the investigation based on its findings that the trucks pose no unreasonable risk (General Motors, *Abbreviated Chronology* 21–22), thus vindicating the trucks' safety and fuel-tank design. On December 2, Secretary Peña announced that GM and NHTSA reached a settlement to close the investigation: the company would fund more than $51-million worth of research and development on auto safety over five years, and the federal agency would drop its investigation and a proposed recall of the pickups ("Auto Safety Groups").

This settlement effectively marked the final purification and redemption of GM. Lawsuits were still pending, but the main drama was over. Public relations activity about GM's 1973-1987 pickups waned considerably after the agreement between GM and NHTSA. Public coverage of continuing litigation had almost no effect on GM's redemption. This pattern tends to reinforce the point that Burke's logological progression, rather than legalistic issues, was the fundamental level in the dramatistic "organization" in this case.

Strictly speaking, one could say that redemption did not cleanse GM of guilt in this case, because it was ultimately determined that GM never sinned in the first place. GM's redemption was to be found to never have sinned. But such considerations are secondary to the fundamental role Burke's logological progression played in structuring the dramatic conflict between GM and its accusers.

A more important consideration is that the applicability of this progression to this case is a strong indication of the universality of Burke's logology. After all, Burke bases his analysis of the logological process from guilt to redemption on his analysis of the "tautological cycle of terms for 'order'" in Genesis, but here we can find evidence of the same process in a public relations battle over an automobile recall dispute. What this suggests is that this logological "organization" reveals something essential about human relations and about what, therefore, had to happen to restore the order in place prior to the August 1992, when GM was first accused. This is an order that is deeper than all the legal issues involved in this case, because it depends on the public trust GM needed to maintain consumer confidence in its products. To regain this trust, GM needed redemption.

NOTES

1. Chesebro is quoting from a transcription of a videotaped interview with Burke at the Kenneth Burke Society convention, May 7, 1990.

2. Studies of organizational discourse based on Burke typically use his later works (i.e., those published after and including *A Grammar of Motives*). Schuetz, for example, dramatistically addresses specific aspects of the symbolic action of corporate advocacy: strategies are acts; advocates are agents; issues, policies and propositions are purposes; symbolic means are agency; contexts are scenes; and motives are teased out from these elements. Cragan and Shields develop an ambitious matrix of three intersecting planes to guide one's analysis in applied communication research; for Burke's dramatism theory, those planes are the master analogue plane for the purification ritual (Burke's terms for order), the structural plane of the hexad (Burke's pentad plus attitude), and the evaluation plane of linguistic vantage point, cyclical standing, quality of motivation and degree of identification. Tompkins, Fisher, Infante, and Tompkins use Burke's concepts of mystery and hierarchy to test people's sensitivity to order in the hierarchy, mystery in the hierarchy, and identification with levels in the hierarchy at a northeastern U.S. university. Foss focuses on Burke's notions of guilt and redemption to investigate the Chrysler bailout by the Federal government and Chrysler's subsequent efforts to redeem itself and "retool" its image. By far the most-used Burkean concept in scholarship about organizational communication is identification. Adler's category of organizational identification refers to one's "buying in to" and, subsequently, participating socially and productively within an organi-

zation. Brown finds that identification "is mediated through symbolic rather than pragmatic motivational states" (354) in a case study of an industrial organization that examines the factors, both symbolic (e.g., achievement) and pragmatic (e.g., money), that motivate people to behave in certain ways in response to their perceived relationship with the organization. Hall and Schneider study "the individual and organizational correlates of identification" (341)—tenure, job challenge, self-image, needs, and satisfaction—concluding that "organizational identification appears to be a process in which some 'right type' of person is most likely to enter an organization (through selection and recruitment) and be ready to identify with it" (349). Rotondi finds that organizational identification is "directly related to the general personality variables of social isolation, or insecurity in social relationships, and incompetence, as reflected by inadequate feelings of mastery over the self and the environment" (99).

3. This treatment of the *in situ* writing process of the "swat" team is admittedly brief and cursory, because while I worked for GM (see note 4), I only came to the case "after the fact" and used textual data for analysis. An ethnographic investigation of such a process could prove to be a fruitful, separate research project.

4. I was a GM employee from 1989 to 1997, and was working in GM's Service Technology Group at the company's Technical Center in Warren, Michigan, when GM began managing the issue of the safety of its 1973–1987 C/K pickup trucks and, subsequently, the controversial story about the trucks that aired on NBC's *Dateline*. I watched the program the evening in November 1992 that it was broadcast. In February of the following year, I listened intently with a few of my fellow employees to a live radio broadcast of GM's response to *Dateline's* story. As I listened to the coverage of the dramatic press conference, I could imagine the scene, the spokesperson from GM, and the material evidence he used to buttress his statements about the story's content. I remember being impressed by the well-crafted, detailed arguments that the speaker presented and being struck by the profound implications this event and the entire issue had—and would have—on GM, NBC, and other organizations, as well as on the practice of public relations. This study had its impetus in that personal experience.

12 Still the King of Queens? Kenneth Burke, *The Rhetoric of Religion,* and the Theorizing of Rhetoric and Religion Now

Benjamin Bennett-Carpenter

Is it a surprise that Kenneth Burke's 1961 book on the rhetoric of religion, by that name, remains the key contemporary text on the topic? Perhaps not. Rhetorical analysis of religious texts of course is widespread. Yet what about the interaction of rhetoric as such and religion as such together at the theoretical level? Does such a question remain viable? If not, does that mean Burke's text should mark an end of what could be dubbed as "essentialist" reflection on the topic? Marjorie O'Rourke Boyle's comments have suggested as much.[1] Burke and Augustine too, in her line, should be left to the side if any advance is to be made; "Augustine," she suggests, "was ultimately, profoundly antirhetorical" ("Religion" 666). In any scenario, when one narrows the field to contemporary reflection on rhetoric and religion, Burke remains king of articulating the analogies between his queen, rhetoric, and Augustine's, theology. Admittedly, there remains something final about this royal position, such that Burke might end up finding his place with Augustine in a pre-historicist theorizing that otherwise is known to some, pejoratively, as classicist, or in neutral or complementary terms, as classical. Indeed Burke's text, like Augustine's, has found its place in what has become a "canonical" rhetorical tradition that now is increasingly replaced by localized studies of particular rhetorical features of particular communications or actions of particular religious bodies. One need only search WorldCat for titles including "the rhetoric of . . ." to get started.

Recent reflection on rhetoric and religion from the rhetoric side has certainly avoided association with disguised theology, which might be equated with something not unlike the occult for rhetoricians. Theologians and theorists of religion still crank out books that find the two not foreign to what Wayne Booth crooned as "essentially wedded" ("Rhetoric and Religion: Are They Essentially Wedded?"). Of course it all depends on what one means by "essentially," whether an open neo-Platonism or something else. If that something else is rooted in the history of religion and the rhetorical tradition, then we might wonder why we would have to use the term "essential." Boyle's pejorative use of this term is indicative of a suspicion of anything that harkens to a Platonist, Augustinian and later Aristotelian Thomistic Christianity that she thinks we are better off without because we are all better off not believing in phantasms. She suggests Calvin's reformation theology along with Erasmus's humanism give us a better chance at eliminating superstition and, insofar as anyone, including Burke, hints at reinstating superstition, we ought to be suspicious.

Yet Burke's take on religion is a bit more sophisticated than Boyle suggests. A big possibility for misunderstanding begins with one's understanding of "analogy," especially Burke's six Analogies in the first chapter of *Rhetoric of Religion,* which still constitute today the main reflection on the interconnected relationship between rhetoric and theology. I say this with some help especially from Walter Jost and Wendy Olmsted's recent collection on the topic, *Rhetorical Invention and Religious Inquiry: New Perspectives.* Of course they are not so reductive as to say that Burke is It. Booth and Walter Ong and a whole range of contemporary scholars play into the current reflection. And while there is not a great deal of attention given to the Analogies, Jost and Olmsted's collection shows an ongoing homage to both Ong and Burke as well as to the tried and true tradition of reflection upon Augustine in a religio-rhetorical tradition that owes an almost overwhelming amount to Christianity.

Before we turn to Burke's Analogies, Booth and Ong merit some attention. For Booth, rhetoric and religion are "inextricably connected," because rhetoric reaches beyond inquiry and epistemology: "rhetoric not only as inquiry, rhetoric not only as epistemic [. . .], but rhetoric as the co-creator of reality itself, rhetoric as the Word that was God and that was with God" ("Rhetoric and Religion" 62, 79). Booth's use of the word "religion" opens up to the pluralistic reality of multiple religions because he is not necessarily taking any one religion as It. Religion and reflection upon it are not necessarily reduced to theology. His understanding of rhetoric not only in terms of inquiry or epistemology but also in terms of human practice more generally brings us to where philosophers of language and communication operate. Booth, however, has not said very much in a systematic fashion, and what he has said remains incomplete.[2]

Meanwhile, Ong's essay "The Word as History: Sacred and Profane" (from Ong's *Presence of the Word*) is included in Jost and Olmsted's reader as a seminal essay for any discussion of rhetoric and religion. To put the matter flatly: Ong takes the Christian doctrine of the Incarnation and the theologies of the mediating role of Christ in human culture as analogous to the historical development of rhetoric and media more generally. Jost and Olmsted say, "Ong views the development of the word as a coming-to-awareness that parallels the coming of humanity to the Logos or Word of God" ("Introduction" 6). Among his strengths, they note, Ong notably combines an historical approach with an ontological one (6). As such, one might suspect that spookiness abounds; on the other hand, all ghostliness gets historicized.

Ong's tracing of the major phases of the history of rhetoric and media in terms of primary orality, visuality (both writing and then print culture), and finally, in the electronic age, secondary orality is well known, and I will not outline it here.[3] Yet I want to note that Ong believes that the major transformations in human communication mean transformations in consciousness. An implication of Ong's theory of the history of media is that as rhetorical practices and theorizing on those rhetorical practices develop, human thought develops, and human culture changes. For Ong the level of change is not only intellectual but has to do with every aspect of culture, including the religious. Ong argues that rhetoric and media are constitutive of fundamental change, or what in religion is often called "conversion."[4] By any account, Ong assumes the interrelationship of rhetoric and religion, or more accurately, theology, both "essentially" in terms of ontology and, we might say, "existentially," in terms of history.

Probably the most explicit treatment of the interrelationship between rhetoric and religion remains Burke's *The Rhetoric of Religion*.[5] His six "Analogies" at the outset of the work are of basic importance. They articulate relationships between the disciplines of theology and of Burke's logology or rhetoric more generally. They also articulate how discourse refers to that which cannot be written or spoken in any ordinary or direct sense (i.e., the "ineffable" or for theology, the supernatural or God). Thus while Burke explicitly asserts brackets around the question or practice of theology, he is all the while asking the questions and doing what theologians, especially so-called "fundamental" (not necessarily fundamentalist nor necessarily "foundationalist") theologians, do or try to do all the time. The attention to *analogy* is something that many Roman and Anglo-Catholic theologians either generally assume as the mode of theological discourse or argue for critically as indispensable to their task. David Tracy's *The Analogical Imagination: Christian Theology and the Culture of Pluralism* is a signature contemporary example.

Booth notes that while Burke explicitly analyzed the rhetoric of religion (i.e., did take religious terminology and analyze it), he also analyzed all terminology in a religious way. For Booth, Burke's dramatistic pentad (purpose / act / agent / agency / scene), his "logology," really his entire project is taken to be a religious activity, though not religious in a conventional sense. Booth at times reveals his missionary tendencies as he keeps wondering whether Burke is really a believer, then affirms that Burke is a believer, and finally qualifies his affirmation by inquiring whether "there's a need for a missionary type like Waxing Wane [a pet name Burke conferred upon Booth] to try to convert a nonbeliever because KB is already converted?—converted, that is, to his religion, the true religion, not to any standard version?" ("Kenneth Burke's Religious Rhetoric" 40). Booth cites Burke's letters (to Booth) that show clearly not only Burke's characteristic eclectic style and sense of humor but also his explicit references to the transcendent: like the "Big Shot"; and "Ennyhow, apparently there is a God—for youenz guys, not us" (employing a bit of Pittsburghese). In the final analysis, Booth takes Burke to be "a modern prophet engaging in a postmodernist, postpositivist revival of religious inquiry" (33).[6]

Burke is clearly no stranger to irony: everywhere in his work we see the enjoyment of its turn. The Analogies could just as easily be read with a twinkle in the eye: Is it not ironic that "words" relate to "The Word" and "The Word" relates to "words" (First Analogy)?[7] To speak of "The Word," one may just as easily be speaking of a word and a rather ordinary word at that! Perhaps we could see Burke chuckling that somehow "G-o-d" relates to "d-o-g" and vice-versa. An irony exists in the fact that "words are to the non-verbal things they name as Spirit is to Matter" (Second Analogy).[8] For example, as Burke points out, "the word is itself material, a 'body,' a meaning 'incarnate'" (16). On the other hand, we might say, if words are like spirit and not so much matter as things are, there is the sense in which words *do not matter;* things matter. Yet words give things life like spirit does matter. The irony of Burke's analogies go right down the line. This brings him into company with professional (and not necessarily confessional) theologians with an eye for dialectic and humor. The University of Iowa's David Klemm, in his "Rhetoric of Theological Argument" for instance, exemplifies the theologian explicitly working out of rhetorical attention to irony.

Meanwhile the familiar theological theme of transcendence plays a crucial role in Burke's analogies. The Fifth Analogy deals with eternity,[9] and the Sixth goes so far as to directly address the Trinity.[10] The Second Analogy notes the symbolic power of words to transcend natural life while the First notes the assent from lower case words to upper case. This brings him into contact with theologians keen not only to the transcendent per se, but to the move from the empirical world "upward" to the symbolic. The Fourth Analogy puts this succinctly in terms of the "linguistic drive towards a Title of Titles, a logic of entitlement that is completed by thus rising to ever and ever higher orders of generalization" (25).[11] Burke adds that a title is not simply a movement "up," but also a *via negativa* and a self-emptying. Moreover the Third Analogy explicitly "concerns the negative."[12] Minimally this brings him into contact with negative theologians but more importantly highlights the negativity of all theological discourse: what God is—no; what God is not—yes.

Burke comes into direct conversation with those theologians who have accepted the "problem of God" as it is at least partially signaled by, among other things, Nietzsche's famous "death of God" in modernity. Burke recognizes that in modernity, where "God" in large measure is practically dead and gone, other terms still function in a god-like way. By addressing the "drive towards a Title of Titles" and calling a title a "god-term" he approaches the problem of God from an interesting spot indeed. Both rhetoric and theology may be, in part, driving towards a God-term of God-terms. Burke's Analogies indicate rhetoric's close involvement with theology in terms of negativity, irony, and transcendence.

Beyond the Analogies, Burke puts Augustine and then chapters one through three of Genesis through a detailed rhetorical analysis, concluding with the fanciful Epilogue: Prologue in Heaven. Of critical importance is his attention to Augustine's conversion in the *Confessions*. Burke shows that the conversion may be located within the structure of the text as the point to which everything leads and everything moves away: the turning point (164). "Augustine's conversion passes its critical point at the mathematical center of the *Confessions* as a whole" (62). Everything in the entire work, Burke rightly claims, is built around that moment (85). Notably, he highlights the relationship between the terms "turned" and "converted" (51). Conversion is taken as "the middle," "the turn," the "peripety" (101ff.). Also, he indicates the relationship of "perversity" to "the 'turn' clan" and the "vert" family (63–64, 81), which is important because of its dialectical (or ironic) relationship to conversion. For Burke the language of the "turn" is closely connected, even at times indistinguishable, from that of conversion (110, 113, 117). Importantly, the conversion language is first used about God and only then applied to Augustine (63). Augustine was convinced "that some power beyond him must have turned in order for him to be turned" (117). Burke writes, "He had the personal sense of the situation which the Old Testament prophet had formulated thus: 'Turn thou me, and I shall be turned' (*converte me et convertar*—Jeremiah 31:18)" (117).

Recent scholarship on rhetoric and religion has continued to highlight Augustine as the classic figure in this area and to put special emphasis upon not only his use of rhetorical devices but on the interrelationship of rhetoric and theology, more specifically the conversion of Augustine itself as rhetorical. The fairly well-known classic work in rhetoric and religion in the West has been Augustine's *De doctrina christiana* (396, 426 C.E.), which makes the case for Christian use of pagan rhetorical education for the purposes of advancing the Gospel.[13] By some accounts he single-handedly provided the example for centuries of medieval Christian preaching and teaching, even though *De doctrina christiana* gained specific attention only in the late medieval period. Among other achievements, his anti-sexuality and his likely misogyny aside, many take him to be no less than the father of semiotics. One may also argue that nowhere in any classical or early medieval writings may be found the level of articulation in theory and in practice of and about rhetoric and religion that we find in *De doctrina christiana,* on the one hand, and on the other, in Augustine's sermons, or, in the work that is more widely known both in general and in scholarship, the *Confessions.*

Of course Augustine is not always read in these terms, as Boyle's work illustrates. For Boyle, Augustine is "profoundly anti-rhetorical" because he puts rhetoric in service to truth and not, in her reading, to love. This interpretation parallels her reading of the theology of Thomas Aquinas as inferior on the one hand to Dante (the theologian as poet) and on the other to Erasmus (the rhetorical theologian), because Aquinas directs the theological task to knowledge and, as she argues, not love. Erasmus is extolled as the first and virtually the only great Christian rhetorician because he directs his project to love.[14] She concludes, "Here is the definitional shift from scholasticism to humanism in theology: from faith seeking understanding to charity seeking charity" ("Rhetorical Theology" 90). Rhetoric in this scenario is a matter of complete assent and even mystical union with the Spirit. Boyle identifies the rhetoric of this era with plenitude, persuasion, and the "lapse of love" as opposed to dialectic, which she identifies with certitude, coercion, and the "grip of logic" (93).

Of course one could reply that we may read Erasmus *with* Augustine, not to mention with Thomas Aquinas. While Augustine did understand rhetoric to be in service to truth, one may not, I think it's safe to venture, separate truth from love in Christian teaching. By implication, Augustine does understand rhetoric in service to love.

It is first necessary to stress that as recent scholars read back through the rhetorical tradition, they note that the *Confessions* is not historical biography but, rather, is epideictic rhetoric (Colish 32, Scanlon 40-41). Boyle herself has specifically argued that the *Confessions,* including the conversion garden scene, may be read as Ciceronian epideictic ("Prudential Augustine" 132ff., 141). Augustine's conversion is to be understood, at least minimally, as linguistically mediated (Colish, Scanlon).[15] Such discussions make a rhetorical (and analytical) observation on the one hand, and on the other, operating along the lines of the twentieth century New Rhetoric, take theology as a participation in that rhetoric. More specifically, as Olmsted observes, until recently rhetorical invention as a constitutive element in Augustine's conversion has largely been overlooked by scholars because of the tendency to take Augustine's view that "'truth comes before the statement of truth'" as a primary emphasis upon dialectic and a regard for rhetoric as simply a "mode of presentation" (65). But as Olmsted argues clearly, rhetoric is constitutive in Augustine's very conversion (73-83). The episode of the garden conversion in Book VIII of the *Confessions* falls into Cicero's categories of instruction, delight, and movement employed by Augustine in Book IV of *De doctrina christiana*.[16] While there is little doubt that Augustine's conversion account aims to instruct and delight, the ultimate purpose is to move or persuade. Olmsted notes the similarity of Augustine's use of delight (*delectet*) toward God and Ciceronian delight (*delectare*) (81). While the account may be read as relating small matters in a restrained style as appropriate to instruction, and to intermediate matters in a mixed style as appropriate for delight, most importantly, this important business of conversion comes in a grand style as appropriate for movement or persuasion.[17]

Augustine, following the epistles of Paul and John in the New Testament, and most notably the gospels themselves, made love the fundamental hermeneutical and rhetorical principle in *De doctrina christiana*.[18] In fact, Augustine made explicit that the point of the scriptures and, by implication, religion, is faith, hope, and ultimately love. Many people, notes Augustine, live without the scriptures yet are not in need of them since they already live these theological virtues.[19] The purpose of the scriptures and, by extension, religion, may be, at least minimally, the instruction of others. Add to this the further purposes of delight and persuasion, or movement, and, in this case, the delight and movement in love. Religion in an Augustinian religious rhetoric informed by late twentieth-century theological thought could be understood as a basic mediation of a gradual—though sometimes sudden or even ecstatic—transformation in love.

This reading of religion follows a line that owes a great deal to Burke. While Boyle's insistence upon attention to the specific original languages of the writers in any rhetorical study remains suggestive for more productive future scholarship ("Religion," "Rhetorical Theology"), her handling of religion runs perhaps more literal than Burke had in mind, overlooking his use of irony and negativity in the context of analogy. Meanwhile, the fact remains that, to date, no one theorizing on rhetoric and religion has matched the influence of Burke's *The Rhetoric of Religion*.

Notes

Special thanks to Stephen J. McKenna, Director of the Rhetoric Program at the Catholic University of America and to the late Stephen P. Happel (1944–2003), former Dean of the School of Theology and Religious Studies, also at CUA, for much work, inspiration, and discussion that helped lead to this essay. A special acknowledgment, too, for the contribution of the editors to the final form of this essay.

1. Boyle criticizes "a [certain] modern theory," one that relies upon an "essentialist definition" that takes "[a]ll religious systems [as] rhetorical . . . because they strive to communicate truth"—"[t]he theory depend[ing] on the conviction that Greek rhetoric conceptualized a universal communicative habit, which historically and culturally exhibited only minor variations of arrangement or style" ("Religion" 662). She is criticizing, among others, both Wayne Booth and Kenneth Burke. She says that Burke misconstrued the term *verbum* in *The Rhetoric of Religion* and that "its premise of a supernatural realm, analogous to a natural one, misconstrues the theological term *supernatural* as a state or condition, whereas it is a mode of action . . ." (669). Boyle says that this "initial major effort at conceptualization" of rhetoric and religion was "seriously flawed," and that "[r]hetorical criticism of specific religious texts has been more illuminating than has general theorizing about the rhetoric of religion" (669–70).

2. Notably, Booth was at the forefront of critical reflection upon rhetoric and religion in the academy. While some of his comments did not take anyone very far, like " . . . that rhetoric and religion are somehow related has been obvious to everyone who has thought about it," other comments did: ". . . *rhetoric,* seen not as a mere way of winning arguments but as an indispensable and universal human practice, the 'art of discovering warrantable beliefs and improving those beliefs in shared discourse' [citing *Modern Dogma and the Rhetoric of Assent,* xiii]; [and] *religion,* seen not as a benighted inheritance from the dark ages but as a universal human need and practice ("Rhetoric and Religion" 63). Other pieces, like Booth's paper for the 75th Anniversary Lecture at the 1984 Annual Meeting of the American Academy of Religion ("Systematic Wonder"), are provocative and inviting yet do not develop beyond the "essentially wedded" question. Meanwhile the mention of a seven-hundred-plus page unpublished manuscript on the subject have had people waiting after Booth's comments at the Rhetoric Society of America meeting at the University of Maryland in 2000. Booth's recent *The Rhetoric of Rhetoric: The Quest for Effective Communication* gives, near its close, minor attention directly to the rhetoric of religion. Perhaps the hesitation had to do with a justifiable anxiety at doing any better than Burke did on the topic? Could the hesitation be due to a potential attack of critics on "essentialism," despite Booth's acknowledged pluralism? Even after Booth's recent passing (in October 2005), I keep hoping we will see some version of that manuscript.

3. See *Orality and Literacy: The Technologizing of the Word; Rhetoric, Romance, and Technology: Studies in the Interaction of Expression and Culture*; and "The Word as History: Sacred and Profane."

4. Some of the most important reflection on conversion in religion includes a classic of religious studies, William James's *Varieties of Religious Experience: A Study in Human Nature* (1901–1902 Gifford Lectures) and more recently Bernard Lonergan's inclusion of it in his "generalized empirical method" in *Method in Theology*. More recent studies posit accounts of conversion in both theoretical and historical studies such as that of Stephen Happel's handling of religious imagery in "Picturing God: The Rhetoric of Religious Images and Caravaggio's *Conversion of St. Paul*."

5. For some further elaboration of issues related to rhetoric and religion, e.g., on negative theology, see Burke's "A Dramatistic View of the Origins of Language."

6. For a related treatment of Burke, see Kevin Hogan, "Kenneth Burke's Postmodern Rhetorical Theological Anthropology."

7. The *First Analogy* is "between 'words' (lower case) and 'The Word' (in capitals)" (11). He lists four realms to which words may refer:

1. words for the natural things, material operations, physiological conditions, animality: "tree," "dog," "sun," "change," "growth";
2. words for the socio-political realm, social relations, laws, right, wrong: "good," "justice," "American," "out of bounds";
3. words about words: dictionaries, grammar, etymology, philology, literary criticism, rhetoric, poetics, dialectics—"logology";
4. words for the "supernatural" or "ineffable": words borrowed by analogy from the three other orders (14–15).

8. Words inspire matter and are analogous to grace and the supernatural. Their symbolic power transcends natural life. Burke offers the example of a news report in which an indigenous islander in the South Pacific had been "hexed by members of his tribe and was dying, despite the efforts of modern science to save him. No actual material harm had been done to him" (17). The very signs of death presented to him in terms of the tribal magic were enough to make him sick.

9. The *Fifth Analogy* deals with "the relation between 'time' and 'eternity'" (27). These are analogous to the relation between words in a sentence and the meaning or essence of the sentence as a whole (27). Burke offers the happy case of the Cheshire Cat in Alice's Wonderland. The cat smiles. At least the cat *appears* to do so: "certain motions, postures and the like take place, and these are interpreted as the signs of a smile." The actual smile is the essence of these elements. "The smile is the *essence* of these material conditions, the *form* or *act* of the sheer motions." The transformation of the

disparate elements into the whole that is now what we recognize as a smile is impossible to picture. These elements are what relate to the temporal, and the smile to eternity (28, emphasis in orignal).

10. Burke's *Sixth Analogy* treats the "likeness between the design of the Trinity and the form underlying the 'linguistic situation.'" Following Augustine, as the Father generates the Son, so the "thing" (symbolized) generates the "word" (symbol). Correspondence, conformity, communion exist between symbolized and symbol (29). The vocabulary of the analogy may be put another way:

> The Trinity: Father as Power
> Son as Wisdom
> Holy Spirit as Love (29).

Burke notes, "the idea of opposition can yield to the idea of counterpart" (30). Father and Son, e.g., may be taken as reciprocal terms: each "makes" the other (32). Together, Love proceeds from them. Love is the relational term that exists between them and makes them both (30). Logology and theology too may be taken as related reciprocally. In the final pages of his analysis of his analogies, Burke goes on to summarize the six analogies, make explicit his theory of "dramatism" as opposed to "scientism," and outline an anthropology that includes the famous definition of "man as [. . .] the symbol using animal" (40).

11. Burke continues, "An ideal title would 'sum up' all particulars of the book. [. . .] Yet the particulars would have all the material reality" (25). Titles are not really positive but are more like questions that allow for an opening that will be filled out, not like an arithmetic but rather like an algebra that provides a central orientation among the diversity of material (26). A title is "a secular summarizing term," a "god-term" (25-26). Titles are what allow theologians to not be reduced to silence.

12. *Third Analogy:* "all words for the non-verbal must, by the very nature of the case, discuss the realm of the non-verbal in terms of what it is not" (18). This "plays a major role in both language and theology" (17). We should note Thomas Aquinas and the Fourth Lateran Council (1215) at this point. The latter said that for every *similitudo* in our language about God there is an even greater *dissimilitude* (DS 806, Denzinger-Schonmetzer, Eds., *Enchiridion Symbolorum, Definitionum et Declarationum de Rebus Fidei et Morum*); meanwhile the former instructed that while we can argue *that God is,* we can not argue for *what God is* (*Summa Theologica,* Pt.1, Q.2). Rather, we must necessarily be content with attempting to discourse upon *what God is not.* For some theologians, this is rather old hat. But for many others, this is controversial, forgotten, or more or less not understood. Burke, however, is on good theological ground here. His principle of the negative includes the

rhetorical devices of irony and metaphor (18–19). He notes, "the negative is a peculiarly linguistic invention and not a 'fact' of nature" (20). Importantly he makes a modification of Bergson's "Idea of Nothing," shifting to the "Idea of No"—a shift that he takes as an avoidance of a quasi-substantial "Nothing" as one might find in Heidegger in favor of an active command as one finds in the Pentateuch (19–23). In his terminology this is a shift from scientism to dramatism.

13. The history of rhetoric here and elsewhere in this essay is indebted in large part to George Kennedy, *Classical Rhetoric and Its Christian and Secular Tradition From Ancient to Modern Times*. Also vital have been Patricia Bizzell and Bruce Herzberg, editors, *The Rhetorical Tradition: Readings from Classical Times to the Present*; James J. Murphy, *Rhetoric in the Middle Ages: A History of Rhetorical Theory from St. Augustine to the Renaissance*; and Thomas Conley, *Rhetoric in the European Tradition*. For a critical account of how histories of rhetoric are done, see Carol Blair, "Contested Histories of Rhetoric." Here I am primarily making use of *De doctrina christiana* and *On Christian Doctrine* as well as Sr. Therese Sullivan, *S. Avreli Avgvstini Hipponiensis Episcopi de Doctrina Christiana, Liber Qvartvs: A Commentary, with Revised Text, Introduction, and Translation*. Augustine explicitly argues that rhetoric is needed in order to make truth more appealing to an audience and thus to bring about conversion to the life of faith. Though *De doctrina christiana* was in fact little known in the early medieval period, the practice of Christian preaching took up the various tools of rhetoric to make itself more effective. Augustine is admired because of his constructive and, by many accounts, largely successful integration of Christian and pagan discourse. Whether one will find his project successful or not owes in large measure to the question of the role of religion and religious discourse more generally and, in this case, the specific relationship between the classical rhetorical cultures and the rhetorical cultures of Christendom since Constantine. By any account, however, his overall project has exerted an enormous influence upon religious discourse ever since.

14. See "Religion" and "Rhetorical Theology: Charity Seeking Charity."

15. I wonder about Michael Scanlon's final points as he asserts that "rhetoric redeemed becomes dialogue" (45) and that "theology is 'redeemed rhetoric'" (47).

16. In terms outlined by Augustine in *De doctrina christiana,* rhetoric incorporates a careful understanding of sign and thing, use and enjoyment, eloquence and wisdom, and, furthermore, the Ciceronian triad of instruction, delight, and movement, or persuasion. Rhetoric is explicitly discussed in Book IV of *De doctrina,* yet Books I-III are crucial for the book that follows and should not be overlooked. James J. O'Donnell and David Tracy have suggested the close connection between *De doctrina* and the *Confessions*.

See O'Donnell's concluding remarks in "Augustine: Elements of Christianity." Tracy notes that the *De doctrina* offers a "central clue for reading other Augustinian texts," and specifically suggests a link between *De doctrina* and *Confessions* ("Charity, Obscurity, Clarity" 257, 259). Burke himself makes explicit the connection between the *Confessions* and *De doctrina* in *The Rhetoric of Religion* (49). On specific classical sources and parallels for *De doctrina*, see Sullivan 8–13.

17. In this sense, Augustine's conversion may be taken as the periscope sitting in front of one's nose as a twenty-first century reader. In my particular case, I depend on the Chadwick translation of the *Confessions* and O'Donnell's commentary on *Confessions*.

18. *De doctrina christiana,* Book I, XXXVI, 40–41—XXXVII, 41 (48–51). Christine Mason Sutherland writes, "Augustine believes that any interpretation may be acceptable if it is consistent with the principle of love [. . .]" (146). And: "Augustine's guiding principle in rhetoric, as in all else, is love. The use of eloquence is legitimate, not because it is good in itself, but because its proper use promotes faith, and faith leads to love" (144). Notably, this love derives from God (147).

19. *De doctrina christiana,* Book I, XXXVIII, 41—XL, 44 (50–55); Book I, XXXIX, 43 (52.)

13 The Revelations of "Logology": Secular and Religious Tensions in Burke's Views on Language, Literature, and Hermeneutics

Christine E. Iwanicki

Is it ever possible to interpret Kenneth Burke too literally? Would such an interpretation be intellectually reckless, or are there legitimate grounds for raising questions about the implications of the tropes that Burke embraces in his later work, particularly in *The Rhetoric of Religion?* Furthermore, can this questioning be done while still paying tribute to Burke's capacious mind, and his inimitable legacy as writer, cultural critic, and philosopher? In his 1974 essay "Kenneth Burke's Way of Knowing," Wayne Booth begins his discussion with an innovative rhetorical gesture: "postscript as preface." Booth writes:

> Postscript as Preface: When I received Kenneth Burke's response to the following piece, I was distressed to find that what was intended as an encomium had given him pain. Teaching his works during the past three years, I have been convinced that he is not just the brilliantly inventive but wrong-headed dogmatist that he had once seemed, but without question, the most important living critic. (1)

In some respects, Booth's puzzlement mirrors some of the emotional and intellectual conflicts that I find myself confronting in my own engagement with Burke. Booth's conundrum arises from finding that words meant one way were read in another altogether contrary to his intention, whereas mine arises from wondering if my reservations about Burke's fascination with religion are compatible with my admiration for his work in general.

Nowhere is this more evident than in my response to Burke's 1961 book, *The Rhetoric of Religion*, in which the humanist, socially grounded, secular accent of so much of Burke's work takes an intriguing detour by virtue of its emphasis on the concept of "logology." While Burke occasionally invokes some religiously inflected themes in earlier works such as *A Grammar of Motives* (1945) and *A Rhetoric of Motives* (1950), his use of religion becomes especially urgent and prominent in *The Rhetoric of Religion*. In the oft-quoted introduction to this volume, Burke notes, "If we defined 'theology' as 'words about God,' then by 'logology' we should mean 'words about words'" (1). From the standpoint of William Rueckert's interpretation of dramatism in *Kenneth Burke and the Drama of Human Relations*, Burke's logology may be seen as a logical step from his earlier work:

> What he has finally done in his dramatistic theory, after many years of moving steadily in that direction, is to systematize a naturalistic, linguistically oriented, secular variant of Christianity. Burke has retained the principal ideas of Christianity and worked out dramatistic equivalents for them with astonishing thoroughness. The whole dramatistic system is laid out on a moral-ethical, Christian-Catholic bias, and is presented in such a way as to make perfectly clear Burke's belief that he has developed a new "scientific" religion which twentieth-century man can "believe" in, but which, unlike the old one it replaces, is designed to save man in this world. (133–34)

But is this possible or even desirable? Why was Burke drawn to issues such as "entelechy" (or "perfection"), the theme of inevitable victimage or "scapegoating," and the notion of "negative theology," as tropes and emphases that he found useful in attempting to explain the phenomenon of language? I agree with many commentators who, like Hugh Dalziel Duncan, suggest that Burke uses the occasion of *The Rhetoric of Religion* to try to break down divisions between the sacred and the secular. Yet this is, I think, a project that produces mixed results— some productive and salutary, others alienating and problematic. In any event, their final impact is almost always provocative and controversial.

In *The Violence of Literacy,* J. Elspeth Stuckey coins a phrase that makes for a good starting point for my critique of Burke. She takes issue with what she calls the twentieth century's "hyperfocus on language as the finest medium of human consciousness" (91). Stuckey is suspicious of those who subscribe to and perpetuate such a "hyperfocus," since she feels that any critical position grounded in *language alone* is somehow insufficient *vis-à-vis* the material conditions that affect communities, schools, families, and other consequential institutions and contexts of human life. As I have already noted, Burke—in both productive but sometimes problematic ways—participates in this trend involving "the hyperfocus on language as the finest medium of human consciousness." In the case of *The Rhetoric of Religion,* this "hyperfocus" manifests itself through the pursuit of an ambitious agenda, ranging from Burke's reading of St. Augustine to his production of a dialogue between Satan and The Lord, which leads Burke to look beyond the context of quotidian, embodied, mortal existence to a supernatural/religious paradigm as a way of understanding the ways in which humans use language. This approach emerges in stunning contrast, I think, to his other work on concepts such as "dramatism" and "terministic screens," and to his efforts to establish a place for various manifestations of rhetorical analysis as integral aspects of hermeneutics and as ways of understanding human existence. While some may see *The Rhetoric of Religion* as part and parcel of these other accents in Burke's work, I suggest that it marks a departure from the general orientations that characterize the *oeuvre* of a figure who has been described by Paul Jay as "the most unorthodox, challenging, and theoretically sophisticated American-born literary critics of the twentieth-century" ("Kenneth Burke" 125).

In his essay "'Too Little Care': Language, Politics, and Embodiment in the Life-World," Kurt Spellmeyer notes that "Man, as Kenneth Burke is rumored to have said, does not live by the *idea* of bread alone. And because reason all too often and too easily prefers ideas over bread itself, its romance conceals a destructiveness that philosophers sometimes prefer to ignore while historians cannot, if they look too closely" (274). Spellmeyer's essay considers the West's tendency to privilege reason over experience, since Western colonialism has deprecated certain forms of ritual, experience, and expression that seem alien or incomprehensible to the colonizer or incompatible with the colonizer's goals. This results in the occlusion—even in the annihilation—of the Husserlian notion of the "life-world," which, as Spellmeyer explains, refers to "the 'horizon,' socially constituted and intersubjective, that each of us takes for granted as we move through our everyday lives" (266).[1] He adds, "Behind the politics of language, or rather, far beneath it, there waits another, long-neglected politics, long-neglected and poorly theorized—a deep politics of experience, 'deep' because it unfolds at the boundary between life-worlds in dialogue or contestation" (270).

Spellmeyer advocates a focus on the politics of language in the light of the "deep" experience of diverse "life-worlds," and much of Burke's work anticipates and answers that call. In so many of his writings, Burke responds to the need to develop a view of language that permits us to explore the *relations* not just between "words" or "language" or "texts," but between people, as people are variously constituted in terms of minds, bodies, voices, ideologies, sociopolitical positions, and even in the form of cultural images/stereotypes. To be sure, a profound element of Burke's legacy is his insistence that language, in both its written and spoken forms, is not merely "descriptive" or "neutral" or "passive," but a *form of action*—a theme that other twentieth-century figures such as Mikhail Bakhtin and J. L. Austin, among others, would explore in their own ways.

Yet even in this emphasis on language as action, there is sometimes a surfacing of the side of Burke that I find problematic. For instance, it is significant that in the *Grammar,* Burke uses the religious example of the Creation as "the ground or scene of human acts" (69), while being careful, however, to qualify that his citation of the Creation is "not as a temporal event, but as the logical prototype of an act" (64). In an effort to understand the anatomy of a human act, Burke has been searching for "the ultimate act," which he finds in the biblical account of the creation of the world: "[This story] 'sums up' action quite as the theory of evolution sums up motion, but with one notable difference: whereas one must believe in evolution literally, one can discuss the Act of Creation 'substantially' or 'in principle'" (61). Burke's interest in the act of "summing up" eerily echoes Marlow's reaction to Kurtz in *Heart of Darkness:* "He had summed up—he had judged. 'The horror!' He was a remarkable man. After all this was the expression of some sort of belief [. . .]" (72). While I don't mean to suggest of course that Burke's interest in "summing up" is on the same plane as Marlow's famous existential pronouncement, nonetheless the examples Burke cites as acts of "summing up" indicate an intriguing demarcation: why grant to one example (the theory of evolution) the condition that it must be taken literally while *exempting* the other example (the biblical account of the Creation) from literal interpretation? While I personally have no interest in advocating the notion of "intelligent design" or other variations on the theme of "creationism," from a rhetorical perspective I am compelled to ask: is this is an instance in which Burke wants to have his cake and eat it too?

For instance, Burke does *not* want his arguments to be distracted by and become embroiled in the theological debates that might ensue if he were to cite religious texts, principles, or images and *require* that they be received as matters of doctrine so as to separate "believers" from "non-believers." Burke disavows any interest in this kind of agenda. Thus, he insinuates that his work goes forth as a secular, intellectual pursuit, yet he cannot resist the impulse to invoke religious references in some of his writings. As these occur, so, too, do the disclaimers that one need not be a "believer" in order to extract the value or purpose of these citations. His insistence that the biblical story of the creation need not be accepted by the reader in a literal way raises the question of why the theory of evolution *must* be viewed as literal. After all, we are well aware that scientific theories and accounts also possess imagistic or metaphorical properties, yet Burke emphasizes the literalism of the example of evolution. In other words—and I make this argument not for any religious agenda of my own—why is Burke unwilling to entertain the tropological implications of the theory of evolution? Even though there is overwhelming *empirical* evidence for the theory of evolution, it is still odd that Burke refuses to recognize its *symbolic* implications.[2]

In other aspects of his work, the discussion of *science* takes place in close proximity to the topic of religion, a coherent move given the fact that many of Burke's most politically overt and "topical" writings take place against the backdrop of the post-World War II years of the "Cold War," as people were struggling to understand two monumental developments that raised terrifying questions about religion and technology: the Holocaust and the development of nuclear weapons. For instance, consider this passage—which I will quote at length—from the 1950 *Rhetoric,* which shows the problematic prominence of religious accents in Burke's thought:

With a culture formed about the idea of redemption by the sacrifice of a Crucified Christ, just what does happen in an era of post-Christian science, when the ways of socialization have been secularized? Does the need for the vicarage of this Sacrificial King merely dwindle away? Or must some other person or persons, individual or corporate, real or fictive, take over the redemptive role? Not all people, perhaps, seek out a Vessel to which will be ritualistically delegated a purgative function, in being symbolically laden with the burdens of individual and collective guilt. But we know, as a lesson of recent history, how anti-Semitism provided the secularized replica of the Divine Scapegoat in the post-Christian rationale of Hitler's National Socialist militarism; and we know how Jews and other minority groups are thus magically identified by other members of our society. [. . .] For the history of the Nazis has clearly shown that there are cultural situations in which scientists, whatever may be their claims to professional austerity, will contrive somehow to identify their specialty with modes of justification or socialization, not discernible in the sheer motions of the material operations themselves. In its transcendence of natural living, its technical scruples, its special tests of purity, a clinic or laboratory can be a kind of secular temple, in which ritualistic devotions are taking place, however concealed by the terminology of the surface. Unless properly scrutinized for traces of witchcraft, these could furtively become devotions to a satanic order of motives. At least such was the case with the technological experts of Hitlerite Germany. The very scientific ideals of an "impersonal" terminology can contribute ironically to such a disaster: for it is but a step from treating inanimate nature as mere "things" to treating animals, and then enemy peoples, as mere things. But they are not mere things, they are persons—and in the systematic denial of what one knows in his heart to be the truth, there is

a perverse principle that can generate much anguish.
(*RM* 31–32)

I find this to be a revealing passage for a number of reasons. In many respects, it represents everything that is appealing in Burke, but it also contains some elements which should give us pause. The passage appears in the section entitled "'Redemption' in Post-Christian Science" in part one of the *Rhetoric*. It is clear from the general tone of this passage that Burke wants to offer a warning about the rhetorics and practices of science—how such rhetorics and practices can be put in the service of reprehensible programs such as the "Final Solution" perpetrated by the Nazi regime. As Burke notes a bit further along: "We know, as a matter of record, that science under Fascism became sinister" (*RM* 35), and Burke goes on to make the very pointed criticisms that "scientific discoveries have always, of course, been used for the purposes of war" (*RM* 35), and that the scientist should "reject and resist in ways that mean the end of 'autonomy,'" or else the scientist "risks becoming the friend of fiends" (*RM* 35).

To be sure, Burke's warning has not become null and void with the passage of more than fifty years. A strong "ethical" voice speaks in this passage, but it is also a voice either unable or unwilling to relinquish the priority it accords to religion as an ultimate touchstone of human motivation and experience. And this is where the passage becomes a more delicate affair. For instance, what are we to make of Burke's assertion that in a "Post-Christian" society—a description that itself needs further commentary, given the tenor of American life in the 1950s—"the ways of socialization have been secularized"? In the first decade of the twenty-first century, given the seemingly ever-increasing influence of the religious right in American politics with its subsequent blurring of the separation between church and state—and the way in which the American presidential elections of 2000 and 2004 put "red states" and "blue states" into the popular lexicon—the assertion that "the ways of socialization have been secularized" seems, in hindsight, to be an almost quaint and defunct characterization of the much more complex matrix of factors that shape social being. The phenomenon of "secularization" that Burke refers to strikes me as an implicitly sentimental *lament* on his part. But even more important, Burke's view seems to be based on an individualist, religiously-inflected nostalgia for saviors and scapegoats. As he observes in the lengthy passage quoted above, "Does the need for the vicarage of this Sacrificial King merely dwindle away? Or must some other person or persons, individual or corporate, real or fictive, take over the redemptive role?" In claiming that "anti-Semitism provided the secularized replica of the Divine Scapegoat in the Post-Christian rationale of Hitler's Nationalist Socialist militarism," Burke seems to be transposing religious, social, and political themes in rather loose ways. *He actually ends up using a piece of anti-Semitic rhetoric as a way of stating his sympathy with the situation of the European Jews during the Nazi regime.* The notion of a "divine" scapegoat is, finally, his own veiled reference to Jesus Christ. For centuries, Christianity has depended upon the existence of a scapegoat (in the form of the Jewish people) as part of its account of the life of Christ.[3] At the same time, though, Christianity also regards Christ as a scapegoat—as someone who was put to death for the sins of others. The notion of scapegoating is inextricably associated with victimage, but what does it mean when Burke calls the Holocaust an instance of the "secularized replica of the Divine Scapegoat"? Does he have in mind the "Divine Scapegoat" of the Crucifixion, Jesus Christ, or some other sense of a scapegoat?[4] And what does it mean to call the Holocaust a "secular replica" (of whom? of what?), when historical evidence shows indisputably that Jews were persecuted and exterminated through a program of genocide motivated expressly by their ethnic-religious identity?[5] If the Holocaust is a "secular replica," then what is or was the "divine original" to which Burke seeks to compare it? Does this analogy do justice to the dimensions of and motivations behind this tragedy?

I do not mean to belabor these points, nor do I mean to engage in some sort of theological debate with Burke, but I hope my point is clear: Burke sometimes has a tendency to use religion as a kind of *master* trope; moreover, when he is in the midst of invoking these kinds of tropes, Burke is at pains to tell us that one need not be inclined to take "such and such" literally. Still in his own rhetoric, Burke's belief in the *priority*—perhaps we could even say in the essential correctness—of his religious examples comes through with a good deal of regularity. In this way, Burke's seemingly "secular," progressive sociopolitical perspective has at least a covert—and sometimes a rather overt—component rooted in a nostalgia for a vision of religion as a desirable touchstone for understanding human existence and human efforts to engage in symbolization and communication. Again, while this religious element does not in and of itself automatically compromise Burke's position, it does raise questions as to the origins of his motivations for presenting his view of language in these terms. It is difficult to keep the emphasis on the material, the worldly, and the "here and now" when there are always echoes of the other-worldly, the supernatural, and the spiritual hovering in the background as the model of, or even as the corrective to, other approaches or explanatory frameworks. As Susan Handelman notes in her critique of the Patristic view of language espoused by the "Church Fathers" (among whom St. Augustine was one of the most prominent): "When language is seen as an external imitation (mimesis) of things, there is an extralinguistic standard of correctness posited for discourse. This standard becomes the true inside of signification, and language itself (as in the theories of Aristotle and Plato) becomes externalized" (89). In Burke, this "extralinguistic standard" manifests itself as "logology," Burke's curious alliance between religious (divine) and secular (mortal) discourse.

An especially revealing example of this alliance appears in the chapter of *Language as Symbolic Action* entitled "What Are the Signs of What?: A Theory of Entitlement," first published in 1962, a year after *The Rhetoric of Religion,* where Burke attempts to bridge the gap between the secular or "natural" and the religious or "supernatural," two concepts which at times have seemed like irreconcilable opposites in his thought. He writes:

> Since language derives its materials from the cooperative acts of men in sociopolitical orders, which are themselves held together by a vast network of verbally perfected meanings, might it not follow that man must perceive nature through the fog of symbol-ridden social structures that he has erected atop nature? Material things would thus be like outward manifestations of forms which are imposed upon the intuiting of nature by language, and by the sociopolitical orders that are interwoven with language (sociopolitical orders that are in turn indicated by the linguistic thou-shalt-not's inhering in a given set of property relationships).
>
> In sum, just as the Word is said by theologians to be a mediatory principle between this word and the supernatural, might words be a mediatory principle between ourselves and nature? And just as the theologian might say that we must think of the Word as the bond

> between man and supernatural, might words (and the social motives implicit in them) be the bond between man and the natural? Or, otherwise put, might nature be necessarily approached by us through the gift of the spirit of words?
>
> If this were possible, then nature, as perceived by the word-using animal, would be not just the less-than-verbal thing that we usually take it to be. Rather, as so conceived and perceived, it would be infused with the spirit of words, and of the social orders that are implicit in any given complex verbal structure. Nature, as the early Greek metaphysical physicist put, would thus be full of gods, gods in essence linguistic and sociopolitical. The world we mistook for a realm of sheerly nonverbal, nonmental, visible, tangible things would thus become a fantastic pageantry, a parade of masques and costumes and guildlike mysteries (such as Carlyle treats of, in his *Sartor Resartus*). (378–79)

In this discussion, Burke seeks to build a bridge between the so-called "non-verbal" natural world and the world of language. *Significantly, his logic here depends upon the replication and transposition of the supernatural model onto the natural world.* That is, just as the supernatural model depends upon the distinction between God and gods, between "the Word" and words, and just as it depends upon the Patristic explanation of "the Word" as a "mediatory principle," Burke now substitutes for that scheme a tableau of human actors who use "secular" words in the effort to elicit from the seemingly inscrutable natural world some measure of connectedness between itself and human life. Burke's scenario here certainly has similarities to and implications for a materialist view of language ("Material things would thus be like outward manifestations of the forms which are imposed upon the intuiting of nature by language . . ."), but I want to suggest that any such potential is undercut by the quasi-religious way in which Burke imagines this animation of nature through language. To this end, this project depends heavily upon the infusion of nature by "the gift of the spirit of words." In this instance, words are still seen by Burke as having an essentially spiritual character; they work their "magic" and perform their "mystery" on the natural world, and thus a material bond between word and world is posited, but not before the alchemy of ethereal language first performs its work, in a replica of the *ex nihilo* moment of the biblical Genesis story: suddenly the human aspiration to the accession of language endows the natural world "full of gods, gods in essence linguistic and sociopolitical . [. . .] [T]angible things [. . .] become a fantastic pageantry, a parade of masques and costumes and guildlike mysteries." Significantly, Burke's "embodiment" of the natural world manifests itself through the conjuring forth of fantastic creatures: gods, nymphs, and other such entities. Burke's effort to embody the natural world seems, on some of these occasions, to be less of a substantive material gesture, anchored decisively in real human culture and history, than a fanciful and exalted gambol in the woods or glance toward the heavens.[6]

"What Are the Signs of What?" reconceptualizes the "commonsense view of the relation between words and things" (360). This view, Burke observes, "favors the idea that 'words are the signs of things'" (360). Burke reverses this assumption, "upholding instead the proposition that 'things are the signs of words.' That is, might words be found to possess a 'spirit' peculiar to their nature as words? And might the things of experience then become in effect the materialization of such spirit, the manifestation of this spirit in visible tangible bodies?" (361).

While this is a fascinating proposition—and one certainly amenable to the notion of the materiality of language—there are reasons for us to pause. Especially curious is Burke's use of an almost "occult" framework for the pursuit of his view of language as a social act. As he puts it:

> If such verbal spirits, or essences, were enigmatically symbolized in nonverbal things, then their derivation (so far as causes within the natural world are concerned) could come *both from the forms of language and from the group motives that language possesses by reason of its nature as a social product.* (361, emphasis added)

Perhaps the most generous interpretation I can give this passage is to say that it reflects a belief in the *interdependence* of language and social life. But Burke's postulation of "spirits" and "essences" strikes me as a counterproductive move, as it introduces a distracting mysticism that threatens to undermine the integrity of Burke's important contributions to the relations between words and world, even in the face of Burke's insistence to emphasize the significance of the temporal and the secular rather than the supernatural. Yet, as Burke observes in 1941 in *The Philosophy of Literary Form,* there is a relationship between magic and religion, between magic and words, and between religion and words. Burke notes: "The magical decree is implicit in all language; for the mere act of naming an object or situation decrees that it is to be singled out as such-and-such rather than as something-other" (4). In positing that a "magical" property is a component of the use of language, Burke again shows his proclivity for attempting to explain human social acts by invoking disembodied, ethereal principles—talking about life on earth by way of talking about a mysterious transcendental realm. For Burke, the emphasis on the magical is indispensable and practically non-negotiable: "I think that an attempt to *eliminate* magic, in this sense, would involve us in the elimination of vocabulary itself as a way of sizing up reality. Rather, what we may need is *correct* magic, magic whose decrees about the naming of real situations is the closest possible approximation to the situation named" (4). Burke's belief in the possibility of a "correct" magic that will preside over the "naming of real situations" reveals his abiding concern to integrate the supernatural with the quotidian. In keeping with his claim that an "entelechial" principle characterizes language use, that is, the urge to search for the "perfect" or "quintessential" title, name, word, or system, or what David Tracy describes as "the drive to perfection seemingly incumbent upon all language use of any terministic screen" ("Charity" 262), Burke's hope is that a "correct magic" will lead to the "closest possible approximation to the situation named" (4).

Ostensibly, Burke's intention, as Duncan explains, is to show that "if we believe that rules are but a crude step on the upward way toward God, then we cannot study society as a game. If we say that art is but a manifestation of the divine, then obviously we must hurry to the divine for our knowledge of society" (407–08). While Duncan notes that *The Rhetoric of Religion* seems to *break down* divisions between the secular and the sacred, I find that to be a somewhat generous claim. If anything, I think the opposite could be ventured; in his effort to look to religion as a system that might help explain the workings of language in the secular realm, Burke ends up unnecessarily "spiritualizing" or even "occulting" his view of language, with my usage of "occulting" in this context suggesting both the sense of the supernatural and the sense of obscuration.

In *The Rhetoric of Religion,* Burke announces, "Our purpose is simply to ask how theological principles can be shown to have usable secular analogues that throw light upon the nature of language" (2). As a result, for Burke, there are "'words' (lower case) and The Word (*Logos, Verbum*) as it were in caps" (7). John Freccero, for instance, notes that Burke's *Rhetoric of Religion* represents an attempt "to observe the formal principles upon which theology is founded in order to learn how those principles operate in all symbol-systems, including those of governance and of language itself, in which more secularized mysteries have yet to be resolved" (54). Thus, Burke characterizes the human inclination to use language as a quest for perfection and purification, since in Burke's universe people are depicted as engaged in a perpetual search to find the ever more precise word, the ever more apt name or title. As Timothy C. Murray points out, the notion of the "god-term"—the illusory, perfect term for which humans search—is tantamount to a "title of titles" (148), which Burke, in *The Rhetoric of Religion,* describes as a phenomenon that requires "a logic of entitlement that is completed by thus rising to ever and ever higher orders of generalization" (25). Burke believed in—and seemed to exalt—the practice of making generalizations, of attempting to identify that which would be the most "universal" or most typically human. As I noted earlier in this essay, the act of "summing up" was, for Burke, a grand gesture and great accomplishment—overtones of Marlow's judgment of Kurtz in *Heart of Darkness* notwithstanding. In explaining the notion of "entitlement," Burke notes that entitlement functions like a process of condensation

> whereby the whole sentence, considered as a title, can be summed up in one word, as were we to sum up the sentence "the man walks down the street" by saying that it had to do with either a "man-situation," or a "walk-situation," or a "street-situation." "Entitling" of this sort prepares for the linguistic shortcut whereby we can next get "universals" such as "man," "dog," "tree," with individual men, dogs, and trees serving as particularized instances or manifestations of the "perfect forms" that are present in the words themselves (which so transcend any particular man, dog, or tree that they can be applied universally to all men, dogs, or trees). (*LSA* 361)

Eventually, Burke refines this classificatory process by adding that the choice of man-, walk-, or street- situation would depend "upon the direction of selectivity of your interests" (*LSA* 371). This line of reasoning is certainly distinguished by its flexibility, by a particular attentiveness to context and to the proclivities of the perceiver who performs the act of naming or "entitling" the situation. But it is important for us to remember that in this scenario, Burke's "perceiver" or "namer" is essentially a disembodied individual, and, moreover, an individual affected by Burke's postulation of larger (supernatural?) forces that go beyond "local contexts of situation." Here again is Burke's supernatural, universalizing impulse at work: "Each language has its peculiar genius, which figures in its modes of entitling, and by suggesting that we entitle some situations rather than others. Also, there is some kind of overall context beyond language, whether natural or supernatural, serving as a nonverbal, or less-than-verbal, or more-than-verbal ground that informs language" (*LSA* 373).[7]

Continuing with this theme, Burke notes that "though one may *scientifically* distinguish between words and things, *philosophically* there must be not only the verbal and the nonverbal, but also the more-than-verbal, since 'Reality' as a whole comprises not only the verbal and the nonverbal, but also the more-than-verbal" (*LSA* 455). In granting the existence of these "extra-linguistic" categories, Burke reveals his penchant for holding out for some sense of renewal—redemption?—for humankind in order to compensate for or ameliorate the limitations, in Burke's judgment, of secular rhetoric. As Rueckert notes,

> So, just as Christians say that all men suffer from "original sin," Burke, in his secularized, dramatistic version of the Genesis "myth," says that all men suffer from "categorical guilt"; and just as all Christians begin in a fallen state, needing and yearning for the redemption made possible by the sacrificial Christ, so all men, according to Burke, *begin in a fallen state, brought on by their distinctive trait—language*—needing and yearning for the redemption made possible by the dramatistic equivalent of the sacrificial Christ, symbolic action and the rhetoric of rebirth. (*Kenneth Burke* 133, emphasis added)

In viewing the human acquisition of language as itself somehow a sad and stigmatizing act, Burke's position, in my judgment, flirts with an essentially anti-social, anti-human perspective: fear and loathing on planet earth among *homo sapiens,* the life-form Burke so curiously and pervasively tends to refer to as "symbol-using animals," "Word-People," "Word-Animals," or "Earth-People" rather than as simply "people." Just as references to the "subject" and "subjectivity" have *sometimes* functioned as elaborate euphemisms in postmodern discourse for references to people, Burke's preferred terms are also euphemistic, and in their way they highlight the binary oppositions that are touchstones of his thought: heaven/earth, divine/mortal, above/below.

In *Language as Symbolic Action,* for instance, Burke offers a definition of what it means to be a "person," but this definition proceeds in the individualist, sexist terms that also typify much of religious discourse.[8] Burke observes:

Man is
the symbol using (symbol-making, symbol mis-using) animal
inventor of the negative (or moralized by the negative)
separated from his natural condition by instruments of his own making
goaded by the spirit of hierarchy (or moved by the sense of order)
and rotten with perfection. (16)

In this famous definition, we again find Burke's religious (or quasi-religious?) impulse infiltrating his theoretical discourse.[9] In contending that "man" is "rotten with perfection," Burke claims that "the principle of perfection is central to the nature of language as motive. The mere desire to name something by its 'proper' name, or to speak a language in its distinctive ways is intrinsically 'perfectionist'" (16). Burke's emphasis on "perfection," along with negativity/negation, as defining properties of the phenomenon of human language—"there is a principle of perfection implicit in the nature of symbol systems" (17)—suggests a view of language that places more emphasis *on the system itself* than on the *social situatedness of its practitioners.* While much of Burke's work has been received as restoring a much needed emphasis on the social aspects of the relationship between language and human experience, I am suspicious of his claim, influenced by his reading of St. Augustine, that a "principle of perfection" inheres in symbol systems and that this principle exerts an influence on speakers and writers in certain ways.

For example, in the "Prologue in Heaven" in *The Rhetoric of Religion,* which consists of a conversation between Satan (S) and The Lord (TL), Burke effects a rather curious shift in terminology in designating the divinity as "The Lord," since throughout the study, his preferred word for the divinity has been "God." More curious, though, is that in the course of this dialogue "The Lord" has a tendency to discourse upon "God," as if referring to "God" as an independent entity, suggesting—at least superficially—that a kind of counter-statement to the Christian doctrine of the Trinity, consisting of the "three-in-one" mystery of Father, Son, and Holy Spirit, is being pursued by Burke. Moreover, in the course of this dialogue, Satan habitually utters the putatively honorific term "milord" in responding to "The Lord," but one cannot help but wonder whether Burke intends for Satan's good manners to be viewed as authentically deferential and exemplary, or as ironic and mocking. Usually, though, Satan exhibits the fawning blandness typical of one of Socrates's interlocutors in a Platonic dialogue. Consider the following exchange on the topic of "perfection," and note the transparency that surrounds The Lord's voice as Burke's theoretical mouthpiece and surrogate:

> **S.** But are not *you* the only conceivable ultimate perfection? [emphasis in original]
>
> **TL.** Exactly.
>
> **S.** Then their idea of you is but a function of *language?* [emphasis in original]
>
> **TL.** All orderly thought will be a function of their symbol-systems.
>
> **S.** I refer not merely to the fact that they must conceive of things in terms of terms. I am asking more specifically whether the principle of perfection upon which they rely in their idea of you is reducible purely and simply to terms of the form underlying all language. Or otherwise put: Is there in all language a principle of perfection which makes all human thought behave as though it had begun in "the one true philosophy," which is still lying about in fragments, and which the

Word-Animals are constantly striving, with partial success, to reconstruct in its entirety?

TL. How exacting do you want their idea of God to be? I am sure you would not be satisfied to let them conceive of God in terms of sheerly natural power (suggested to them by their experience as animals). We have already agreed that their confusing of God and money is regrettable. Later in our discussions we shall consider the objections to the conceiving of God in terms of human personality. *And now you would deny them the right to conceive of God in terms of a perfection which is identical with an underlying principle of language* [emphasis added]. Are not such strictures as haughty in their way as the Earth-People will accuse you of being? Are you not in effect rebelling against them as absolutely as they will accuse you of rebelling against me? Would you not, in effect, be denying them the resources of their own minds, in effect be demanding that they think without thought?

S. I pray, milord, don't ask me; tell me. (297–98)

In positing the relationship between theology and logology in these terms, Burke shows how it is impossible, in his judgment, to separate words about words from words about God. As "The Lord" remarks: "all doctrine is by its very nature a system of words, or symbols—and so, there is always the wise possibility of using [. . .] theological nomenclatures for purely logological purposes" (301). Then comes an astonishing turn: The Lord suggests, at least to some extent, that "God" is a human creation: "the idea of supernatural God is built out of human components" (304). This, as "The Lord" explains, is because "as the perfected projection of human personality," God, who "is built out of human components," is considered by humans as "the perfect exemplar of natural powers, as the ultimate of verbal perfection" (304).

In contrast to this view of God, Burke appeals to the concept of negative theology to describe humans. The Lord comments on the human contribution to the creation of the idea of "God" and of religion:

TL. In their societies, they will seek to keep order. If order, then a need to repress the tendencies to disorder. If repression, then responsibility for imposing, accepting, or resisting the repression. If responsibility, then guilt. If guilt, then the need for redemption, which involves sacrifice, which in turns allows for substitution. At this point, the logic of perfection enters. Man can be viewed as perfectly depraved by a formative "first" offense against the foremost authority, an offense in which one man sinned for all. The cycle of life and death intrinsic to the nature of time can now be seen in terms that treat natural death as the result of this "original" sin. And the principle of perfection can be matched on the hopeful side by the idea of a perfect victim. The symmetry can be logologically rounded out by the idea of this victim as also the creative Word by which time was caused to be, the intermediary Word binding time with eternity, and the end towards which all words of the true doctrine are directed. As one of their saints will put it: "The way to heaven must be heaven, for He said, I am the way."

(TL rises. S also rises immediately after.)

TL (continuing). The way to heaven (the means to the end, the agency for the attainment of purpose) must be heaven (scene), for He (agent) said (act as words): I am the way (act as Word). Here is the ultimate logological symmetry!

S. Formally, it is perfect. It is perfectly beautiful!

TL. It is truly cumulative!

S. Words could do no more! (RR 314–315)

In this closing section of *The Rhetoric of Religion*, Burke identifies humans as the "other half," so to speak, in the dialectic of perfection: "man is rotten with perfection." That is, for Burke the human condition is characterized by a relentless striving toward forms of perfection, an aspiration which is inevitably compromised by the fact that "man can be viewed as perfectly depraved by a formative 'first' offense against the foremost authority, an offense in which one man sinned for all" (314). The notion that people are "perfectly depraved," then, becomes the way in which Burke uses the principle of negativity to bring the human condition into a dialectical relationship with perfection.

As the dialogue between The Lord and Satan comes to its conclusion, we find Burke creating his own quasi-scriptural text by using the terminology of dramatism. Although dramatism as an analytical apparatus stands as one of Burke's greatest contributions to a view of the materiality of language, the above synthesis of the stories of the creation and of the appearance of God's son, in the form of the Christian Savior, explained by Burke in dramatistic terms, is a problematic exegesis. For the closing section of the dialogue between The Lord and Satan represents the triumph of logology as well as a *perfectly* self-indulgent moment for Burke. For in this moment, Burke seeks to "prove" his dramatistic and logological tenets by associating them with major biblical themes that have had a decisive influence on Western civilization. The "ultimate of logological symmetry" that "The Lord" and Satan eventually celebrate is the ability of an explanatory system devised by a human "rotten with perfection" to highlight the intertwining of the mortal who is "perfectly depraved" with the divinity who is, as I will put it, "perfectly perfect."

David Tracy, in "Mystics, Prophets, Rhetorics: Religion and Psychoanalysis," remarks that the role of the negative in Burke's system is closely related to the principle of perfection. In summing up Burke's position, Tracy observes that people "learn by learning negatives (the prophetic negatives 'thou shalt not') in order to create once they learn that they cannot stop going to the end of the line—the line of the widest possible generalization, the most perfect language for the truly creative act—to god-terms" (264–65). Tracy continues his reading of Burke by noting that "The basic necessity for the symbolic animal is to speak, to learn negatives, to create and *not* to stop. Perfection is our *telos*—which seems to mean, paradoxically, that end *is* origin" (265). As Burke explains in *The Rhetoric of Religion,* the tradition of negative theology pertains to "defining of God in terms of what he is not, as when God is described in words like 'immortal,' 'immutable,' 'infinite,' 'unbounded,' 'impassive' and the like" (22). From Burke's perspective, this process of naming occurs almost by default, and it is based on paradox. Burke entertains this conundrum, as when words such as "Love" or "Father" are used to describe God. He notes: "By 'love' we don't mean such love as people have for one another, for that would be merely human. And by 'father' we don't mean father in the literal, legal or naturalistic sense of the term" (22). In this case, it's as though Burke is telling us that language operates on multiple wavelengths and that it achieves a variety of results depending upon the context and purposes of its mortal practitioners—or to put it in purely Burkean terms: dramatism and terministic screens inexorably shape our relationships to language and its effects.

Robert McMahon sees *The Rhetoric of Religion* as a comic send-up of the Platonic and Christian themes of hierarchy, order, guilt, and victimage, arguing that the book pursues a connection between the religious realm and the secular: "For Burke the rhetoric of politics is deeply informed by the principle of perfection, which is most clearly illustrated in the rhetoric of religion. He teaches us that politics and religion have long been and still are more deeply interconnected than our conventional categories lead us to think" (61).[10] McMahon makes some revealing observations about Burke's claim that the discourse of religion sometimes bears affinities to the discourse of politics and economics, noting that "[t]he rhetoric of the cold war was much on Burke's mind as he wrote *The Rhetoric of Religion,* first published in 1961" (61). McMahon notes: "Cold-war rhetoric simplified the world into two opposing ideologies" (61), just as some religious perspectives embrace variations on the "Us" versus "Them" way of looking at the world. McMahon observes:

> In politics, the principle of perfection tends toward the reduction of the opposition. In its ultimate forms, it anathematizes and seeks to eliminate the opposition. For Burke, as we have seen, the principle of perfection inherent in symbols generates hierarchy and order, hence guilt and victimage. The entelechy of language tends to convert distinctions into oppositions, and these, in the political realm, imply the sacrificial principle as an ever-present danger. Hence, comic charity and true irony prove tools for tolerance and understanding: they would make the counterconversion, to render the opposition apposite. (60)

As I have indicated, McMahon's reading of *The Rhetoric of Religion* strikes me as an incisive analysis, especially in its highlighting of the rhetorical similarities between religious and political discourse, but McMahon seems to fall short, in my judgment, by not putting more pressure on Burke's claim that "theological principles can be shown to have usable secular analogies that throw light upon the nature of language" (*RR* 2).

Yet it is perhaps by virtue of this theme that Burke's work, despite what I consider the problematic aspects of *The Rhetoric of Religion,* offers an alternative to the possibility of silence in a post-Holocaust world—indeed, in a world that had become more conscious than ever, if not of the death of God as Nietzsche had once observed, then of the *absence* of God. At one point, in trying to "sum up" the capaciousness of his *oeuvre* in "Dancing with Tears in My Eyes," which is Burke's response to Booth's "Kenneth Burke's Ways of Knowing," Burke offers a revealing moment of self-analysis:

> I guess the truth is that, even more urgently than trying to help people "get along with people," I was trying to get along with myself. Since I was too pigheaded (or possibly too arrogant despite my timidities) to seek the guidance of any psychologist, and I couldn't fold up in the Church despite my great love of theology, I worked out a way of getting along by dodges, the main one being a concern with tricks whereby I could translate my self-involvements into speculations about people. (26)

Is it possible, therefore, to characterize Burke's approach in *The Rhetoric of Religion* as one of these so-called "dodges" or "tricks" that he employs as a way to explore the larger implications of social life, of *people's* lives, of human consciousness? Within this same essay, he notes: "Above all, I guess, I am engrossed by the great range of *ingenuities* which the study of symbolic action allows us to contemplate" (27). If that is the case, then Burke here sheds some light on the appearance of the elaborate conceits that pervade *The Rhetoric of Religion*. For Burke, it is preferable to be involved in a world permeated by utterances and significations of all kinds, even if they emanate from the mouths of extraordinary figures such as The Lord and Satan. Like Stephen Dedalus in Joyce's *Ulysses,* Burke's motto could very well be:

"Ineluctable modality of the visible. [. . .] Signatures of all things I am here to read. [. . .] Limits of the diaphane. But he adds: in bodies" (37). While, of course, the palpable, visceral human body does seem to be a missing element in *The Rhetoric of Religion,* we cannot forget that Burke's ultimate goal was to use this text as an occasion to reconceptualize the understanding of human language, and that he does attend to the material conditions of human existence more saliently in some of his other works, such as *Permanence and Change (1935)* and *Attitudes Toward History* (1937), among others.

In *Ineffability: The Failure of Words in Philosophy and Religion,* Ben-Ami Scharfstein observes that "every culture appears to have recognized and even exalted the power of words" (50). Yet he acknowledges the gaps and contradictions that surround any effort to explain or critique the workings of language:

> There is always the residue, what has not been said, what one has forgotten or cannot remember, what one has not conceived or conceived clearly, or what escapes because it is too delicate or quick. For such reasons, we should speak not of ineffability, but of the many ineffabilities—neurological, synesthetic, musical, logical, philosophical and religious, personal, familial, and tribal, childish and adult, normal, abnormal, and outright pathological—that make our speech less regular and more human. These ineffabilities are the demons (and maybe angels) of incompleteness and incompletability. They are also our rest, after and between speech, in silence, which derives its possible eloquence from the speech that surrounds it. The gaps themselves of speech translate our intermittency into still another of its complex perfections. (219–220)

Theodor Adorno, in his essay, "Cultural Criticism and Society," observes famously—or infamously?—that "Cultural criticism finds itself faced with the final stage of the dialectic of culture and barbarism. To write poetry after Auschwitz is barbaric" (34). In the face of Sharfstein's reflections on the inevitability of ineffability and the pessimism of Adorno's pronouncement about the transgressive nature of the attempt to write poetry after the Holocaust, where do we situate Burke? His particular "hyperfocus on language as the finest medium of human consciousness," to again quote Stuckey, finds its apex in *The Rhetoric of Religion*'s preoccupation with the theme of perfection. For perfection, in one sense, can be understood as a form of "completeness," as a manifestation of the ultimate, most satisfying form of expression, as well as of the unimpeachable, incontestable comprehension of such expression. Yet certainly Burke was not so naïve as to fail to acknowledge that moments of ineffability, incompleteness, and ambiguity characterize the experience of life and the significations we encounter and create. Perhaps what *The Rhetoric of Religion* and Burke's definition of man as "rotten with perfection" (*LSA* 16) show us, however, is his tenaciousness in resisting the impulse to surrender to silence and incompleteness, and the lengths to which he would go in order to avoid such an outcome. With his "tricks" and "dodges," Burke refuses to become just another Prospero, who at one point in *The Tempest* announces: "But this rough magic / I here abjure . . . / I'll break my staff . . . / And deeper than did ever plummet sound / I'll drown my book" (V. i. 51–57). Unwilling to settle for silence, Burke, I think, insists on keeping a few tricks up his sleeve in his quest to understand life, language, literature, and symbolism as fully and imaginatively as possible. Perhaps this accounts for some of the histrionic legerdemain I take issue with in *The Rhetoric of Religion?*

I began this discussion by invoking the notion of "conundrum," with its connotations of riddle, paradox, mystery, and puzzlement, to characterize my response to some elements of Burke's work. Perhaps my effort to puzzle out this conundrum by casting Burke as a sort of "anti-Prospero" exemplifies the fashion in which Burke's work, in a way analogous to the dynamics of Schleiermacher's "hermeneutic circle," compels us to remain in perpetual motion, trying to reconcile the part with the whole, the extraordinary with the ordinary, as he challenges us to embrace his *mélange* with all of its risks, paradoxes, provocations, and pleasures.

NOTES

1. See Husserl, especially 48–53.
2. For an interesting discussion of the sociopolitical effects of the tropes that characterize the discourse of evolution—and of science in general—see Gross and Averill.
3. In this regard, one need only consider the controversy surrounding Mel Gibson's release of the film *The Passion of the Christ* in 2004.

4. In attempting to explain the levels of symbolic action that occur in a literary text, Burke in *Philosophy of Literary Form* remarks on the impact of this process on characterization, as characters are depicted in the act of forming and transforming their roles. Burke writes:

> Even if one would symbolically form a role by becoming "most thoroughly and efficiently himself," he must slough off ingredients that are irrelevant to this purpose (ingredients that are "impure," if only in the chemical sense). So we watch, in the structural analysis of the symbolic act, not only the matter of "what equals what," but also the matter of "from what to what." And we detect, under various guises, the abandonment of an old self, in symbolic suicide, parricide, or prolicide. [. . .] Since the symbolic transformation involves a sloughing off, you may expect to find some variant of killing in the work. [. . .] So we get to the "scapegoat," the "representative" or "vessel" of certain unwanted evils, the sacrificial animal upon whose back the burden of these evils is ritualistically loaded. (38–40)

By tying the notion of the scapegoat so centrally to the process of the transformation of literary characters through symbolic action, Burke seems to be suggesting that there is a certain *inevitability* that attends the phenomenon of scapegoating. In addition, René Girard's observations in *Violence and the Sacred* are of relevance, since Girard associates the scapegoat with religious ritual. Girard observes:

> All religious rituals spring from the surrogate victim, and the great institutions of mankind, both secular and religious, spring from ritual. [. . .] It could hardly be otherwise, for the working basis of human thought, the process of "symbolization," is rooted in the surrogate victim. Even if no example taken alone offers conclusive proof of my theory, their cumulative effect is overwhelming; all the more so because they coincide with archetypal myths that tell, in apparently "naïve" fashion, how all man's religious, familial, economic, and social institutions grew out of the body of an original victim. (306)

In a manner somewhat analogous to Burke, then, Girard argues for the scapegoat as a central source in the founding of myths that account for the rise of various sociopolitical institutions; but unlike Burke, Girard does not seem to view scapegoating as a necessary inevitability, although he does acknowledge it as a decisive feature of human social life. The difference I want to call attention to, then, could be described as a "teleological" one: Burke views the scapegoat as a *necessity* of human experience; Girard views it as an *aspect* of human experience. See also Girard's *The Scapegoat*.

5. The documents that indisputably support this point are too numerous to mention. But consider in particular Hitler's *Mein Kampf* (1924), the Nuremberg Laws (1935), the First Ordinance to the Reich Citizenship Law (1935), various documents pertaining to "Kristallnacht" (1938), the Protocols of the Wannsee Conference (1942), and the diaries of Joseph Goebbels—among the multitude of other documents that testify to this fact. See Rubin.

6. It should be added that in "What Are the Signs of What?" Burke envisions the linguistic universe as consisting of

> Four terministic pyramids, each of which contains words for a certain realm, or order. These four are: (1) words for the sheerly natural (in the sense of the less-than-verbal, the realm of visible tangible things and operations, the realm that is best charted and described in terms of motion and position); (2) words for the verbal realm itself, the terms of grammar, rhetoric, poetics, logic, dialectic, philology, etymology, semantics, symbolism, etc.; (3) words for the sociopolitical realm, for personal and social relations, including terms like "justice," "right," and "obligation," etc.; (4) words for the supernatural. (373–74)

Significantly, Burke acknowledges that these four categories "are not mutually exclusive." He offers, as an example, a word such as "person," which, he maintains, participates simultaneously in all four categories:

> A word such as "person" belongs in the sheerly *natural* insofar as a person must have a living body subject to the laws of motion; it is in the *verbal* order inasmuch as the rationality of a person is involved in kinds of mental maturity that require a high degree of aptitude at symbol-using; it is in the *sociopolitical* order because of the sociopolitical relationships and roles involved in personality; and it is in the *supernatural* order at the very least to the extent that it involves attitudes towards words for this order and towards the institutions representing this order, *while furthermore the person is often said to be derived from some transcendent principle of pure personality that is designated by whatever term may be the Title of Titles in this fourth realm*. (374, emphasis added)

While I have no question as to the applicability of aligning the word "person" with the first three categories, I find Burke's effort to demonstrate the "supernatural" properties of the word to be a very strong instance of the quasi-religious, mystical bent that characterizes elements of his work. The fact that Burke supposes, for instance, that some sort of "transcendent principle of pure personality" is designated by some sort of "Title of Titles" suggests that Burke ends up perpetuating the transcendental and ineffable values that are incompatible with a view of the materiality of language. (Later in this essay, I look at Burke's usage of the "god-term" as further evidence of this trend.)

7. As Burke observes in *The Rhetoric of Religion,* putting a slightly different spin on the notion of God as the "title of titles":

> Instead of looking upon "God" as the title of titles in which all is summed up, one could look at all subclasses as materially "emanating" or "radiating" from this "spiritual source." And thus, just as religion could be viewed as central, with all specialized fields such as law, politics, ethics, poetry, art, etc. "breaking off" from it and gradually becoming "autonomous" disciplines, so there is a technical sense in which all specialization can be treated as radiating from a Logological center. Logology could properly be called central, and all other studies could be said to "radiate" from it, in the sense that all -ologies and -ographies are guided by the verbal. (26)

In this passage Burke gives evidence of the extent to which he subscribes to the same sort of hierarchical thinking he features in his memorable "definition of man," inasmuch as he is compelled to posit logology as having a certain *priority* in relationship to other disciplines, because logology is concerned with the workings of language and, in turn, logology can be applied to the "special idioms" of the various sciences and branches of the humanities. The central, vexing question is why logology—"words about words"—should be granted this priority in the first place? Why construct this hierarchy with logology occupying the most privileged position, especially given Burke's impulse to transcend the temporal and the verbal, as these final moments in the conversation between Satan and The Lord in *The Rhetoric of Religion* suggest:

> **TL.** The way to heaven (the means to the end, the agency for the attainment of purpose) must be heaven (scene), for He (agent) said (act as words): I am the way (act as The Word). Here is the ultimate of logological symmetry!
> **S.** Formally, it is perfect. It is perfectly beautiful!
> **TL.** It is truly cumulative!
> **S.** Words could do no more!
> *(Pause.)*
> **S.**(*pensively*). In some ways they will be dismal, in some ways they will have a feeling for the grandeurs of form. But

> when these Word-People are gone, won't the life of words be gone?
>
> **TL**. Unfortunately, yes.
>
> **S**. Then, what of us, the two voices in this dialogue? When words go, won't we, too, be gone?
>
> **TL**. Unfortunately, yes.
>
> **S**. Then of this there will be nothing?
>
> **TL**. Yes . . . nothing . . . but it's more complica—.(315)

At this point, the dialogue between the two abruptly concludes, with The Lord hinting that something more may be behind the scene—possibly the appearance of some sort of extra-linguistic, supernatural "moment" destined to manifest itself after the death of mortal language and the death of the "Word-People." In this way, *The Rhetoric of Religion* concludes with a decidedly eschatological emphasis, again suggesting the teleological accent behind so much of Burke's work.

8. While I have not commented up to this point on the sexism of Burke's discourse, it is quite clear that his work reveals the bias of a white, Western man. Burke writes from a privileged androcentric perspective; his literary touchstones are most often the classics of Western literature in the Greco-Christian tradition. References to Homer, Aristotle, St. Augustine, Shakespeare, Goethe, and Coleridge regularly appear in Burke's works, but this is counterbalanced by Burke's very pointed commentaries on sociopolitical issues. Burke's engagements with Marx, Freud, the perniciousness of Nazi ideology, the ethical questions raised by modern technology, and the politics of the cold war show that he was no rarified aesthete but a politically-engaged individual. See Burke, *Permanence and Change* and *Attitudes Toward History;* and Jameson, "Symbolic." In a 1978 "response" forum in *Critical Inquiry,* Burke and Jameson engage each other in dialogue. See Burke, "Methodological Repression and/or Strategies of Containment," and Jameson, "Ideology and Symbolic Action."

9. In what may be simply a coincidence, Burke's contemporary M.M. Bakhtin also was influenced—*to an extent*—by his relationship to the Russian kenotic tradition of Christianity. See Katrina Clark and Michael Holquist's biography, *Mikhail Bakhtin.* This aspect of Bakhtin's background strikes me as significant since I feel that Bakhtin, along with Burke, both explore innovative territory in the understanding of language and hermeneutics during the twentieth century.

10. This claim seems especially pertinent, as one need only consider the theme that Bill Clinton announced for his administration upon accepting the Democratic party's nomination for the presidency in July 1992 at the Democratic National Convention in New York City: the "New Covenant." With more controversial results, the administration of President George W. Bush has been assailed for its blurring of the lines between church and state.

14 Burkean Perspectives on Prayer: Charting a Key Term through Burke's Corpus

William T. FitzGerald

If one may advance something uncontroversial about Kenneth Burke it is this: he was a consummate artist of definition, a wordsmith of the highest order ever formulating new coinages or refashioning old terms to serve fresh critical purposes. Indeed, Burke illustrates, copiously, the falsity of Samuel Butler's adage, "For all the rhetorician's rules / Teach nothing but to name his tools" (*Hudibras* I.i.89). In the case of Kenneth Burke, his contributions to our lexical "toolbelt" have reinvigorated rhetoric as an intellectual discipline to an extent impossible, now, to imagine otherwise. *Dramatism, identification, logology, symbolic action, trained incapacity, perspective by incongruity:* a list of Burkean "key terms" goes productively on and on.

Among any such set of terms, this essay argues, is *prayer*, a term whose significance for Burke (and, by extension, for contemporary rhetorical studies) has yet to be adequately appreciated. Throughout his long career and rich corpus, Burke has significant things to say about prayer and even, in several key places, through the language of prayer. While references to prayer appear only sporadically throughout Burke's corpus, they do so always at critical moments where Burke seeks to characterize the rhetorical dimension of language. The cumulative effect of these references is to establish prayer as an especially telling marker of our character as linguistically endowed, rhetorically motivated beings.

I propose, then, to consider Burkean perspectives on prayer, doing so in two complementary directions: first, by charting Burke's specific uses of "prayer" as a critical term; second, by applying Burkean principles to the discourse of prayer, in particular to "prayers" of Burke's own composing. Indeed, Burke's prayers exemplify rhetorical features that make Burke's attention to prayer (recognized here as a heading for various modes of symbolic activity that ostensibly engage significant non-human audiences) an important, if largely heretofore overlooked, aspect of his development of rhetorical theory. Such modes of symbolic activity, Burke helps us to realize, are especially illustrative of language's rhetorical resources and effects. To take a perspective on prayer, as Burke does, involves characterizing the motives for prayer. That is, it involves *saying* what we or others are *doing* in and through the discourse of prayer. How to characterize such discourse, accurately, emerges as a crucial concern in pluralist cultures such as our own, where prayer is experienced as a contested activity; Burke's incorporation of "prayer" into his critical lexicon thus presents opportunities to examine common, deeply held assumptions about the nature of discourse in both its secular and religious stirrings. While a thorough accounting of Burkean perspectives on prayer would chart the place of prayer within an associative cluster of terms at the heart of Burke's rhetorical concerns (e.g., *ritual, form, appeal, hierarchy, pure persuasion, transcendence,* and *piety*), this present account, of necessity, presents a sketch of only the most significant linkages.

These last terms, *transcendence* and *piety,* indicate the extent to which Burke's critical project, over his entire corpus, proceeds from a strong affinity for the religious dimension of language. Among the major intellectuals of the twentieth century, few take religion as seriously as does Burke. To understand Burke's approach to and use of "prayer," it is important to recognize Burke's larger project with respect to secularity and religion. Even casual acquaintance with Burke reveals the degree to which such convenient binaries are effectively undermined through Burke's demonstration of the analogs operating between ostensibly opposed domains. For Burke, such binaries are themselves dependent upon some conceptually prior, ultimately unifying ground. In the case of the binary opposing the secular with the religious, Burke explores its analogs most thoroughly in *The Rhetoric of Religion,* where he advances principles of logology, "words about words," as the secular analog to theology, or "words about God" (*RR* 1). Long before this project, however, in works of literary and social criticism, Burke devotes considerable attention to—and borrows substantially from—the lexicon of religion. These acts of borrowing, Burke acknowledges, are an important component of his critical method, one to which he refers to at one point as "verbal 'atom cracking'" (*ATH* 308). As Burke explains, "a word belongs by custom to a certain category—and by rational planning you wrench it loose and metaphorically apply it to a different category" (308). This is Burke's characteristic method with respect to the term "prayer." Rather than consider the discourse of prayer "head on" in an expected context of religious belief and practice, Burke achieves "perspective by incongruity" by examining secular activities *in terms of* a corresponding religious nomenclature (308). In doing so, Burke invites us to see something essentially "prayer-like" in secular activities seemingly removed from contexts of faith or scenes of devotion.

This is Burke's approach in *Attitudes Toward History,* the occasion of his earliest "perspectivizing" through a critical lens of "prayer." In his "Dictionary of Pivotal Terms" and under the heading "Secular Prayer—or, extended: Character-building by Secular Prayer" (*ATH* 321-27), Burke expounds upon his chosen term, "secular prayer," through a series of definitional moves. The first of these moves is Burke's association of secular prayer with "word magic," the use of words for some incantatory effect. As Burke observes, charges of "word magic" can always be leveled against the verbal strategems of others by critics of a debunking streak who, discovering in another's rhetoric something false, would "propose contrivances for its elimination" (*ATH* 321). In contrast to such critics, Burke claims that the net effect of all such debunking strategies, rather than to eliminate verbal magic, is to introduce some counter-magic. Such contrivances, according to Burke, "are examples of prayer, albeit in disguise" (321). At the heart of Burke's observation here is an insight, to be developed more thoroughly in later works, that what others would disparagingly call "magic," blind to their own forms of counter-magic, is best understood as prayer "in disguise," prayer being a more valorous term for such verbal ministrations. In Burke's formulation, then, "prayer" is a pervasive discursive phenomenon, a dimension of language operative in human affairs even in cases where its practitioners are ignorant of or resistant to its use.

Recognizing that much is at stake in resisting a thoroughly debunking attitude, one that would "see through" all verbal appeals, Burke makes a positive case for "secular prayer":

> Any mimetic act is prayer. Even "psychogenic illness" may be a prayer, since it is the "substantiation of an attitude" in a bodily act. All mimetic procedures in the dance, the plastic or graphic arts, music and verbalization are aspects of "prayer" in our technical sense of the term. And they have a great deal to do with the building of character. In fact, the man who does not "pray" cannot build his character. (*ATH* 321–22)

What Burke touches upon in this provocative statement are the profound connections that exist between thought and action, between matters verbal and physical, between the symbolic and the real. Each of these binaries is effectively transcended through a "prayerful" process by which attitude, as incipient action, becomes performance and, vice-versa, performance shapes subsequent attitudes. Burke proceeds from this eye-opening analogy—prayer *has* a secular counterpart—to a statement of breathtaking scope: *all* poetic and symbolic activities, including those of which we are often dimly cognizant, are forms of "prayer" insofar as they shape our character in and through performance.

Technically defined, "[s]ecular prayer, as a 'moral act,' is the *coaching of an attitude* by the use of mimetic and verbal language" (322). Burke illustrates with examples of decree and petition—and by extension their non-verbal, yet equally symbolic, counterparts in gesture—as instantiations of attitude. He cites an example, after Piaget, of young children *"naming the essence* of their play objects [. . .] thus, picking up a block of wood, the child decrees by legislative fiat: 'This is a train'" (322); and *so,* a particular block of wood *becomes* a train. For Burke, such exhortations are not strictly the province of childhood, something to be outgrown upon reaching maturity. Rather, there exists a human propensity to name essences, to decree that something *is* such-and-such. For Burke, this propensity is itself an essential property of our linguistic ordination. Moreover, even in the face of a recalcitrant physical world, our strategic acts of naming have profound consequences.

What matters for Burke, therefore, is not an eradication of "word magic"—something impossible—but purification of the magical decree. With respect to verbal magic, Burke professes that we "must simply eradicate the wrong kinds and coach the right kinds" (323). Whether Burke speaks tongue-in-cheek about how "simply" this objective may be accomplished, he is nonetheless quite serious about the end itself, the coaching of the "right kinds" of attitude. Such inducements, Burke suggests, are tantamount to prayer. Referring to the "secular prayers" of "propaganda," Burke observes that we are ever engaged in exhortations, addressing both ourselves and others, to accept some partisan, motivated account of the way things are. These exhortations, Burke reminds us, "can be extremely accurate, just as they can be extremely inaccurate" (324). Their accuracy, an accuracy not easily achieved, depends on the degree to which verbal decrees reflect the "full realities of the situation" (324). Burke notes that it is all too easy to adopt a "polemic, pamphleteering attitude," an attitude that amounts to praying "on too simple a level" (327). By contrast, a quest for accuracy in one's prayers is a process by which one seeks "the exact names for all the relationships and interrelationships," a process that Burke, citing Socrates as a figure exemplifying the quest for exactitude, finds to be salient (327). Although he counters the notion that one can mount a platform of objectivity from which to identify false rhetoric from true, Burke nonetheless suggests in *Attitudes* that it is indeed possible to articulate better, that is, more complex, prayers, provided one is sufficiently engaged in constructive dialogue with surrounding situations. Burke seems to suggest that mimetic acts that seek to name their situation must necessarily approach their task "asymptotically," coming ever closer to, if never entirely achieving, their desired goal. The less "simple" one's prayer, the closer one comes to accurately representing a situation's "full realities" (324).

That Burke refers to all mimetic acts as "prayer" is more than an ironist's rhetorical move. That is, Burke aspires to something more than exposing hidden religious motives in ostensibly secular activities or revealing crassly secular motives in the outwardly religious act. As is apparent here, Burke's characterization of "secular prayer" moves some distance from conventionally religious scenes of reverent address to divine beings. Yet rather than focus on the character of prayer's addressees, Burke emphasizes the *formal* character of such address, seeing in prayer a paradigmatic scene for all acts of address. At the level of form, Burke thus identifies a default scene for prayer among his definitional moves: "The essence of prayer is *petition*. Its simple reverse, we might say its grotesque *caricature,* is denunciation, invective, excommunication, ostracism, the pronouncing of anathema. It is *polemic.* Such prayer-upside-down has been used profusely by both clerical and secular antagonists" (325). Burke understands prayer, then, not only in terms of its character-building, character-revealing instantiations of attitude, but also as a matter of rhetorical action in the social sphere. Specifically, prayer is an act of verbal appeal directed, explicitly or implicitly, toward some audience. It is an act seeking to remake the constitution of human communities. In positive terms, prayer is a symbolic gesture of communion or solidarity toward an audience. Expressed negatively, prayer is a statement of division or separation. A key insight of Burke's in this regard is that prayer can function both positively and negatively, even at the same time.

What prayer is not, for Burke, is a static, merely declarative discourse. To the contrary, "prayer" expresses the fundamentally dynamic character of discourse. Thus, there exist exhortations and decrees of all kinds, even acts of cursing as a form of anti-prayer. Such verbal activities underscore for Burke the thoroughly motivated character of discourse, since all verbal acts, including apparently "neutral" acts of description, are nonetheless manifestations of the hortatory. Linguistically, we might say, the deictic *there is* shades into the optative *let there be*. Indeed, one might understand Burke's descriptive efforts in *Attitudes* as themselves fundamentally exhortative. He invites us to "own up" to the prayerful character of our discourse whenever we "size up" situations, which is in most every case. It is through such acts in which we aspire to align our verbal pronouncements with corresponding extra-verbal realities, Burke argues, that we effectively shape our character.

Incisive as his employment of "secular prayer" as a terministic screen for revealing the hortatory in language, Burke's later use of "prayer"—having now dropped "secular" as a modifier—reflects a further evolution of his thought on the rhetorical dimension of symbolic action. In the title essay of *The Philosophy of Literary Form*, in particular, Burke recognizes that poetry, understood here as "any work of critical or imaginative cast," involves the "adopting of various strategies for the encompassing of situations" (1). As a scheme for analyzing these strategies, Burke proposes a critical triad of terms—*dream, prayer* and *chart*—to serve as shorthand for "subdivisions for the analysis of an act in poetry" (5). Under Burke's formulation, dream represents "the unconscious or subconscious factors in a poem" and chart stands for "the realistic sizing-up of situations that is sometimes explicit, sometimes implicit, in poetic strategies" (5). Under the heading of prayer, Burke places the "communicative functions of a poem," a characterization, Burke suggests, that leads to "the many considerations of form, since the poet's inducements can lead us to participate in the poem only in so far as his work has a public or communicative structure" (5–6). In "Philosophy of Literary Form," the dimension "prayer" is now characterized as orthogonal to the expressive character of the poetic act and even to those specific articulations that aspire to name one's situation accurately. While any of these "axes" may be singled out for analysis (or otherwise elevated to a position of primacy) in the interpretation of a poetic act, no act is *purely* expressive (dream) or *purely* referential (chart). Absent an additional dimension of "prayer," neither "dream" nor "chart" fully encompasses the situation to which the poetic act is a strategic response.

But why "prayer" as a strategic label for a symbolic act's public, or communicative, structure? What purchase does Burke gain by identifying communicative structure, in general, with prayer? Here, again, Burke's use of "prayer" achieves perspective by incongruity, revealing aspects of symbolic action that would otherwise go unnoticed. Nowhere in "Philosophy of Literary Form" does Burke state explicitly why a mode of language typically understood as extraordinary, even marginal, should be held up as representative of the communicative act writ large. Nonetheless, the choice to do so makes sense given that prayer, in all its variety—individual or corporate, vocalized or silent, scripted or extemporaneous—is (or aspires to be) an idealized communicative scene consisting of (human) speaker, speech, and (divine) spoken-to. Burke's identification of prayer as a paradigmatic communicative act recognizes the extent to which prayer is communication in its "purest" form, an audience-focused address "awaiting" the exigencies arising from experience to be "filled in" along the axes of "dream" and "chart."

Burke comes closest to explaining the significance of his choice of term in "Freud—and the Analysis of Poetry":

> Prayer would enter the Freudian picture in so far as it concerns the optative. But prayer does not stop at that. Prayer is also an act of communion. Hence the concept of prayer, as extended to cover also secular forms of petition, moves us also into the corresponding area of communication in general. We might say that, whereas the expressionistic emphasis reveals the

> ways in which the poet, with an attitude, embodies it in appropriate gesture, communication deals with the choice of gesture for the inducement of corresponding attitudes. (*PLF* 281)

As the domain of the optative, Burke observes, prayer derives from a capacity to desire and express some counter-reality, a hoped-for future. Yet such expression and its motivating attitudes are not, for Burke, prayer's *essential* function. Rather, its essence is the inducement of "corresponding attitudes" in an audience, effects only possible through a choice of formal means appealing to the "psychology of the audience" (*CS* 31). For Burke, such formal means of appeal are epitomized in scenes of petition, in both secular and religious contexts. Locating such scenes within a context of prayer allows Burke to emphasize the range of formal appeals, a range that includes audiences of all kinds— including audiences of self, other, and "other"—as well as the fundamentally abstract character of this appeal. Such strategic inducements, with their mixture of base and noble motives, achieve their paradigmatic expression in scenes of prayer.

In attending to the definitional moves Burke employs in his treatment of "secular prayer" in *Attitudes Toward History* and, later, of "prayer" in *Philosophy of Literary Form,* one can chart a significant development in Burke's thought about the rhetorical character of symbolic action, a development that will find its culmination in *A Rhetoric of Motives*. In that development, one thing especially stands out. Burke's term "prayer" in *Philosophy* enjoys a narrower, or more refined, reference than does his use of "secular prayer" in *Attitudes*. In *Attitudes,* aspects of the symbolic that Burke later comes to identify as "dream" and "chart" fall under his heading of "secular prayer," e.g., the naming of essences. Likewise, although he wishes to identify as "prayer" what some might term magic, Burke does not, in *Attitudes,* distinguish between the categorical domains of magic and prayer. By *Philosophy,* however, Burke is working out what emerges as a crucial distinction between magic and "religion," with religion now a more generalized term for prayer.

As Burke observes in a key passage, "If magic says, '*Let there be* such and such,' religion says, '*Please do* such and such.' The decree of magic, the petition of prayer" (*PLF* 4). For Burke, prayerful discourse emphasizes rhetoric's invitational character, its cooperative, rather than coercive nature. In sharp contrast to a magical, instrumental view of language, in which saying something effectively makes it so, the petitionary appeal is always a matter of persuasion, finding the correct words to move some audience. For Burke it is possible to distinguish, at least in theory, the "coercive command" from the "conducive request," even though Burke observes that in actual practice these strands are necessarily intertwined. And they may take both positive and negative form: "the spell and the counter-spell, the curse; the prayer and the prayer-in-reverse, oath, indictment, invective; the dream, and the dream gone sour, nightmare" (*PLF* 5).

This distinction between spell and prayer, between magic and religion, marks a significant way forward in Burke's characterization of rhetorical action. Interestingly, however, when Burke turns, in *A Rhetoric of Motives,* to rhetoric *per se,* he chooses not to do so through a terministic screen of "prayer." Rather, in what I contend is a highly significant re-formulation, the "offices" Burke has previously assigned to "prayer" and "secular prayer" are now largely subsumed into Burke's characterization of rhetoric itself. That is, the symbolic strategies involved in inducing an audience, strategies previously discussed in terms of "prayer," are brought together under the heading of rhetoric and its cognates, e.g., identification, persuasion. In some sense, Burke's pronouncements on "prayer" can be understood as anticipatory sketches on the nature of rhetorical action awaiting adequate scope within a comprehensive treatment of situations and strategies.

These pronouncements on prayer can thus be recognized as "pontifical." Indeed, they serve as a sort of bridge between Burke's earliest statement on rhetoric in *Counter-Statement* and his eventual return to rhetoric within the context of human motivation. Specifically, Burke's "Lexicon Rhetoricae" in *Counter-Statement,* which serves as a series of elaborations and refinements of his essays "Psychology and Form" and "The Poetic Process," can be understood as an effort to chart the rhetorical dimension of the aesthetic by identifying the principles informing the "contract" between artist and audience. "Form," Burke observes, involves "the creation of an appetite in the mind of the auditor, and the adequate satisfying of that appetite" (*CS* 31). Without abandoning his interest in the aesthetic, Burke broadens his inquiry beyond the literary, narrowly conceived, to embrace the full range of symbolic acts, including social acts of propanganda and other suasory discourse. In that expansion, prayer serves as a particularly appropriate touchstone, for it is a discourse at once highly formulaic (and as such concerned with the proper form of expression) and highly invested in efficacious results. Arguably, prayer is the discourse that most powerfully manifests the rhetorical character of language. Though Burke does not make this claim, it seems clear that prayer manifests the range of discursive features and effects that Burke will consider the province of rhetoric. While nowhere does Burke make such an assertion about prayer explicitly, his use of "prayer" to speak of matters he will later consider within the province of rhetoric suggests that such associations are implicit to his terminological practices. So if "rhetoric" goes underground in Burke's critical project, only to resurface later as Burke's term of terms, it is "prayer" that carries its terminological burdens in the interim.

When Burke finally returns to rhetoric, his ground-clearing task is to reclaim an intellectual tradition, one now grown suspect, and to reinvigorate that tradition in light of contemporary modes of inquiry. In securing space for rhetoric within contemporary disciplinary domains, Burke considers, once again, the issue of magic, particularly the widely shared perception that magic is a counter-logic to modern science. As a preparatory step to rhetoric's reclamation, Burke critiques a magic/science binary that would see in primitive practices of magic some failed and flawed effort now superseded by science, with its greater accuracy and objectivity. Specifically, Burke challenges an historical narrative whereby "magic is treated as an early uncritical attempt to do what science does, but under conditions where judgment and perception were impaired by the naively anthropomorphic belief that the impersonal forces of nature were motivated by personal designs" (*RM* 41). Under this scheme, Burke notes, "'rhetoric' has no systematic location" (41). And Burke seeks to "locate" rhetoric, whose "basic function" is "the use of words by human agents to form attitudes or to induce actions in other human agents" (41). This function, neither scientific nor magical in Burke's view, finds its epitome in the call for help. "The call for help," argues Burke, "is quite 'prejudiced'"; it is a form of "wishful thinking," one that is "hortatory" and "rhetorical" (41). As Burke further observes, a choice only between magic and science is a false dichotomy, for it offers "no bin in which to accurately place such a form of expression" (42).

This "call for help," of course, is nothing other than prayer's essential character as petition. Thus does rhetoric as a "third" way, as an antidote to an inaccurate dualism, emerge as a near-perfect synonym to

Burke's previous use of "prayer." Burke would have us see in magic an "erroneous and derived use of language" (*RM* 44). That is, for Burke

> the magical use of symbolism to affect natural processes by rituals and incantations was a mistaken transference of a proper linguistic function to an area for which it is not fit. The realistic use of addressed language to *induce action in people* became the magical use of addressed language to *induce motion in things* (things by nature alien to purely linguistic orders of motivation). (*RM* 42)

Rather than see rhetoric as a surviving component of primitive magic, Burke believes we come closer to an accurate account in seeing "the socializing aspects of magic" in terms of a "primitive rhetoric" (42). That is, magic performs vital regulative functions for the societies in which it is practiced, notwithstanding the misattribution of human agency on which magical thought depends.

The degree to which Burke fusses over the interplay among notions of rhetoric, magic, and science merits careful attention. For Burke, the stakes attendant to an ascendant *mythos* of scientific progress are, quite simply, enormous. Modern science enjoys the privilege of a dominant epistemology. Burke, therefore, approaches rhetoric from a perspective that sees in it an effective challenge to reigning orthodoxies of rationalistic objectivity, what Burke characterizes as "scientific realism," a habit of thinking that would reduce all effects to that of the material, to states of motion (*RM* 44). Burke claims for rhetoric a status he regards as equally realistic, "a realism of the *act*" (*RM* 44). That is, the essence of language is not ultimately referential, but rather, performative. In what is Burke's central statement on *homo rhetoricus*, rhetoric is envisioned in the widest terms possible as a binding force holding communities and selves together: "*For rhetoric as such is not rooted in any past condition of human society. It is rooted in an essential function of language itself, a function that is wholly realistic, and is continually born anew; the use of language as a symbolic means of inducing cooperation in beings that by nature respond to symbols*" (*RM* 43). Given present concerns to examine Burke's ideas in relation to prayer, his statement on the rhetorical function of language invites, indeed implicitly poses, a provocative question. What, precisely, is this range of beings whose cooperation may be induced by symbols, who "by nature" respond to symbols? What, for Burke, is the proper circumference of this linguistic circle?

A page earlier, Burke defines the "realistic use of addressed language to *induce action in people*" as a function that slides over into magic when language is employed to induce motion in things. Is it, therefore, surprising that Burke chooses "prayer" as a touchstone for the rhetorical character of language, given the "otherness" of prayer's prototypical audience: some non-human entity? Nowhere does Burke explicitly discuss prayer's apparent strangeness as a use of language to address non-human audiences. Instead, and significantly, Burke focuses on prayer's character as a language of address to *some* audience, human or otherwise. To the extent that prayer's audiences are experienced in anthropomorphic terms, the scene of prayer is one that extends outward the linguistic circle of human to human communication. For Burke prayer epitomizes the functionality of rhetoric, its capacities to forge identities, to sustain (or divide) communities, and to frame (or reframe) situations. Consequently, the character of the audiences addressed in prayer, even the specific content of such prayers, is not as significant for Burke as the character of the relationships enacted through prayer. Rather than eliminate such practices in an enlightened age (in which there remains fewer non-human entities to meaningfully address), Burke would, where their effects prove pernicious, see those practices reformed, so that prayer's utterances might become more accurate, more realistic responses to their encompassing situations.

Another way to frame this observation is to say that nowhere does Burke challenge the legitimacy of prayer on the basis of any failure to address "realistic" audiences. To the contrary, Burke's "agnostic" silence on this point suggests that it is the performative effects embodied in the formal acts of address that invest prayer with its significance as a "realistic" rhetorical act. To appreciate this significance, to understand prayer's role as a sign within a wider circle of linguistic acts, it is useful to follow Burke's suggestive lead. For Burke, prayer possesses a certain abstract quality. That is, prayer is already an abstracted scene of communication, one set apart from ordinary discourse. Though set apart, prayer nonetheless exemplifies language's most characteristic function as a medium of communication. Burke thus looks past specific ministrations of prayer, its wide range of illocutionary and perlocutionary effects, to recognize the degree to which prayer manifests the linguistic motive itself in especially potent form. That is, Burke is ultimately concerned with prayer as an epitome of the principle of communication embodying all scenes of communication.

Burke takes up this principle and teases out its implications most thoroughly in the latter stages of the *Rhetoric,* when he turns to an extensive treatment of "pure persuasion." Exploring how far one can go in ascertaining motives for rhetoric, Burke examines scenes of communication that come closest to owing their existence to a goal of maintaining communion, a communion established by discourse itself. Burke realizes that at the level of principle there is a type of communication that does not primarily seek advantage, whatever the motives that may have led, initially, to a communicative act. Burke likens such scenes of pure persuasion to the inherent pleasures of the game, in which winning is, often, less the object than is playing.

Burke stresses that "pure persuasion" is best understood *as* a principle, a tendency to which any rhetorical act may lean and never an absolute condition. As Burke observes, while "pure persuasion in the absolute sense exists nowhere, it can be present as a motivational ingredient in any rhetoric, no matter how intensely advantage-seeking such rhetoric may be" (269). Burke proceeds to illustrate how such rhetoric typically embodies a telltale "self-interference," that is, a principle of "standoffishness" that resists some final consummation. In a particularly eloquent passage, Burke observes that

> Pure persuasion involves the saying of something, not for the extra-verbal advantage to be got by the saying, but because of a satisfaction intrinsic to the saying. It summons because it likes the feel of the summons. It would be nonplused if the summons were answered. It attacks because it likes the syllables of vituperation. It would be horrified if, each time it finds a way of saying, "Be damned," it really sent a soul to rot in hell. It routinely says, "This is so," purely and simply because this is so. (269)

Here one finds echoes of Burke's earlier observations on the world-creating powers of language in the hands of children (or adults) who would ordain that *this* is *that* by linguistic fiat. In this case, however, it is not the aspect of magical thought (a matter of naming essences) implicit in the verbal decree that Burke highlights, but the possibilities for perfection embodied within the form. In contrast to mere "phatic communion," or talk for the sake of talking, "pure persuasion" is more intensely purposive. It becomes an end in itself.

Approached from this avenue, prayer can be understood as a discursive space in which it is possible to practice a perfection, or purity, of expression only rarely granted within other scenes. As Burke argues, this is a purity of purpose achieved through awareness of and continual maintenance of some distance between speakers and addressees, a distancing that depends upon the preservation of what Burke describes as the mysteries of courtship. Burke identifies the essential ingredient of courtship as the recognition of difference *in kind* between classes of beings, e.g., royal persons and subjects, lovers and their beloved, gods and humans, actors and their audiences. For Burke, the maintenance of this categorical, social distance is fundamental to the operations of rhetoric. As Burke explains in a key passage:

> In its essence, communication involves the use of verbal symbols for the purposes of appeal. Thus, it splits formally into the three elements of speaker, speech, and spoken-to, with the speaker so shaping his speech as to "commune with" the spoken-to. This purely technical pattern is the precondition of *all* appeal. And "standoffishness" is necessary to the form, because without it the appeal could not be maintained. For if union is complete, what incentive can there be for appeal? Rhetorically, there can be courtship only insofar as there is division. Hence only through interference can could one court continually, thereby perpetuating genuine "freedom of rhetoric." (271)

Rhetoric, for Burke, thus depends upon the internal checks imposed upon our impulses to acquire, which find their motive and expression in acts of interference. As Burke puts it, a principle of interference gives rise to a "feeling that one should not 'take things,' but should court them, show gratitude for them, apologize for killing them" (271). Self-interference gives rise, Burke claims, to attitudes of piety and acts of ritual that serve to frustrate the purely self-interested motives that might otherwise attend.

To be clear, Burke is not suggesting that prayer, as a form of "pious" communication, is necessarily more pure, less selfish, than other persuasive practices of language, any more than lovers are always disinterested in the objects of their affection or hunters in the objects of their pursuit. What Burke is saying, however, is that the motive of persuasion itself can aspire, by a process of dialectic, to a purity of interest in which communication serves as an end unto itself, an end thus requiring "interference" for its perpetuation, since successful persuasion "dies" (274). Various forms of self-interference in any activity are for Burke an indication of the motive of pure persuasion at work.

At the heart of Burke's pronouncements on pure persuasion is the key insight that the act of persuasion is "implicit in language itself" (274). Proceeding from this starting point, Burke can point to necessary correspondences between the linguistic and the social, correspondences that take the form of categories—a principle of division—separating people, things and abstractions into not only different kinds but also a hierarchically ordered range of differences. Once a hierarchical principle is admitted, there must be admitted as well some ultimate term, some "god-term" as a completion of the linguistic process. As Burke puts it, given that language is "essentially a means of transcending brute objects, there is implicit in it the 'temptation' to come upon the idea of 'God' as the *ultimate* transcendence" (276). Put differently, the eventual "discovery" of ultimates, which properly speaking exist nowhere in nature, is for Burke a necessary outcome of our linguistic inheritance, a "dialectical transcending of reality through symbols" that reaches its culmination in "pure persuasion, absolute communication, beseechment for itself alone, praise and blame so universalized as to have no assignable object" (275). In an explicit reference to prayer, Burke further observes that "considered dialectically, prayer, as pure beseechment, would be addressed not to an *object* (which might 'answer' the prayer by providing booty) but to the *hierarchic principle itself,* where the answer is implicit in the address" (276).

Thus does Burke chart the dialectical "leap" by which it becomes possible to transcend the physical order, and even the human social order, by expanding the range of entities, abstractions, powers, and principles—all anthropomorphized to one degree or another—that one discovers it is now possible, at least for someone, to address. Proceeding by this "verbal route," Burke observes, "from words for positive things to titles, thence to an order among titles, and finally to a title of titles, we come as far as rhetoric-and-dialectic can take us" (277). Consequently, prayer is addressed to some "title of titles," for the inherent satisfaction attendant upon doing so would be, in principle, persuasion at its most pure. But note that Burke does not claim that all prayer is a type of pure persuasion or that prayer, because it is addressed to various divine entities, is necessarily purer than other forms of discourse. To the contrary, Burke recognizes that all symbolic acts, prayer included, are a complex of motives. One of those motives, however, never to be discounted (Burke is at pains to stress), is inherent in the formal act of appeal itself. While this appeal is implicit in all communicative acts, it is especially prominent in the performance of prayer, given prayer's highly ritualized and formal character. As Burke observes of pure persuasion in general, "the important consideration is that, in any device, the ultimate form (paradigm or idea) of that device is present, and is acting. And this form would be the 'purity'" (273–74).

If the essence of prayer is, as Burke claims, a scene of petition, the verbal appeal in all its purity, then clearly too prayer is a scene in which its performers recognize themselves as lower-ordered beings appealing to certain higher-ordered beings within a structure of hierarchy. While this scene is familiar to most anyone, what is less obvious, apart from Burke's speculative insights here, is the implication of this scene for understanding the operations of rhetoric in wider, more "diluted" contexts. For if prayer and rhetoric function as nearly synonymous terms, for the reasons Burke supplies, the implication to be made is that rhetors, when being wholly realistic, must realize the extent to which they necessarily persuade "upward." The object of one's appeal, if that appeal is truly rhetorical and not, finally, magical, is always higher up the ladder of hierarchy. To say this is to go beyond the observation that one should demonstrate (or actually have respect) for one's audience. It is also to claim, as Burke implicitly does, that absent a fundamental sense of reverence, piety, mystery in our attitudes toward the objects of our address, we are as rhetoricians quite lost.

Perhaps such Burkean perspectives on rhetoric's prospects find apt illustration in Burke's own composing efforts in the medium of prayer. As Burke observes in *Attitudes,* it is possible to utter prayers both better and worse, more accurate and less accurate. Indeed, Burke himself provides what he certainly expects to be taken as instructive instances of each. Consider, first, Burke's "Dialectician's Hymn," where Burke provides an eloquent, if also a vaguely satiric, example of prayer's formal character as a language of appeal. Addressed to the "Logos," that most ultimate of ultimate terms, this hymn exhibits a range of optative statements (in the form of "let" and "may") that both recognize and reinforce an ongoing relationship between this prayer's speakers and its addressee:

> May we be Thy delegates
> In parliament assembled,
> Parts of Thy wholeness.
> And in our conflicts
> Correcting one another. (*LSA* 55)

Although formally in the mode of petition, effectively seeking "divine" assistance for its desired end, this hymn's primary speech act is arguably that of a declaration of intention to do or to become something, since the hymn's intrinsic purpose is to reinvest in a system of perceived obligations that define a dialectician's service to dialectic's "god," the Logos.

This reinvestment is accomplished through the symbolic resources actualized in the formal strategies of appeal, above all, through the rhetorical power of appeal itself, since appeals, whether in the form of requests or commands, "logically" necessitate a response. Secondly, the appeal articulates the very situation it would hope to enact; in reviewing perceived obligations to the Logos, the hymn is already engaged in meeting those obligations. Indeed, its specificity in naming those obligations contributes persuasively to the seriousness of the appeal. Finally, the appeal must be performed by this hymn's human speakers. At the level of form, this hymn requires that its speakers enter into a scene of address, dramatically performing the "we" that would address a "thee"; how fully this "we" may do so depends upon the degree of intentionality motivating each of its performer's words. Like all hymns, this is one that may be performed piously, albeit mechanically, or one delivered with great intensity of feeling and commitment. It can be strictly ceremonial or quite purposive.

An additional overlay of rhetorical action implicit in this scene is the presence, whether explicitly figured as addressee or not, of additional human audiences who effectively "overhear" a hymn addressed to another audience. Whatever the ontological status of prayer's addressee, at least one audience, the audience of the prayer's speakers themselves, is always present in the scene of prayer. At a minimum, of course, this audience can be understood as a locus of rhetorical action, whereby one's prayer serves as a form of "roundabout appeal" ultimately addressed to oneself (*RM* 44). This is certainly the case, but admitting this does not admit the entire story, for the performance of prayer cannot simply be reduced to indirect strategies of auto-suggestion. If Burke's attention to form tells us anything, it is that prayer is always something more than merely a stylized form of talking to oneself.

As the textual record of Burke's hymn suggests, prayer admits of a public character as well as a private character, even where it is performed individually or in silence. Invariably, prayer owes its formality to some imagined scene of auditors who may stand in judgment of its propriety. Where prayer *is* public, its audience is a complex construction consisting of prayer's speakers, various other over-hearers who may (or may not) vicariously participate in the prayer, and, of course, prayer's explicitly figured addressee. Where prayer is also communal, a collective enterprise, as is the case with hymns—whose speakers experience themselves as a chorus—prayer's speakers ideally achieve solidarity through their performance. Without simplifying the complexities attendant to such scenes, Burke's identification of rhetoric as address summarizes the identities by which speakers and audiences are multiply configured in and through acts of address.

Burke's contributions to a theory of prayer find further embodiment in this hymn, which reflexively dramatizes the interplay between dual logics of appeal and statement. Its implicit narrative is one of ever-developing integration of human speakers (and those for whom they would speak) and divine addressee—configured here as the "Logos," the spirit of discourse that makes prayer itself possible—into an harmonious whole as well as ever-evolving movement toward an imagined state of linguistic perfection. By seeking to articulate its objectives as accurately as possible, this hymn presents itself as counterpart to the inevitable disputation that marks human conduct. Here, at least, this prayer (and all prayer) suggests, purpose is pure; and where not yet pure, it will strive to become so. In this respect, one may see in this prayer a tendency for prayer in general to function as a discursive space in which possible futures are worked out prior to their final enactment. In this sense, prayer is something of a "rehearsal for living," to paraphrase Burke's characterization of literature as "equipment for living" and to echo Burke's famous essay on the role of proverbial wisdom (*PLF* 293)

So, given Burke's concerns, ought we to regard this particular prayer as ultimately serious? In commenting on this "Dialectician's Hymn," Burke warns us that here "the distinction between belief, make-believe, and mock-belief is left fluctuant" (*PLF* 448). It is thus important to recognize that Burke's serio-comic disclaimer presents a characteristically Burkean dialectic of attachment and detachment, one that enables Burke (and quite a few others) to embrace the *form* of prayer, its linguistic structure, its performative possibilities, its moral energies, without necessarily subscribing to any particular credo. In the act of performing this hymn, one effectively believes it, even if, under different contexts, a critical distance obtains about its theology. Of course, it is useful to note as well that Burke relies here upon a distinctly dramatic persona of the dialectician rather than presenting this prayer as one possessed of an authentic Burkean voice. This is a prayer an ardent dialectician might utter, albeit one filtered through the ironic distancing of a playful rhetor such as Burke. And yet is there not something discernibly heartfelt and urgent here in Burke's dramatized appeal to the Logos? Is this not a prayer that Burke himself, as dialectician, could conceivably offer?

Indeed, as this example demonstrates, a Burkean approach to prayer provides a means for avoiding cynicism with respect to religious stirrings as the inevitable price for a critical perspective. In this respect, a second prayer penned by Burke provides an instructive contrast to his hymnal offering. In the opening to his "Newspaper Editor's Prayer," Burke presents a praying voice quite different in spirit from the dialectician, if also not an unfamiliar one:

> I pray thee, God,
> Send us for tomorrow's copy
> Some great flood or earthquake or disastrously erupting volcano
> Or picturesquely havoc-bearing storm
> Or other natural calamity such as we
> In piety
> Call "acts of God."
>
> Or may there transpire some big new step forwards toward
>   greater global malice
> Or may the peaceful work of the U.N.

Be disrupted by a new flare-up, with corresponding walk-out.
("Thinking of the Body" *LSA* 330–31)

Here remains the formal appeal—it is unmistakably a prayer in form—but the attitude embodied in the text could not be more different from that of the previous case. Resolutely self-absorbed, the praying subject revealed by this text is never more than the sum of its acquisitive wants. Bad news sells newspapers. Here, however, there exists no expectation for genuine communication, no possibility for personal transformation. While this prayer will inevitably be answered—for it wants only what it is entitled to expect in any case—we can also say that this is a prayer that will forever remain unheard, not least of which by its speaker. As a genuine act of address, it fails miserably. Moreover, while we may take comfort in the discovery that we are not a suggestible audience for its particularly incantatory appeal, we likely do so in the realization that there exist a great many similar prayers, in both secular and religious guise, that would prove equally contemptible were we to accurately hear them. Yet here, however, this prayer points to the very real possibility that we, like the newspaper editor, will not hear many prayers accurately, that, being blind to the partisan nature of our petitions, we will also be deaf to what distinguishes a good prayer from a bad and thus prayer on what Burke identifies as too simple a level. Indeed, as is often the case, for one's particular prayer to be answered, it is also necessary that someone else's prayer remain unanswered.

Missing from this prayer-in-reverse is, in a word, piety. For Burke, piety is a sense of "*what properly goes with what*" (*PC* 74). As Burke observes in *Permanence and Change*, "Santayana has somewhere defined piety as loyalty to the sources of one's being. Such a notion should suggest that piety is not strictly confined to the religious sphere. It would be present when the potter molds the clay to exactly the form which completely gratifies his sense of how it ought to be" (71). Clearly, a sense of piety is akin to the attitudes instantiated by prayer. For Burke, prayer distills the motive of piety, in the absence of which the prayerful appeal becomes barbarous. Yet as the "Newspaper Editor's Prayer" reveals, we are easily deaf to the impiety of our petitions. As a formal vehicle for the linguistic embodiment of attitudes, then, prayer is morally neutral. One can pray for good or for ill. By juxtaposing these two particular prayers, Burke suggests that the poorest prayers, the least accurate, suffer from a lack of imagination of some greater, as yet unrealized possibilities. With a spirit of piety, one that does reduce one's audience to the merely instrumental, the language of prayer is capable of transcending present conflicts and travails through an enlightened vision of some greater whole.

Whether it is possible to achieve transcendent effects in a language of secular prayer—that is, through acts of address that do not call upon ultimate audiences such as divine beings—is one issue Burke does not directly address. However, Burke's own stylized prayers, dramatizing fundamental stances toward piety and purpose, suggest what his analysis of pure persuasion concludes: that *some* god-term must inevitably occupy the title slot for our prayers, secular or religious, if they are to have fully transformative effects. If not "God" or "Beauty," then something else will call out to be addressed in tones reverent and plaintive. At least, it seems, this appears to be Burke's hope, for the alternative to imperfect prayer is no prayer at all, in a cosmos denuded of all mystery, the source from which prayer ultimately springs.

Consider, finally, one last Burkean voice, this time that of John Neal, the narrator of *Towards a Better Life,* who concludes one of his extended meditations with this sober musing:

> If that day comes when all humanity is busied with its prosperity in human terms, and the miraculous thread of prayer is broken, then will our ingratitude have snapped the continuity of existence. In ages of dwindling piety, let adept worshippers keep long vigil, lest there arise some fatal moment of lapse when no thread of prayer joins us to vital forces and the props and underpinnings of the universe are thus removed. (206)

For what if the Burkean voice in *Towards a Better Life* is correct? Burke's critical attention to prayer reminds us that our bonds of connection with one another are fragile indeed, and that it is through honest, pious prayer, of one form of another, that those bonds are held together.

Works Cited

Adell, Sandra. "The Big E(llison)'s Texts and Intertexts: Eliot, Burke, and the Underground Man." *CLA Journal* 37 (1994): 377–401.

Adler, Barbara J. "'They Are Us': Identification Strategies in the Rhetoric of Two Lutheran Church Organizations." Diss. Wayne State University, 1993.

Adorno, Theodor. "Cultural Criticism and Society." *Prisms*. Trans. Samuel and Shierry Weber. Cambridge, MA: MIT UP, 1982. 19–34.

—. "On Lyric Poetry and Society." *Notes to Literature*. Vol 1. Trans. Shierry Weber Nicholsen. New York: Columbia UP, 1991. 37–54.

Albrecht, James M. "Saying Yes and Saying No: Individualist Ethics in Ellison, Burke, and Emerson." *PMLA* 114.1 (January 1999): 46–63.

Ammons, A. R. "Information Density." Conference. Seton Hall University. South Orange, NJ, Dec. 1986.

—. "Information Density." *Sumerian Vistas*. New York and London: Norton, 1987. 71.

Apollinaire, Guillaume. "Horse Calligram." *Poems for the Millennium: The University of California Book of Modern and Postmodern Poetry*. Vol. 1. Ed. Jerome Rothenberg and Pierre Joris. Berkeley: U of California P, 1995. 119.

Aristotle. *On Rhetoric: A Theory of Civic Discourse*. Trans. George Kennedy. New York: Oxford UP, 1991.

—. *Politics*. Trans. T. A. Sinclair. New York: Penguin, 1985.

Augustine. *Confessions*. Commentary by James J. O'Donnell. 3 Vols. Oxford: Clarendon Press; Oxford: Oxford UP, 1992.

—. *Confessions*. Trans, and Introd. Henry Chadwick. Oxford: Oxford UP, 1991.

—. *De doctrina christiana*. Ed. and Trans. R. P. H. Green. Oxford: Clarendon Press, 1995.

—. *On Christian Doctrine*. Trans. D. W. Robertson, Jr. Macmillan/Library of Liberal Arts, 1958.

"Auto Safety Groups Want GM C-K Pickup Truck Deal Scuttled." *NewsEDGE*. Waltham, MA: Desktop Data, 2 July 1996.

Bailey, Bill. *Spin Tactics: A Guide to Guerrilla Media Relations.* Saginaw, MI: Glovebox Guidebooks of America, 2000.
Benston, Kimberly W., ed. *Speaking for You: The Vision of Ralph Ellison.* Washington: Howard UP, 1990.
Bewley, Marius. *The Complex Fate: Hawthorne, Henry James, and Some Other American Writers.* New York: Golden Press, 1967.
Bizzell, Patricia, and Bruce Herzberg, eds. *The Rhetorical Tradition: Readings from Classical Times to the Present.* 2nd ed. Boston: Bedford-St. Martins, 2001.
Blair, Carol. "Contested Histories of Rhetoric: The Politics of Preservation, Progress, and Change." *Landmark Essays on Contemporary Rhetoric.* Ed. Thomas B. Farrell. Mahwah, New Jersey: Hermagoras Press, 1998. 181–213.
Blake, William. *The Complete Poetry and Prose of William Blake.* Rev. ed. Ed. David V. Erdman. New York: Doubleday, 1988.
Blum, W. C. "A Poetry of Perspectives: A Review of the Book of Moments." *Poetry* 86.1 (March 1956): 362–66.
Booth, Wayne. "Kenneth Burke's Religious Rhetoric: 'God-Terms' and the Ontological Proof." Jost and Olmsted 25–46.
—. "Kenneth Burke's Ways of Knowing." *Critical Inquiry* 1.1 (Sept. 1974): 1–22.
—. *Modern Dogma and the Rhetoric of Assent.* Chicago: University of Chicago, 1974.
—. *The Rhetoric of Fiction.* Chicago: U of Chicago P, 1983.
—. "Rhetoric and Religion: Are They Essentially Wedded?" *Radical Pluralism and Truth: David Tracy and the Hermeneutics of Religion.* Ed. Werner G. Jeanrod and Jennifer Rike. New York: Crossroad, 1991. 62–80.
—. *The Rhetoric of Rhetoric: The Quest for Effective Communication.* Malden, MA: Blackwell, 2004.
—. "Richard McKeon's Pluralism: The Path between Dogmatism and Relativism." Garver and Buchanan 213–30, 265–70 (notes).
—. "Systematic Wonder: The Rhetoric of Secular Religions." *Journal of the American Academy of Religion* 53.4 (1985): 677–702.
Boyle, Marjorie O'Rourke. "The Prudential Augustine: The Virtuous Structure and Sense of His *Confessions.*" *Recherches Augustiniennes* 22 (1987): 129–50.
—. "Religion." *Encyclopedia of Rhetoric.* Ed. Thomas O. Sloane. Oxford: Oxford UP, 2001. 662–72.
—. "Rhetorical Theology: Charity Seeking Charity." Jost and Olmsted 87–96.
Brown, Michael E. "Identification and Some Conditions of Organizational Involvement." *Administrative Science Quarterly* 14 (1969): 346–55.

Burke, Kenneth. *Attitudes Toward History.* 2 vols. New York: New Republic, 1937.
—. *Attitudes Toward History.* 1937. Rev. 3rd ed. Berkeley: U of California P, 1984.
—. "Auscultation, Creation, Revision." *Extensions of the Burekeian System.* Ed. James W. Chesebro. Tuscaloosa: U of Alabama P, 1993. 42–172.
—. *Book of Moments: Poems 1915–1954.* Los Altos, CA: Hermes, 1955.
—. *Collected Poems, 1915–1967.* Berkeley: U of California P, 1968.
—. *Counter-Statement.* 1931. Berkeley: U of California P, 1968.
—. "Dancing with Tears in My Eyes." *Critical Inquiry* 1.1 (Sept. 1974): 23–31.
—. "Dialectician's Hymn." *Language as Symbolic Action: Essays on Life, Literature and Method.* Berkeley: U of California P, 1966. 55-57.
—. *Dramatism and Development.* Barre, MA: Clark UP, 1972.
—. "A Dramatistic View of the Origins of Language." *Language as Symbolic Action: Essays on Life, Literature and Method.* Berkeley: U of California P, 1966. 419-79.
—. "Fact, Inference, and Proof in the Analysis of Literary Symbolism." *Terms for Order.* Ed. Stanley Edgar Hyman. Bloomington: Indiana UP, 1964. 145–72.
—. "Freud—and the Analysis of Poetry" *The Philosophy of Literary Form: Studies in Symbolic Action.* 1940. 3rd ed. Berkeley: U of California P, 1973. 258–92.
—. *A Grammar of Motives.* Berkeley: U of California P, 1969.
—. *The Humane Particulars: The Collected Letters of William Carlos Williams and Kenneth Burke.* Ed. James H. East. Columbia: U of South Carolina P, 2003.
—. "Ideology and Myth." *Accent* 7 (Summer 1947): 195–205.
—. *Language as Symbolic Action: Essays on Life, Literature, and Method.* Berkeley: U of California P, 1966.
—. *Late Poems, 1968–1993: Attitudinizing Verse-wise, While Fending for One's Own Selph; And in a Style Somewhat Artificially Colloquial.* Ed. Julie Whitaker and David Blakesley. Columbia: U of South Carolina P, 2005.
—. Letter to Denis Donoghue. 1 Jan. 1980. Kenneth Burke Papers, Rare Books and Manuscripts, Special Collections, The Pennsylvania State University Libraries.
—. Letter to Howard Nemerov. 2 September 1974. Kenneth Burke Papers, Rare Books and Manuscripts, Special Collections, The Pennsylvania State University Libraries.
—. Letter to Malcolm Cowley. 8 September 1933. Kenneth Burke Papers. Rare Books and Manuscripts, Special Collections, The Pennsylvania State University Libraries.

—. Letter to Malcolm Cowley. 16 March 1955. Kenneth Burke Papers. Rare Books and Manuscripts, Special Collections, The Pennsylvania State University Libraries.
—. Letter to Matthew Josephson. 27 December 1921. Matthew Josephson Papers. Beinecke Rare Book and Manuscript Library, Yale University.
—. *Letters from Kenneth Burke to William H. Rueckert, 1959–1987.* Ed. William H. Rueckert. West Lafayette, IN: Parlor P, 2003.
—. Letters to Richard McKeon. 24 October 1934, 19 May 1942, 6 June 1976, and 24 December 1979. Richard McKeon Papers, Joseph Regenstein Library, University of Chicago. Carbon copies of the 1976 and 1979 letters are in the Kenneth Burke Papers at the Pattee Library at Pennsylvania State University.
—. "Methodological Repression and/or Strategies of Containment." *Critical Inquiry* 5.2 (Winter 1978): 401–17.
—. "Musical Chronicle." *The Dial* Dec. 1927: 535–39.
—. "Musical Chronicle." *The Dial* Apr. 1928: 356–58.
—. "Musical Chronicle." *The Dial* Dec. 1928: 529–32.
—. *Permanence and Change: An Anatomy of Purpose.* 1935. Rev. 3rd ed. Berkeley: U of California P, 1984.
—. *Permanence and Change: An Anatomy of Purpose.* New York: Bobbs-Merrill, 1965.
—. *The Philosophy of Literary Form: Studies in Symbolic Action.* 1940. 3rd ed. Berkeley: U of California P, 1973.
—. "Poetics and Communication." *Perspectives in Education, Religion, and the Arts.* Ed. Howard E. Kiefer and Milton K. Munitz. Albany: State U of New York P, 1970. 401–18.
—. "Ralph Ellison's Trueblooded *Bildungsroman.*" Benston 349–59.
—. "Rhetoric and Poetics." *Language as Symbolic Action.* Berkeley: U of California P, 1966. 295–307.
—. *A Rhetoric of Motives.* 1950. Berkeley: U of California P, 1969.
—. *The Rhetoric of Religion: Studies in Logology.* 1961. Berkeley: U of California P, 1970.
—. "Semantic and Poetic Meaning." *The Philosophy of Literary Form.* 3rd ed. Berkeley: U of California P, 1973. 136–67.
—. "Sensation, Memory, and Imitation / and Story." Henderson and Williams 202–5.
—. "The Study of Symbolic Action." *Chimera* 1 (Spring 1942): 7–16.
—. "Terministic Screens." *Language as Symbolic Action.* Berkeley: U of California P, 1966. 44-62.
—. "The Thinking of the Body." *Psychoanalytic Review* 50 (Fall 1953): 25–68. Rpt. in *Language* as Symbolic Action. 308–43.
—. *Towards a Better Life: Being a Series of Epistles, or Declamations.* 1932. 2nd ed. Berkeley: U of California P, 1966.

—. "The Unburned Bridges of Poetics, Or, How Keep Poetry Pure?" *The Centennial Review* 8 (Fall 1964): 391–97.
—. "'Watchful of Hermetics to Be Strong in Hermeneutics': Selections from 'Poetics, Dramatistically Considered.'" 1958. Henderson and Williams 35–80.
—. "William Carlos Williams: A Critical Appreciation." *William Carlos Williams*. Ed. Charles Angoff. Rutherford, N.J.: Fairleigh Dickinson UP, 1974. 15–19.
—. "Words as Deeds." *Centrum* 3.2 (Fall 1975): 147–68.
—, et al. "Dramatism as Ontology or Epistemology: A Symposium." *Communication Quarterly* 33.1 (1985): 17–33.
Butler, Samuel. *Hudibras*. Ed. John Wilders. Oxford: The Clarendon Press, 1967.
Bygrave, Stephen. *Kenneth Burke: Rhetoric and Ideology*. London: Routledge, 1993.
Cameron, Sharon. *Lyric Time: Dickinson and the Limits of Genre*. Baltimore: Johns Hopkins UP, 1979.
Cheney, George. "The Corporate Person (Re)presents Itself." *Rhetorical and Critical Approaches to Public Relations*. Ed. Elizabeth L. Toth and Robert L. Heath. Hillsdale, NJ: Erlbaum, 1992. 165–83.
—. "On the Facts of the Text as the Basis of Human Communication Research." *Communication Yearbook*. Vol. 11. Ed. J. A. Anderson. Newbury Park, NJ: Sage, 1988. 455-81.
—. "On the Various and Changing Meanings of Organizational Membership: A Field Study of Organizational Identification." *Communication Monographs* 50 (1983): 342–62.
—. *Rhetoric in an Organizational Society: Managing Multiple Identities*. Columbia: U of South Carolina P, 1991.
—. "The Rhetoric of Identification and the Study of Organizational Communication." *Quarterly Journal of Speech* 69 (1983): 143–58.
—. "Toward an Ethic of Identification." Kenneth Burke Conference. Kenneth Burke Society. Philadelphia. March, 1984.
Cheney, George, and Greg Frenette. "Persuasion and Organization: Values, Logics, and Accounts in Contemporary Corporate Public Discourse. *The Ethical Nexus*. Ed. C. Conrad. Norwood, NJ: Ablex, 1993. 49–74.
Cheney, George, and J. J. McMillan. "Organizational Rhetoric and the Practice of Criticism." *Journal of Applied Communication Research* 18 (1990): 93–114.
Cheney, George, and Philip K. Tompkins. "Coming to Terms with Organizational Identification and Commitment." *Central States Speech Journal* 38 (1987): 1–15.
Cheney, George, and Steven L. Vibbert. "Corporate Discourse: Public Relations and Issue Management. *Handbook of Organizational Communica-*

tions: An Interdisciplinary Perspective. Ed. Fredrick M. Jablin, Linda L. Putnam, Kenneth H. Roberts, & Lynn W. Porter. Newbury Park, CA: Sage, 1987. 165–94.

Chesebro, James W. "Extensions of the Burkean System." *Quarterly Journal of Speech* 78 (1992): 356–68.

Clark, Katrina, and Michael Holquist. *Mikhail Bakhtin.* Cambridge, MA: Harvard UP, 1984.

Colish, Marcia. *The Mirror of Language.* Rev. ed. Lincoln: U of Nebraska P, 1983.

Conley, Thomas M. *Rhetoric in the European Tradition.* New York: Longman, 1990.

Conrad, Joseph. *Heart of Darkness.* Ed. Robert Kimbrough. NY: Norton, 1963.

Cowley, Malcolm. Letter to Kenneth Burke. 1 February 1924. Jay 155–56.

Crable, Bryan. "Race and *A Rhetoric of Motives:* Kenneth Burke's Dialogue with Ralph Ellison." *Rhetoric Society Quarterly* 33.3 (2003): 5–25.

Cragan, John F., and Donald C. Shields. *Symbolic Theories in Applied Communication Research: Bormann, Burke and Fisher.* Cresskill, NJ: Hampton, 1995.

Crusius, Timothy W. "Kenneth Burke on his 'Morbid Selph': The Collected Poems as Comedy." *CEA Critic* 43.4 (May 1981): 18–32.

Damon, S. Foster. *A Blake Dictionary: The Ideas and Symbols of William Blake.* Rev. ed. Hanover: UP of New England, 1988.

Davidson, Donald. "The White Spirituals and Their Historian." *The Sewanee Review* 51 (1943): 589–98.

Davies, Donald. "Review of *Book of Moments.*" *Shenandoah* 7 (Autumn 1955): 93–95.

Derrida, Jacques. *Of Grammatology.* 1967. Trans. Gayatri Chakravorty Spivak. Baltimore: Johns Hopkins UP, 1976.

de Tocqueville, Alexis. *Democracy in America.* 2 vols. New York: Vintage, 1990.

Donoghue, Denis. *Adam's Curse.* Notre Dame: U of Notre Dame P, 2001.

—. *Being Modern Together.* Richard Ellmann Lectures in Modern Literature. No. 2.Atlanta: Scholar's Press, 1991.

—. *Connoisseurs of Chaos.* New York: Macmillan, 1965.

—. "K.B.—In Memory," *Sewanee Review* 102.3 (Summer 1994): 443–46.

—. *Reading America.* New York: Knopf, 1987.

—. *Speaking of Beauty.* New Haven: Yale UP, 2003.

Duffey, Bernard I. "Reality as Language: Kenneth Burke's Theory of Poetry." *Western Review* 12 (Spring 1948): 132–45.

Duncan, Hugh Dalziel. "Communication in Society." *Critical Responses to Kenneth Burke, 1924–1966.* Ed. William Rueckert. Minneapolis: U of Minnesota P, 1969. 407–20.

DuPlessis, Rachel Blau. *Genders, Races, and Religious Cultures in Modern American Poetry, 1908–1934.* Cambridge: Cambridge UP, 2001.
Eagleton, Terry. *The Ideology of the Aesthetic.* Cambridge, UK: Blackwell, 1990.
Eaton, Robert J., Alex Trotman,, and John F. Smith Jr. Letter to the President of the United States. 1994, Nov. 10.
Eddy, Beth. *The Rites of Identity: The Religious Naturalism and Cultural Criticism of Kenneth Burke and Ralph Ellison.* Princeton: Princeton UP, 2003.
Ellison, Ralph. *The Collected Essays of Ralph Ellison.* Ed. John F. Callahan. New York: Random House, 1995.
—. *Invisible Man.* New York: Signet, 1952.
—. *Juneteenth.* Ed. John F. Callahan. New York: Random House, 1999.
Ellison, Ralph, and David L. Carson. "Ralph Ellison: Twenty Years After." *Studies in American Fiction* 1 (1973): 1–23.
Ellison, Ralph, Ishmael Reed, Quincy Troupe, and Steve Cannon. "The Essential Ellison: An Interview." *Y'Bird Reader* 1 (1977): 130–59.
Ellison, Ralph, Robert B. Stepto, and Michael S. Harper. "Study and Experience: An Interview with Ralph Ellison." *Massachusetts Review* 18 (1977): 417–35.
Empson, William. *Seven Types of Ambiguity.* Norfolk: New Directions, 1953.
Essick, Robert N. *William Blake and the Language of Adam.* Oxford: Clarendon, 1989.
Farrell, Thomas. "From Semantics to Praxis: Some Old Tricks for the New Pluralism." Garver and Buchanan 189–212, 263–65 (notes).
"Feds Want GM Pickup Probe." *Detroit News* 3 December 1992: 1.
Fish, Stanley. *Doing What Comes Naturally: Change, Rhetoric, and the Practice of Theory in Literary and Legal Studies.* Durham: Duke UP, 1989.
Forrest, Leon. "Luminosity from the Lower Frequencies." Benston 308–21.
Foss, Sonja K. "Retooling an Image: Chrysler Corporation's Rhetoric of Redemption." *Western Journal of Speech Communication* 48 (1984): 75–91.
—, Karen A. Foss, and Robert Trapp. *Contemporary Perspectives on Rhetoric.* Prospect Heights, IL: Waveland P, 1985.
Frank, Armin Paul. *Kenneth Burke.* New York: Twayne, 1969.
Freccero, John. "Logology: Burke on St. Augustine." White and Brose 52–67.
Frye, Northrop. "Approaching the Lyric." *Lyric Poetry: Beyond New Criticism.* Eds. Chaviva Hošek and Patricia Parker. Ithaca: Cornell UP, 1985. 31–37.
Garver, Eugene. *Aristotle's Rhetoric: An Art of Character.* Chicago: U of Chicago P, 1994.

Garver, Eugene, and Richard Buchanan, Eds. *Pluralism in Theory and Practice: Richard McKeon and American Philosophy.* Nashville: Vanderbilt UP, 2000.

The Gene Harris Trio Plus One. Concord 4303. Perf. Gene Harris, Piano; Ray Brown, bass; Mickey Roker, drums; with Stanley Turrentine, tenor saxophone. Recorded at The Blue Note in New York City, 1985. NPR. KUER, Salt Lake City. 12 Sept. 2001.

General Motors Corporation. *Abbreviated Chronology of Key Events that Occurred Regarding GM's 1973–1987 Full-size C/K Pickups.* Detroit: General Motors Corporation, 25 Jan. 1995.

—. *General Motors Statement on Data Submitted to NHTSA.* Detroit: General Motors Corporation, 2 Dec. 1992.

Gilbert, Sandra L., and Susan Gubar. *The Madwoman in the Attic: The Woman Writer and the Nineteenth-Century Literary Imagination.* New Haven: Yale UP, 1979.

Girard, René. *The Scapegoat.* Trans. Yvonne Frecerro. Baltimore: The Johns Hopkins UP, 1986.

—. *Violence and the Sacred.* Trans. Patrick Gregory. Baltimore: The Johns Hopkins UP, 1977.

Greimas, Algirdas Julien. *On Meaning: Selected Writings in Semiotic Theory.* Trans. Paul J. Perron and Frank H. Collins. Minneapolis: U of Minnesota P, 1987.

Gross, Michael, and Mary Beth Averill. "Evolution and Patriarchal Myths of Scarcity and Competition." *Discovering Reality: Feminist Perspectives On Epistemology, Metaphysics, Methodology, and Philosophy of Science.* Ed. Sandra Harding and Merrill B. Hintikka. Dordrecht, Holland: D. Reidel, 1983. 71–96.

Hall, Douglas T., and Benjamin Schneider. "Correlates of Organizational Identification as a Function of Career Pattern and Organizational Type." *Administrative Science Quarterly* 17 (1972): 340–50.

Handelman, Susan. *The Slayers of Moses: The Emergence of Rabbinic Interpretation in Modern Literary Theory.* Albany, NY: SUNY P, 1982.

Happel, Stephen. "Picturing God: The Rhetoric of Religious Images and Caravaggio's *Conversion of St. Paul.*" Jost and Olmsted 323–55.

Hawhee, Debra. "Burke and Nietzsche." *Quarterly Journal of Speech* 82 (1999): 129–45.

Heath, Robert L. *Realism and Relativism: A Perspective on Kenneth Burke.* Macon, GA: Mercer UP, 1986.

Henderson, Greig. "A Rhetoric of Form: The Early Burke and Reader-Response Criticism." Henderson and Williams 127–42.

Henderson, Greig, and David Cratis Williams, eds. *Unending Conversations: New Writings by and about Kenneth Burke.* Carbondale: Southern Illinois UP, 2001.

Hogan, Kevin. "Kenneth Burke's Postmodern Rhetorical Theological Anthropology." Diss. Catholic University of America, 2002.
Holmes, David G. "The Fragmented Whole: Ralph Ellison, Kenneth Burke, and the Cultural Literacy Debate." *CLA Journal* 43.3 (2000): 261–75.
Husserl, Edmund. *The Crisis of the European Sciences and Transcendental Phenomenology.* Trans. David Carr. Evanston, IL: Northwestern UP, 1970.
Hyman, Stanley Edgar. *The Armed Vision: A Study in the Methods of Modern Literary Criticism.* Rev. Ed. New York: Vintage, 1955.
Jack, Jordynn. "'The Piety of Degradation': Kenneth Burke, the Bureau of Social Hygiene, and *Permanence and Change*." *Quarterly Journal of Speech* 90 (2004): 216–34.
Jackson, Lawrence. "The Birth of the Critic: The Literary Friendship of Ralph Ellison and Richard Wright." *American Literature* 72.2 (2000): 321–55.
—. *Ralph Ellison: Emergence of Genius.* New York: John Wiley & Sons, 2002.
James, William. *Varieties of Religious Experience: A Study in Human Nature.* 1901–1902 Gifford Lectures. New York: Modern Library, 1994.
—. *Varieties of Religious Experience.* New York: New American Library, 2003.
Jameson, Fredric. Foreword. Greimas vi-xxii.
—. "Ideology and Symbolic Action." *Critical Inquiry* 5.2 (Winter 1978): 417–22.
—. "The Symbolic Inference; or Kenneth Burke and Ideological Analysis." *Critical Inquiry* 4.3 (Spring 1978): 507–23.
Jay, Paul. "Kenneth Burke." *The Johns Hopkins Guide to Literary Theory and Criticism.* 1st ed. Ed. Michael Groden and Martin Kreiswirth. Baltimore: The Johns Hopkins UP, 1994. 125–27.
—, ed. *The Selected Correspondence of Kenneth Burke and Malcolm Cowley, 1915–1981.* New York: Viking, 1988.
Jordan, Jay. "Dell Hymes, Kenneth Burke's 'Identification,' and the Birth of Sociolinguistics." *Rhetoric Review* 24 (2005): 264–75.
Jost, Walter, and Wendy Olmsted. "Introduction." Jost and Olmsted 1–7.
—, eds. *Rhetorical Invention and Religious Inquiry: New Perspectives.* New Haven: Yale UP, 2000.
Joyce, James. *A Portrait of the Artist as a Young Man.* New York: Penguin Books, 1999.
—. *Ulysses.* 1922. 1934 edition. NY: Vintage International, 1990.
Kennedy, George. *Classical Rhetoric and Its Christian and Secular Tradition From Ancient to Modern Times.* Chapel Hill: U of North Carolina P, 1980.
Klemm, David. "The Rhetoric of Theological Argument." *Rhetoric of the Human Sciences: Language and Argument in Scholarship and Public Affairs.*

Ed. John S. Nelson, Allan Megill and Deirdre M. McCloskey. Madison: U of Wisconsin P, 1987. 276–98.
Knox, George. "The Negro Novelist's Sensibility and the Outsider Theme." *Western Humanities Review* 11.2 (1957): 137–48.
Langer, Suzanne. *Feeling and Form.* New York: Scribner, 1953.
—. *Philosophy in a New Key.* Cambridge, MA: Harvard UP, 1942.
Lear, Jonathan. *Love and Its Place in Nature: a Philosophical Interpretation of Freudian Psychoanalysis.* New Haven: Yale UP, 1990.
Lechtzin, Edward S. "One Year after the Infamous Dateline NBC Test-Crash Show, GM Executive Tells How Automaker 'Swatted' Back." *TJFR Business News Reporter* 7 (1993): 1, 4–5, 8.
—. Personal interview transcript. 25 Aug. 1997.
Leval, Gaston. *Collectives in the Spanish Revolution.* Trans. Vernon Richards. London: Freedom P, 1975.
Levinas, Emmanuel. "The Other in Proust." Trans. Seán Hand. *The Levinas Reader.* Ed. Sean Hand. Oxford: Basil Blackwell, 1989. 160–65.
—. *Totality and Infinity.* Trans. Alphonso Lingis. Pittsburgh: Duquesne UP, 1969.
Lewis, R. W. B. "The Ceremonial Imagination of Ralph Ellison." *The Carleton Miscellany* 18.3 (1980): 34–38.
Lonergan, Bernard J. F., S.J. *Method in Theology.* 1971. Toronto: U of Toronto P, 1999.
MacIntyre, Alisdair. *After Virtue: A Study in Moral Theory.* Notre Dame: U of Notre Dame P, 1984.
McKeon, Richard. "Being, Existence, and That Which Is." *Selected Writings* 244–55.
—. "Discourse, Demonstration, Verification, and Justification." *Essays* 37-55.
—. *Essays in Invention and Discovery.* Ed. Mark Backman. Woodbridge, CT: Ox Bow P, 1987.
—. "Imitation and Poetry." *Though, Action, and Passion.* Chicago: U of Chicago P, 1954.
—. Letters to Kenneth Burke. 12 December 1934 and 24 June 1976. Kenneth Burke Papers, Rare Books and Manuscripts, Special Collections, The Pennsylvania State University Libraries. Carbon copy of the 1976 letter is in the Richard McKeon Papers, Special Collections Research Center, University of Chicago Library.
—. "A Philosopher Meditates on Discovery." *Essays* 194–220.
—. "Philosophic Semantics and Philosophic Inquiry." *Selected Writings* 209–21.
—. "Philosophy of Communications and the Arts." *Essays* 95–120.
—. *Selected Writings of Richard McKeon.* Vol. 1. Ed. Zahava K. McKeon and William G. Swenson. Chicago: U of Chicago P, 1998.

—. "The Subject Matter of Philosophy and the Processes of Philosophizing." Philosophic Semantics and Philosophic Inquiry. Department of Philosophy, University of Chicago. 2 Oct. 1967.

McKeon, Zahava K. "General Introduction." Richard McKeon, *Selected Writings* 1–21.

McMahon, Robert. "Kenneth Burke's Divine Comedy." *PMLA* 104.1 (Jan. 1989): 53–63.

Mill, John Stuart. "What Is Poetry?" *Essays on Poetry*. Ed. F. Parvin Sharpless. Columbia: U of South Carolina P, 1976. 3–22.

Murphy, James J. *Rhetoric in the Middle Ages: A History of Rhetorical Theory from St. Augustine to the Renaissance.* Berkeley: U of California P, 1974.

Murray, Timothy C. "Kenneth Burke's Logology: A Mock Logomachy." *Glyph 2*. Baltimore: The Johns Hopkins UP, 1977. 144–61.

Nelson, Cary. *Revolutionary Memory: Recovering the Poetry of the American Left*. New York: Routledge, 2001.

—. "Writing as the Accomplice of Language," *The Legacy of Kenneth Burke*. Ed. Herbert W. Simons and Trevor Melia. Madison: U of Wisconsin P, 1989: 156–73.

Nemerov, Howard. "A Day on the Big Branch." *New and Selected Poems*. Chicago: U of Chicago P, 1960.

The New Princeton Encyclopedia of Poetry and Poetics. Ed. Alex Preminger and T. V. F. Brogan. Princeton: Princeton UP, 1993.

O'Brien, Dennis. "One Mind in the Truth: Richard McKeon, a Philosopher of Education." Garver and Buchanan 77–91, 244–46 (notes).

O'Donnell, James J. "Augustine: Elements of Christianity." *Augustine of Hippo*. November 2000. June 2003 <http://ccat.sas.upenn.edu/jod/augustine.html>.

O'Gorman, Ned. "Reading Kenneth Burke's 'Marxism' in *Permanence and Change* with Lewis Mumford." National Communication Association Convention. Chicago. 11–13 Nov. 2004.

Olmsted, Wendy. "Invention, Emotion, and Conversion in Augustine's *Confessions*." Jost and Olmsted 65–86.

O'Meally, Robert G. "On Burke and the Vernacular: Ralph Ellison's Boomerang of History." *History & Memory in African-American Culture*. Ed. Genevieve Fabre and Robert O'Meally. Oxford: Oxford UP, 1994. 244–60

—. "The Rules of Magic: Hemingway as Ellison's 'Ancestor.'" Benston 245–71.

Ong, Walter, S.J. *Orality and Literacy: The Technologizing of the Word*. London: Methuen, 1982.

—. *Rhetoric, Romance, and Technology: Studies in the Interaction of Expression and Culture*. Ithaca: Cornell UP, 1971.

—. *The Presence of the Word: Some Prolegomena for Cultural and Religious History*. New Haven: Yale UP, 1967.

—. "The Word as History: Sacred and Profane." Jost and Olmsted 15–24.
Oppenheimer, Judy. *Private Demons: The Life of Shirley Jackson.* New York: Fawcett Columbine, 1988.
Parrish, Timothy L. "Ralph Ellison, Kenneth Burke, and the Form of Democracy." *Arizona Quarterly* 51.3 (1995): 117–48.
Pease, Donald. "Ralph Ellison and Kenneth Burke: The Nonsymbolizable (Trans)Action." *boundary 2* 30.2 (2003): 65–96.
Perelman, Chaim, and Lucie Olbrechts-Tyteca. *The New Rhetoric: A Treatise on Argumentation.* Trans. John Wilkinson and Purcell Weaver. Notre Dame: U of Notre Dame P, 1969.
Public Relations Society of America Foundation. *The National Credibility Index: Making Personal Investment Decisions.* New York, NY: Public Relations Society of America Foundation, 2000.
Rorty, Richard, ed. *The Linguistic Turn: Essays in Philosophical Method.* Chicago: U of Chicago P, 1992.
Rotondi Jr., Thomas. "Organizational Identification: Issues and Implications." *Organizational Behavior and Human Performance* 13 (1975): 95–109.
Rubin, Alexis. P., ed. *Scattered Among the Nations: Documents Affecting Jewish History 1949 to 1975.* Toronto, Canada: Wall and Emerson, 1993.
Rueckert, William. *Kenneth Burke and the Drama of Human Relations.* 2nd ed. Berkeley: U of California P, 1982.
—. "Some of the Many Kenneth Burkes." *Encounters with Kenneth Burke.* Urbana: U of Illinois P, 1994. 3–28.
Rutland, Laura E. "Hindrance, Act, and the Scapegoat: William Blake, Kenneth Burke, and the Rhetoric of Order." Diss. U of Tennessee. 2003.
Scanlon, Michael. "Augustine and Theology as Rhetoric." *Augustinian Studies* 25 (1994): 37–50.
Scharfstein, Ben-Ami. *Ineffability: The Failure of Words in Philosophy and Religion.* Albany, NY: SUNY P, 1983.
Schuetz, Janice E. "Argumentation and Corporate Advocacy: A Synthesis." *Corporate Advocacy: Rhetoric in the Information Age.* Ed. Judith D. Hoover. Westport, CT: Quorum Books, 1997. 237–52.
Scruggs, Charles. *Sweet Home: Invisible Cities in the Afro-American Novel.* Baltimore: Johns Hopkins UP, 1993.
Seigel, Marika. "'One little fellow named Ecology': Ecological Rhetoric in Kenneth Burke's *Attitudes Toward History.*" *Rhetoric Review* 23 (2004): 388–404.
Selzer, Jack. *Kenneth Burke in Greenwich Village: Conversing with the Moderns, 1915-1931.* Madison: U of Wisconsin P, 1996.
Smudde, Peter M. "A Practical Model of the Document-development Process." *Technical Communication* 38 (1991): 316–23.
—. "Implications on the Practice and Study of Kenneth Burke's Idea of a 'Public Relations Counsel with a Heart.'" *Communication Quarterly* 52 (2004): 420–32.

Southwell, Samuel B. *Kenneth Burke and Martin Heidegger, with a Note against Deconstruction.* Gainesville: U of Florida P, 1987.

Spellmeyer, Kurt. "Too Little Care: Language, Politics, and Embodiment." *College English* 55 (1993): 265–83.

Stuckey, J. Elspeth. *The Violence of Literacy.* Portsmouth, NH: Boynton-Cook Publishers, 1991.

Sullivan, Therese, Sr. "S. Avreli Avgvstini Hipponiensis Episcopi de Doctrina Christiana, Liber Qvartvs: A Commentary, with Revised Text, Introduction, and Translation." Diss. The Catholic University of America, 1930.

Sutherland, Christine Mason. "Love as Rhetorical Principle: The Relationship Between Context and Style in the Rhetoric of St. Augustine." *Grace, Politics, and Desire: Essays on Augustine.* Ed. Hugo A. Meynell. Calgary: U of Calgary P, 1990.

Thompson, E. P. *Witness Against the Beast: William Blake and the Moral Law.* New York: New P, 1993.

Tompkins, Phillip K., Jeanne Y. Fisher, Dominic A. Infante, and Elaine L. Tompkins. "Kenneth Burke and the Inherent Characteristics of Formal Organizations: A Field Study." *Speech Monographs* 42 (1975): 135–42.

Tracy, David. *The Analogical Imagination: Christian Theology and the Culture of Pluralism.* New York: Crossroad, 1981.

—. "Charity, Obscurity, Clarity: Augustine's Search for Rhetoric and Hermeneutics." *Rhetoric and Hermeneutics in Our Time: A Reader.* Ed. Walter Jost and Michael J. Hyde. New Haven: Yale, 1997. 254–74.

—. "Mystics, Prophets, Rhetorics: Religion and Psychoanalysis." *The Trial(s) of Psychoanalysis.* Ed. François Meltzer. Chicago: U of Chicago P, 1988. 259–72.

Warren, R. S., and L. B. Kaden. *Report of Inquiry into Crash Demonstrations Broadcast on Dateline NBC November 17, 1992.* Unpublished manuscript, 21 March 1993.

Watson, Walter. "McKeon: The Unity of His Thought." Garver and Buchanan 10–28, 231–39 (notes).

Watten, Barrett. *The Constructivist Moment: From Material Text to Cultural Poetics.* Middletown, CT: Wesleyan UP, 2003.

Weiser, Benjamin. "Does TV News Go Too Far? A Look Behind the Scenes at NBC's Truck Crash Test." *Washington Post* 23 Feb. 1993.

Wess, Robert. *Kenneth Burke: Rhetoric, Subjectivity, Postmodernism.* Cambridge: Cambridge UP, 1996.

Whitaker, Thomas R. "Spokesman for Invisibility." Benston 386–403.

White, Hayden, and Margaret Brose, eds. *Representing Kenneth Burke.* Selected Papers from the English Institute. No. 6. Baltimore: Johns Hopkins UP, 1982.

Wright, John. "Shadowing Ellison." Benston 63–88.

Contributors

Benjamin Bennett-Carpenter (PhD, Catholic University of America, 2008) is Special Lecturer in the Rhetoric Program at Oakland University (Rochester, Michigan) and Research Associate at Sacred Heart Major Seminary (Detroit). His work analyzes rhetoric and religion in media or information culture, with a particular focus upon theories and methods. Recently he completed a dissertation entitled "Moving *Memento Mori* Pictures: Documentary, Mortality, and Transformation in Three Films," which argues that documentary films operate as *memento mori* pictures— or images that bring mortality to consciousness —and that the experience of them is transformative, not simply informative.

Gregory Clark is Professor of English at Brigham Young University and serves as Associate Dean of the College of Humanities. He teaches and writes about American rhetoric and culture. His most recent book is *Rhetorical Landscapes in America: Variations on a Theme from Kenneth Burke* (University of South Carolina Press, 2004). He has been editor of *Rhetoric Society Quarterly* and serves now as executive director of the Rhetoric Society of America. His current project is a study of relationships of rhetoric and jazz in America.

Miriam Marty Clark is Associate Professor of English at Auburn University, where she teaches courses in American literature and world literature in English. She has published on modern and contemporary writers from William Carlos Williams and Ernest Hemingway to Alice Munro, William Trevor, and A. R. Ammons. She is currently completing a book, *Kenneth Burke and American Poetry*, which addresses Burke's extended conversations with twentieth century poets and poetry critics, dialogues that include not only Williams, Theodore Roethke, Howard Nemerov, Ammons and Susan Howe but also John Crowe Ransom, Denis Donoghue, Frank Lentricchia, and Cary Nelson.

Bryan Crable (PhD, Purdue University, 1998) is Associate Professor and Chairperson in the Communication Department at Villanova University. His research places Burke's rhetorical theory in dialogue with existential phenomenology and communication theory. Some of his current work explores Burke's personal and intellectual relationship with African-American novelist and critic, Ralph Ellison—a portion of which earned the 2003 Charles Kneupper Award from the Rhetoric Society of America. In addition, he has published a dozen other chapters and articles in such journals as *Rhetoric Society Quarterly, Quarterly Journal of Speech, Rhetoric Review, Argumentation & Advocacy, Human Studies*, and *Western Journal of Communication*.

William FitzGerald is Assistant Professor of English at Rutgers University - Camden, where he teaches rhetoric, writing studies, and literature, including courses in genre, figurative language, and the history of media. His manuscript in progress, tentatively titled *Rhetoric and Reverence: Prayer and the Human Imaginary* extends Burke's use of "prayer" as a key term in his lexicon to a wider account of prayer as rhetoric, rhetoric as prayer.

Melissa Girard is a PhD candidate in modern American poetry and poetics at the University of Illinois at Urbana-Champaign. Her dissertation focuses on popular American poetry of the first half of the twentieth century and argues for the aesthetic sophistication of these mass cultural forms.

Greig Henderson is Professor of English at the University of Toronto. He is the author of *Kenneth Burke: Literature and Language as Symbolic Action* (1988) and the co-editor of and a contributor to *Unending Conversations: New Writings by and about Kenneth Burke* (2001).

Christine E. Iwanicki is Associate Professor of English at Western Illinois University, where she teaches courses in literary and rhetorical theory and British Literature. She is especially interested in issues that focus on the intersection of language, ideology, culture, hermeneutics, and epistemology. Her work explores connections between continental and Anglo-American philosophy and contemporary practices of reading, writing, and other forms of representation and communication.

Michael Jackson is Lecturer at the University of New Hampshire. His research interests include visual rhetoric, rhetoric of science, rhetorical theory, and rhetorical criticism.

James Kastely is Associate Professor of English at the University of Houston, where he directs the Creative Writing Program. He has published numerous essays in the history and theory of rhetoric and also *Rethinking the History of Rhetoric: From Plato to Postmodernism* (Yale UP).

Cary Nelson is Jubilee Professor of Liberal Arts and Sciences and Professor of English at the University of Illinois at Urbana-Champaign. His numerous authored or edited books include *The Incarnate Word: Literature as Verbal Space* (1973), *Marxism and the Interpretation of Culture* (1987), *Cultural Studies* (1992), *Higher Education Under Fire: Politics, Economics, and the Crisis of the Humanities* (1994), *Revolutionary Memory: Recovering the Poetry of the American Left* (2001), and *Office Hours : Activism and Change in the Academy* (2004). Nelson took office as the 49th President of the American Association of University Professors in June 2006.

Laura E. Rutland is Assistant Professor of English and Director of Freshman Composition at Gannon University, where she teaches a variety of courses in writing, literature, and literary criticism. Her primary field of specialization is British Romanticism, but her scholarly agenda focuses on the scapegoating process as it appears both in literature and in public rhetoric, an interest which sometimes leads her to explore texts outside that primary teaching field. Both William Blake and Kenneth Burke remain central to her research efforts.

Jack Selzer has taught graduate and undergraduate courses on rhetoric and composition, technical and scientific communication, and Kenneth Burke at Penn State since 1978. He is the author of *Kenneth Burke in Greenwich Village* (Wisconsin, 1996) and coauthor (with Ann George) of the recently published *Kenneth Burke in the 1930s* (University of South Carolina Press). He was awarded the Kenneth Burke Society's Lifetime Achievement Award in 2005.

Peter M. Smudde (PhD, Wayne State University) is Assistant Professor in the School of Communication at Illinois State University. He came to academe in 2002 after sixteen years in industry in the fields of public relations, marketing communications, and technical writing. He received a Wisconsin Teaching Fellowship for 2005-2006 from the University of Wisconsin System while on the faculty at the University of Wisconsin-Whitewater. His primary research and teaching interest is the application of Burke's ideas (and contemporary theories of rhetoric) to pedagogy and industry. He has published articles and presented papers in communication, rhetoric, and other topics in regional, national, and international venues.

Robert Wess is the author of *Kenneth Burke: Rhetoric, Subjectivity, Postmodernism* and has also published articles on Burke and other theorists, as well as a number of literary works. His recent work on ecocriticism includes editing a special issue of *KB Journal* on Burke and ecocriticism. Trained at the University of Chicago, where studies under Richard McKeon evolved later into his interest in Burke, Wess has taught at the University of Texas at Austin and Oregon State University, where he continues as a member of the Emeritus faculty. He was awarded the Kenneth Burke Society's Distinguished Service Award in 1999 and served as the Society's President from 2005 to 2008.

Index of Names and Titles

Adams, Leonie, 28
Adell, Sandra, 24
Adorno, Theodor, 45, 144-145, 195
Albrecht, James M., 24
Ammons, A. R., xii, xv, 46-48
Apollinaire, Guillaume, 140, 148
Aristotle, xvi, xvii, xviii, 71, 81, 86, 87, 88, 89, 94, 97, 103, 110, 182, 200
Ashbery, John, 40, 41
Attitudes Toward History (Burke), ix, xix-xx, 29, 35, 70, 133, 149, 195, 200, 203, 208
Augustine, St., 161, 162, 166-168, 171-173, 176, 182, 188, 200; *Confessions*, 166-167, 172-173; *On Christian Doctrine* (*De doctrina Christiana*), 166, 168, 172-173
Austen, Jane, 67
Averill, Mary Beth, 196

Bachelard, Gaston: *The Poetics of Space*, 123
Bailey, Bill, 154
Bakhtin, Mikhail, xiii, 79, 177, 200
Bateson, Gregory, xiii
Belitt, Ben, xiii, xiv, xxi, 27-28, 37
Bennett-Carpenter , Benjamin, xix, 161

Bergson, Henri, xiii, 172
Bewley, Marius, 147
Bizzell, Patricia, 172
Blackmur, R. P., x, 42
Blair, Carole, 172
Blake, William, xviii, 109-119; *Songs of Experience*, 113; *The Book of Ahania*, 110, 118; *The Book of Thel*, 119; *The Book of Urizen*, 109, 118; *The Marriage of Heaven and Hell*, 117
Blakesley, David, x, 147
Bloom, Harold, xxi, 46
Blum, W. C., 138, 140, 147
Book of Moments (Burke), 134, 136-140
Booth, Wayne, xii, xv, xix, 42, 51-52, 54, 68-70, 73, 77-79, 82, 83, 84, 162, 164, 169, 174, 194; *Modern Dogma and the Rhetoric of Assent*, 169; *The Rhetoric of Fiction*, 68, 77-78, 82; *The Rhetoric of Rhetoric*, 169
Boyle, Marjorie O'Rourke, 161-162, 167-169
Brose, Margaret, 41
Brown, Michael E., 45, 72, 160
Bureau of Social Hygiene, ix
Burke, Kenneth, *Attitudes Toward History*, ix, xix, xx, 29, 35, 70, 72, 84, 133, 149, 195, 200,

203-204, 208; *Book of Moments*, 134, 136-140; *Collected Poems*, xxi, 27; *Counter-Statement*, xiii, xx, 7, 8, 42, 43, 70, 85, 98-99, 103, 107, 111, 117, 147, 209; *Dramatism and Development*, 67; *Essays Toward a Symbolic of Motives, 1950-1955*, 120; *A Grammar of Motives*, xvi, 4, 36, 43, 54, 72, 159, 175; *Language as Symbolic Action*, x, 70, 182, 188; *Late Poems, 1968-1993*, x, 147; *Permanence and Change*, x, 28, 36, 39, 53, 70, 140, 143, 147, 195, 200, 220; *The Philosophy of Literary Form*, xvi, xviii, xx, 66, 70, 103, 185, 197, 206, 207, 208; *A Rhetoric of Motives*, xiv, xx, 4, 24-25, 59, 70, 118, 175, 208-209; *The Rhetoric of Religion*, xiii, xviii, xix, 36, 42, 70, 75, 109-111, 118-119, 124, 153, 161-163, 168-169, 173-176, 182, 185-186, 189, 191-194, 196, 199-200, 202; *Towards a Better Life*, xiii, xviii, 7, 42, 47, 109-112, 114-118, 221

Burke, Libbie, 9, 17, 25, 26, 66
Burks, Virginia, ix
Butler, Samuel, 201
Bygrave, Stephen, 111

Caldwell, Erskine, 70
Cameron, Sharon, 134
Cannon, Steve, 6, 25
Chekhov, 29
Cheney, George, 149; *Rhetoric in an Organizational Society*, 150
Chesebro, James, 149, 159
Cicero, 51, 168
Clark, Gregory, xvi, xvii, 96
Clark, Katrina, xiii, xiv, xvii, 40, 66, 200
Clark, Miriam Marty, xiii, 40, 66
Coleridge, Samuel Taylor, 7, 30, 33, 48, 110, 200
Colish, Marcia, 167
Collected Poems (Burke), xxi, 27
Conley, Thomas M., 172
Conrad, Joseph, *Heart of Darkness*, 177, 186; *Lord Jim*, 72
Counter-Statement (Burke), xiii, xx, 7, 8, 42, 43, 70, 85, 98-99, 103, 107, 111, 117, 147, 209
Cowley, Malcolm, xii, xiv, xxi, 5, 22, 32, 111, 119, 131, 138, 146-147
Crable, Bryan, xiii, xiv, 3
Cragan, John F., 159
Crusius, Timothy W., 139
Culler, Jonathan: *Structuralist Poetic*, 121

Damon, Foster S., 119
Dangerous Drugs, x
Davidson, Donald, 11, 26
Davies, Donald, 134, 138, 140
Day, Dorothy, xii
De Certeau, Michel, 42
De Man, Paul, 42
Derrida, Jacques, 42, 63, 121, 122
Dial, The (magazine), xiii, 34, 67, 107, 119
Donoghue, Denis, xii, xiii, xiv, 40-48; *Reading America*, 41; *Speaking of Beauty*, 43
Duffey, Bernard I., 134
Duncan, Hugh Dalziel, xii, 175, 185
DuPlessis, Rachel Blau, 145

Eagleton, Terry, 106; *The Ideology of the Aesthetic*, 106
Eaton, Robert J., 158
Eddy, Beth, xiv, 24

Eliot, T. S., 19, 20, 22, 143
Ellison, Fanny, 4, 15, 17, 25
Ellison, Ralph, xii, xiii, xiv, 3-26, 46; *Invisible Man*, xiv, 3, 4, 5, 9, 11, 15, 17, 19, 22-25; *Juneteenth*, 25; *Shadow and Act*, 4, 12, 15, 21, 25
Empson, William, xii, 44
Enoch, Jessica, x
Erasmus, Desiderius, 162, 167
Essays Toward a Symbolic of Motives, 1950-1955 (Burke), 120
Essick, Robert N., 118
Eves, Rosalyn, x

Farrell, James T., xii
Farrell, Thomas, 51, 52
Ferguson, Francis, xii
Fielding, Henry, 67
Fish, Stanley, 73, 83, 121-122
Fisher, Jeanne Y., 159
FitzGerald, William, xx, 201
Forrest, Leon, 24
Forster, E. M.: *Aspects of the Novel*, 68, 70
Foss, Sonja, 32, 159
Foss, Karen, 32
Foucault, Michel, xiii, 121, 128
Frank, Armin Paul, xii, xv, 122, 147
Frank, Waldo, xii
Frazer Sir James, xiii
Freccero, John, 186
Frye, Northrop, 121, 122, 135

Garver, Eugene, 94
Gene Harris Trio Plus One, The, 102, 108
Gilbert, Sandra L., *The Madwoman in the Attic*, 109
Girard, René, 197
Grammar of Motives, The (Burke), xvi, 4, 7-8, 36, 43, 53-54, 58, 62, 67, 72, 159, 175, 177
Greimas, Algirdas Julien, 72
Gross, Michael, 196
Gubar, Susan, *The Madwoman in the Attic*, 109

Hall, Douglas T., 45, 107, 160
Hall, Stuart, 126
Handelman, Susan, 182
Happel, Stephen, 169, 170
Harding, D. W., 44
Hartman, Geoffrey: *The Unmediated Vision*, 123
Hawhee, Debra, 142
Heath, Robert L., 138
Heidegger, Martin, 172
Henderson, Greig, xv, 68
Hill, Geoffrey, 29, 44
Hogan, Kevin, 170
Hoggart, Richard, 126
Holmes, David G., 24
Holquist, Michael, 200
Hook, Sidney, xii
Husserl, Edmund, 196
Hyman, Stanley Edgar, xii, xiv, xvi, 5-10, 12, 15-26, 29, 147
Hymes, Dell, x

Infante, Dominic A., 159
Ivie, Robert L., xxi
Iwanicki, Christine E., xix, 174

Jack, Jordynn, ix
Jackson, Lawrence, 6
Jackson, Michael, xiii, xiv
Jackson, Shirley, 9, 15, 16, 19, 24, 25, 26, 27
James, William, 96, 107, 170; *The Varieties of Religious Experience*, 96, 170
Jameson, Fredric, 41, 42, 71, 122, 131-133, 146, 200
Jay, Paul, x, xii, 5, 46, 140, 141, 176

Jordan, Jay, x, xi, 114
Josephson, Matthew, xii, 50-51, 66
Jost, Alter, 162, 163
Joyce, James, xvi, 69, 70, 73, 76-78, 194; *Portrait of the Artist as a Young Man*, xvi, 69, 73, 84; *The Dead*, xvi, 69, 70, 73, 76, 77, 78, 194; *Ulysses*, 81, 194

Kaden, L. B., 155
Kafka, Franz, 70
Kastely, James, xvi, xvii, 86
Kennedy, George, 172
Klemm, David, 165
Knox, George, 19, 20-21, 26
Kristeva, Julia, 72
Kunitz, Stanley, 29

Langer, Suzanne, 42, 44, 47
Language as Symbolic Action (Burke), x, 70, 182, 188
Lear, Jonathan, 72, 91, 92
Lechtzin, Edward S., 151-157
Leval, Gaston, 137
Levinas, Emmanuel, 42, 48
Lewis, R. W. B., 24, 25, 147
Lonergan, Bernard, 170
Lubbock, Percy: *The Craft of Fiction*, 68
Lucretius, xiii

MacIntyre, Alisdair, 44
Mann, Charles, xi, 70
Mann, Thomas, 70
Mansfield, Katherine, 29
McClatchy, J. D., xxi
McKeon, Richard, xii, xiii, xv, 49-58, 60-61, 64-67
McKeon, Zahava, 55, 66
McMahon, Robert, 193-194
Mill, John Stuart, 135
Mills, C. Wright, xiii
Moore, Marianne, xii, 129

Munson, Gorham, xii
Murphy, James J., 172
Murrary, Timothy C., 186

Nation, The (magazine), xiv, 27, 28, 34, 36
Nelson, Cary, xv, xviii, xix, xxi, 41, 42, 45, 120, 137, 139
Nemerov, Howard, xii, xxi, 29, 37, 46, 50, 66
New Republic, The, ix
Nietzsche, Friedrich, xiii, 142, 165, 194

Olbrechts-Tyteca, Lucie, 103, 106
Olmsted, Wendy, 162, 163, 167
Ong, Walter S.J., 162-163; *Rhetoric, Romance, and Technology*, 170
Oppenheimer, Judy, 25

Parrish, Timothy J., 24
Pease, Donald, 24
Perelman, Chaim, 103, 106
Permanence and Change: An Anatomy of Purpose (Burke), x, 28, 36, 39, 53, 70, 140, 143, 147, 195, 200, 220
Philosophy of Literary Form, The (Burke), xvi, xviii, xx, 66, 70, 103, 185, 197, 206, 207, 208
Plato, 51, 162, 182
Porter, Katherine Anne, xii
Poulet, Georges: *The Metamorphoses of the Circle*, 123
Pound, Ezra, 140
Provincetown Players, xii

Ransom, John Crowe, x, xii
Reed, Ishmael, 6, 25
Rhetoric of Motives, A (Burke), xiv, xx, 4, 24, 25, 59, 70, 118, 175, 208, 209

Index   245

Rhetoric of Religion, The (Burke),
   xiii, xviii, xix, 36, 42, 70, 75,
   109-111, 118-119, 124, 153,
   161-163, 168-169, 173-176,
   182, 185-186, 189, 191-194,
   196, 199-200, 202
Rhetorical Landscapes in America
   (Clark), 97
Roethke, Theodor, xii, 29
Rorty, Richard, xxi
Rosenblatt, Louise M., 44
Rotondi Jr., Thomas, 160
Rubin, Alexis, 198
Rueckert, William H., xii, xxi, 46,
   51, 55, 120, 175, 187; *Kenneth Burke and the Drama of Human Relations*, 175; *Letters from Kenneth Burke to William H. Rueckert, 1959-1987*, 55

Sabre, Jeanette, x
Scanlon, Michael, 167, 172
Scharfstein, Ben-Ami, 195
Schneider, Benjamin, 160
Schuetz, Janice E., 159
Scruggs, Charles, 24
Sears, Paul, ix; *Deserts on the March*, ix
Seigel, Marika, ix, xi
Selzer, Jack, ix, 32, 35, 51, 67, 111, 119, 135
Shakespeare: *King Lear*, 72
Shields, Donald C., 159
Slochower, Harry, 6, 7
Smith, Jr., John F., 158
Smudde, Peter M., xix, 149-150, 152
Southwell, Samuel B., 59
Spellmeyer, Kurt, 176, 177
Stevens, Wallace, 45, 48
Stuckey, J. Elspeth, 176, 196
Sullivan, Therese, Sr., 172, 173

Sutherland, Christine Mason, 173

Tate, Allen, x, xii, 135
Tell, David, x
Thompson, E. P., 111; *Witness Against the Beast; William Blake and the Moral Law*, 111
Tocqueveille, Alexis de, xvii, 106
Tompkins, Philip K., 159
Toomer Jean, xii
Towards a Better Life (Burke), xiii, xviii, 7, 42, 47, 109-118, 221
Tracy, David, 164, 172, 185, 192
Trotman, Alex, 158
Troupe, Quincey, 6, 25
Troy, William, 28
Tzara, Tristan, 140

Veblen, Thorstein, 143

Walton, Eda Lou, 27, 28
Watson, J(ames) S(ibley), xii, 147.
   See also Blum, W. C.
Watten, Barrett, 145
Warren, Austin, xii
Warren, R. S., 155, 160
Watson, Walter, 55, 57, 67
Weiser, Benjamin, 151
Wess, Robert, ix, xiii, xv, 49, 67
Whitaker, Julie, x, 147
Whitaker, Thomas, 24
White, Hayden, 41
Wible, Scott, x
Williams, Raymond, 126
Williams, William Carlos, xii, xiv, xxi, 46, 50, 108, 129
Wilson, Edmund, xii
Woods, (Colonel) Arthur, x
Woolf, Virginia, *Mrs. Dalloway*, 70
Wright, Richard, 3, 8, 14, 16, 24
Zappen, James, xxi

www.ingramcontent.com/pod-product-compliance
Lightning Source LLC
Chambersburg PA
CBHW032020230426
43671CB00005B/153